BAD
REPUTATION

BAD
REPUTATION

The Unauthorized Biography of
JOAN JETT

DAVE THOMPSON

Backbeat
Books

An Imprint of Hal Leonard Corporation

Published in 2011 by Backbeat Books
An Imprint of Hal Leonard Corporation
7777 West Bluemound Road
Milwaukee, WI 53213

Trade Book Division Editorial Offices
33 Plymouth St., Montclair, NJ 07042

Printed in the United States of America

Book design by Publishers' Design and Production Services, Inc.

Library of Congress Cataloging-in-Publication Data

Thompson, Dave, 1960 Jan. 3–
     Bad reputation : the unauthorized biography of Joan Jett / Dave Thompson. — 1st pbk. ed.
          p. cm.
     Includes bibliographical references and index.
     ISBN 978-0-87930-990-9
     1. Jett, Joan. 2. Rock musicians—United States—Biography. 3. Guitarists—United States—Biography. I. Title.
     ML419.J48T46 2011
     782.42166092—dc23
     [B]
               2011027282

www.backbeatbooks.com

To Poly Styrene (1957–2011) and Ari Up (1962–2010) . . .
without whom Joan would have been even more alone

Contents

Preface

Nobody lives their entire existence in the spotlight, doing remarkable things all the remarkable days of their remarkable lives. Which is wonderful for them, because we all need some downtime. But it's a bitch for the biographer, who takes a thirty-plus-year fascination with an artist and tries to tell his or her story.

It's not true that people become less interesting as they grow older. In fact, the opposite is probably the case, as experience and knowledge build around enthusiasm and talent. But there is a tradeoff. Without a single, solitary exception, artists, and especially rock 'n' roll artists, are at their most energetic and active in the years before they make it big.

Those are the years during which they create their mythologies; those are the years during which they write their stories. The decades after that may not always flow smoothly and will certainly have their own tales to tell. But in terms of a cohesive narrative that doesn't simply bound from one stadium tour to the next, via an album that may or may not be as good as the first few, it's the years of struggle, acceptance, and consolidation that paint the conquering hero, whereas those that follow simply bring the portrait up to date.

The Joan Jett story is different. For sure, it is the first six years of her career that hold the most interest and saw the most action, but what is remarkable about Jett, and what made this book such a joy to write, is the way she has constantly succeeded in renewing not only herself but also (to use that most hateful of modern marketing terms) her "brand."

In 1988, with the chart-topping "I Love Rock 'n' Roll" already six years' worth of underperforming singles behind her, it would have been easy for Jett to have bowed to the inevitable and joined the rest of the early '80s hit parade on the set of *Where Are They Now?* Instead, she turned around and had one of the biggest hits of her life.

She could have lined up there again in 1994, when "I Hate Myself for Loving You" was equally buried beneath half a decade of underachievement. Instead, she reemerged as the figurehead for one of the most crucial musical movements of the postpunk era.

And so on. Whenever it seems safe for history to finally draw a line beneath Joan Jett's career, she turns the tables on the doomsayers and reminds them not why she was so important way back when, but why she continues to be important today.

It's not because she's a woman, or even because she's a gay woman. Unlike so many of her peers, Jett has never defined herself by what she is. She has no need to—there are almost forty years' worth of music critics who have done that for her.

It's not because she's one of the best American rock songwriters of her age, nor because she has a talent for turning out cover versions that are often as good as, or stronger than, the originals. Again, those are observations that the critics can either make or not make, and besides, few artists can ever be truly subjective about their own work.

Joan Jett is important because it doesn't matter when you started listening to her music: in 1976, with the Runaways hurling cherry bombs out of the radio; in 1980, when she had a bad reputation; or in 1982, when all that was suddenly forgiven; later in the decade or early in the '90s; onstage or on Broadway or even on the silver screen . . . *Whenever* it was, she was making the music that you grew up with, and the kind of music that you wished you could listen to forever.

It doesn't matter that it wasn't always what the industry would call "commercially successful," because the industry was saying that about her right up until the moment "I Love Rock 'n' Roll" went into the Top 40. The fact was, in one corner of that industry, away from all the bullshit and bluster that normally surrounds the superstar machine, Jett never stopped dropping a dime into her private jukebox and then playing along with what came out.

In June 2010, Jett took the stage at Wembley Stadium in London, one of the largest venues that the United Kingdom has to offer. Twenty-eight years earlier almost to the day, she was preparing to take the stage at the

Milton Keynes Bowl, *another* of Britain's biggest concert arenas. And in between times . . .

Whenever she toured, whether stadiums or clubs, theaters or casinos, there would be a roomful (literally, *full*) of people of every generation, and all were there to hear their youth come back to life . . . or to experience their youth for the first time, because Jett's appearance on the Warped tour in 2005 proved that age and status mean nothing whatsoever. What matters is what artists put into their music and what they're willing for the crowd to take away from it. Jett has always put everything in, and her audience has always taken it away.

Since the days of the Runaways, Joan Jett has literally created the soundtrack to our lives, and if this story seems to spend more time on the years when she was building her own life, then that—to return to my opening thoughts—is simply the nature of the beast in general, and Joan Jett in particular.

She gets on with her job. There have been (with one storm-in-a-teacup exception) no vividly sensational tabloid headlines with which to while away a few chapters. There have been no high-profile explosions or behind-the-scenes implosions (or none that anybody wants to talk about, anyway). There has been no gradual mellowing, or slackening of fury— onstage in 2011, Joan Jett is the same ball of energy that she was back in 1976, and because she often plays the same songs she did back then, it's easy to compare the two.

Offstage, too, she just gets on with her life, overseeing the vast business empire that she and longtime manager Kenny Laguna launched from the trunk of his Cadillac in 1980—writing and recording for the next CD; rehearsing for the next tour; and the rest of the time, living as quietly and normally as anybody else. In fact, there are probably times when even she forgets that she's Joan Jett, which means that when one of her records comes on the radio, she can get as excited about it as the rest of us.

That is what this book is about. It is a celebration of an artist who remains as vital and vibrant at fifty-plus as she was when she was sixteen or less. Because if Joan Jett wasn't writing, recording, and playing the best goddamned straight-ahead, down-the-line, and in-your-face rock 'n' roll music in the world . . . who would?

—*Dave Thompson*
Delaware, June 2011

Introduction

The fact that The Runaways picked up guitars was not accepted. And me, being one of the louder ones with the leather jacket and the heavy eye makeup, I was just pushing the envelope. We were called sluts, whores, and dykes all the time. And we were constantly laughed at by bands we played with, by the crews, and by the press. It was just totally frustrating. I didn't get it.

—Joan Jett (PopCult.com)

"If you want to know who Joan Jett is, Joan is the child star who never had to grow up." Journalist and promoter Randy Detroit, one of the founding fathers of the Los Angeles punk scene, spoke with almost paternal pride of the girl—because she *was* a girl back then, barely out of her midteens and as bemused by what was happening as she was belligerently protective of all she had created.

Think about it. She was sixteen when she met Kim Fowley, and that was an education in itself. She was seventeen and she was touring the world in a rock 'n' roll band, and it doesn't matter that the Runaways were never superstars in the hit records and lots of money sense, they were treated like superstars because the music press had never seen anything like them. So all those years that most teenagers spend being teenaged, she was already out there learning how to be a star as well, which meant that when she was old enough to grow up, she'd already lived a life that most adults could only dream of having lived. And she was already Joan Jett, which sometimes was a bad thing, but most of the time, it was a good thing. Well, she's still Joan Jett and, when she wants to be, she's still fifteen years old.

"Joan Jett frightened me, to be honest," Hollywood scenester Skye Zalimit confessed. In 1976, "or somewhere round there," Skye was one of the several hundred California teenagers who descended as often as they could upon Hollywood, bussing, driving, or sometimes even hitch-hiking in from all across the valley, all around the city, for the pleasure of . . . what?

> What do you think? Why does any teenager travel halfway across the city, simply to get someplace else.
>
> She was in a band, she had a record deal, she was working with Kim Fowley, she had all this going for her, and she was six months younger than me; I'd look at her and think "Fuck, if she's this self assured now, what's she going to be like when things really take off for her?" I mean, she wasn't mean or anything, she was still dancing at the same clubs and hanging out with the same friends, but when you're that age, and you don't know what you want to do with your life, seeing someone the same age as you who has already answered all of those questions can be really intimidating.

"Joan was just Joan," said another old friend. "She didn't have a mean bone in her body. She was too busy being determined." And if nobody was certain what she was determined about, then that would come quickly enough as well.

"A lot of people love rock 'n' roll," Randy Detroit punned. "But Joan has lived it as well."

PART ONE

QUEENS OF NOISE

ONE

American Nights

Kim Fowley has never been one to mince words. He is an amazing person. He knows that, we know that, so why should anyone even bother burying that knowledge away beneath modesty or politeness? Resplendent in whichever colored suit he has pulled on to his outsized frame today, documenting his achievements in a voice that is all the more audible for the measured tones with which he employs it, Kim Fowley has been described as a force of nature, and he would probably agree. He might even have been the one who said it in the first place.

Kim Fowley was born on July 21, 1939, the son of the actor Douglas Fowley and the actress Shelby Payne. Growing up in Los Angeles, attending the same university high school as Nancy Sinatra, Jan and Dean, and Beach Boy Bruce Johnson, he shared the same fascination with the infant rock 'n' roll as the rest of his school friends, and the same desire to make his mark on it as some of them.

Fowley didn't have the easiest apprenticeship, but he learned from everything. He was stricken with polio in his late teens, enduring months of hospitalization and treatment; he served in the American armed forces and was still looking back on boot camp with affection two decades later. He worked in some undisclosed capacity within the LA sex industry for a time. And he not only developed a sharp eye for potential opportunities, he had the balls to leap into them as well.

He worked publicity for a local band called the Sleepwalkers, whose drummer, Sandy Nelson, would go onto a chain of massive hits a few years later; then moved into record production with a string of other area acts—including Skip and Flip, a University of Arizona duo who ran up a pair of Top 20 hits in 1959 before Flip (Gary Paxton) and Fowley formed a nonexistent group of their own, the Hollywood Argyles. "Alley Oop," their debut single, went to #1 in 1960, and Fowley was off and running.

In 1961, Fowley cowrote "Like, Long Hair" for Paul Revere and the Raiders; in 1962, he topped the British chart with B Bumble and the Stingers' classical boogie "Nut Rocker." He discovered songwriter David Gates, later to spearhead Bread to early '70s fame, and produced the future soft rocker's first hit, the Murmaids' version of his "Popsicles and Icicles."

He moved to London and recorded with Rolling Stones manager/ producer Andrew Loog Oldham, he managed P. J. Proby, he wrote for Cat Stevens, and he produced the first single by the Soft Machine. He even scored a massive—and massively controversial—hit with the galloping madness of "They're Coming to Take Me Away, Ha! Ha!" released under the guise of Napoleon XIV, and according to one legend, he saw his record banned from British radio after a hapless listener repeatedly played its B-side, "!Ah !Ah Yawa Em Ekat Ot Gnimoc Er'yeht," and promptly went insane.

"We met Kim Fowley completely by accident," recalled another of the myriad future superstars to pass through his hands, English singer Noddy Holder. Holder's band, the N'Betweens, were playing a rare London show at the time, venturing down from their native midlands city of Wolverhampton to headline Tiles, one of the hottest nightclubs on the swinging London scene. "Halfway through our set, we noticed this incredibly tall, streaky figure in the middle of the crowd."

In fact, Holder wrote in his autobiography, it would have been hard to miss him. "Not only was he wearing a cowboy hat, which made him stick out head and shoulders above everyone else, but he was doing this freaky dancing. When we came offstage, he appeared in our dressing room. He just strolled through the door. 'I'm going to make you guys stars,' he said. That was his opening line."

That was always his opening line—either that or something like it. It usually worked, as well, at least inasmuch as it convinced his prey to go with him. Which is how the remainder of Fowley's 1960s blasted past with the same undying élan as they began.

The N'Betweens didn't make it, but five years later, Noddy Holder did, as his new band, Slade, set about midwifing the glam rock scene in Britain. But Fowley didn't care about past failures. He would discover talent and give it what he could. And then it was up to the artist. Fowley had no interest at that time in nursemaiding his charges' careers, in wiping their noses and patting their heads through the trials and tribulations of their unfolding careers. But he would lead them to the gate and make sure they got a good start.

He made a handful of records under his own name, and is duly honored in the Psychedelic Hall of Fame for the megamagnificent "The Trip." He worked with Frank Zappa, and when the classic '50s rocker Gene Vincent attempted a comeback in 1969, he turned to Fowley to produce it.

He reunited with Skip and Flip's Skip, bassist Skip Battin, and they cowrote a clutch of songs for the Byrds. He produced the earliest sessions by Jonathan Richman and the Modern Lovers; he reinvented the 1950s with Flash Cadillac and the Continental Kids' contributions to the *American Graffiti* soundtrack.

And it didn't even matter that few of these projects ever became household names. An evening spent listening to Kim Fowley namedrop was an education in the history of rock 'n' roll.

So it was really just another day at the office, the night Fowley got back to his Hollywood home with Joan Larkin's phone number tucked securely away in one of his pockets. He collected phone numbers just like every other impresario on the Sunset Strip. The difference was, he usually followed through on them, because you never knew which of the hopefuls that strutted their stuff on the streets every evening might just have the wherewithal to translate that strutting into something more valuable.

Plus, he had a feeling about Ms. Larkin that he simply couldn't shake. He was going to help make her a star. But what excited him even more than that was the knowledge that she didn't actually need any help. She may have been a mere fifteen years of age, she may never have strummed a guitar in anger. He wasn't even sure whether or not she could sing.

But she had the kind of toughness and determination that adults twice her age would have killed for, because it wasn't forced, it wasn't bitter, it wasn't even visible most of the time. When she smiled, she lit up the room; when she laughed, the room fell in love. And when she talked, all the bullshit in the world packed its bag and vacated the premises. Kim Fowley had met a lot of wannabe rock stars over the years, and he'd given a helping hand to a few of them. Joan Larkin made them all look like amateurs.

The name would have to go, of course. But she had already figured that out for herself, was already introducing herself to people as Joan Jett, and what a magnificent name that was.

Fowley knew where she got it from of course. Nightly at the English Disco, which is where he met her and where she always hung out, the dance floor shook to the hit sounds of the island that gave the nightclub its name. Gary Glitter and Barry Blue were huge; Freddie Mercury once recorded as Larry Lurex—alliteration was hot in pop right then because it made a name memorable and could foist an impression upon people as well. Gary did glitter; Barry did wear blue. And Jett had the kind of drive that only a jet could rival. And she'd powered it up singlehandedly.

She was a Philadelphia girl, born on September 22, 1958, in the Lankenau Hospital on Lancaster Avenue in Penn Wynne, northwest of the city as it fades toward Bryn Mawr. She was the first of three children—Joan Marie Larkin was followed into the world by brother James and sister Anne—and her father was an insurance salesman, which was why the family always seemed to be on the move.

New positions would open up around the country, and Mr. Larkin would be sent to fill them. Not long after Joan was born, the family relocated to Pittsburgh, on the other side of Pennsylvania; and in 1967 they moved again, to Rockville, MD, within gig-going distance of Washington DC. And by 1974, the family was in Brentwood, a suburb of Los Angeles that left the girl just a couple of bus rides away from the place she really wanted to be. Hollywood.

Which is where Kim Fowley first saw her.

Hollywood is a weird town. It's best known for the movie industry that settled there at the end of the 1910s, a story that itself is emblematic of the hopes and dreams and faded tinsel that Hollywood embraces. New York used to be the center of the American film industry, but it was the heart of the vice trade as well, and in 1908, New York Mayor McClellan launched the most vigorous clean-up campaign that either the city or the infant industry had ever seen. There was talk that if the movies did not clean up their acts directly, they might be banned altogether.

Immediately, the largest and most successful movie producers and distributors of the day banded together to form the Motion Picture Patents Company, the industry's first concerted attempt to prove that it could be trusted not to corrupt the American people. And together, they wrested control of every aspect of the filmmaking business, from the patents applied to the necessary equipment, through the usages to which that equipment could be put, and onto the venues in which it could be utilized. Furthermore, it allowed nonmembers less than two months, until the end of January 1909, in which to comply with all of its regulations and demands or face immediate closure.

Most of the other filmmakers filed into their clutches. A bunch of smaller operators, however, opted not to heed their new master's voice. Foreshadowing the controversies that rage today around the policing and financing of the Internet, they saw the infant medium of film as a wide-open prairie, unfenced and ungoverned and free for all to use as they saw fit, and they were determined that it should remain that way.

So they fled across the country to the West Coast, far from their tormentors' reach, and there, amid the palm trees on the fringe of Los Angeles, they established a new renegade community where movies could be made without fear of interference. Within a decade, a sparsely populated patch of farmland had been transformed into a glittering dreamland, whose very name was synonymous with the silver screen, and which acted as a magnet for every starstruck kid in the country. Some of them even made it big.

That much was still true. But by the mid-1970s, it was also synonymous with a lot of other things—including many of the sins that Mayor McClellan had been so set on cleaning up. Vice, crime, violence, juvenile delinquency—there were only so many openings in the mainstream movie industry, even at its peak, but there were an infinite number of kids out there chasing the Hollywood dream.

They had to find some way of living, and when the first rock 'n' rollers made their own presence felt in Hollywood in the mid-1950s, clambering out of the local high schools or taking Greyhound buses from all points east, so a whole new youth army descended likewise, to share in the lifestyle that they believed was synonymous with the stars. It wasn't, so they added their desires and demands to the melting pot of perversion and disillusion that paved the city streets, and watched as fickle fate descended to snatch somebody else entirely to glory.

Phil Spector was a local boy, the archetypal high-school-nerd-made-good, and he opened the door to a host of followers. Then came Jan and Dean and the Beach Boys, architects of a California sound that had Hollywood as its epicenter. Psychedelia blossomed there, and so did an entire army of "West Coast" soft rockers: the Eagles, Linda Ronstadt, and Warren Zevon. Clubs opened up on (or at least within a cheap cab ride of) Sunset Strip: legendary joints like the Whisky a Go Go, where the Doors made their debut; and the Troubadour, which gave us James Taylor. And they too attracted hopefuls by the horde, all of them armed with their own slice of talent, in the hope that somebody might be impressed by it.

Kim Fowley was one of the names that the more ambitious among them sought out. He was approaching his midthirties by the time he met Joan Jett in 1975, and a lot of his greatest achievements were the kind of things that, at this late date, really only excited record collectors. But his reputation preceded him, so when he sought out Jett, it was probably only a matter of time before she would find him. Individually, Kim Fowley and Joan Jett both had dreams.

Collectively, they could transform them into reality.

TWO

Queen of Noise

It was through the auspices of *Who Put the Bomp* that Kim Fowley first voiced his latest ambition. More than a fanzine but not quite a magazine, *Who Put the Bomp* was the five-year-old baby of journalist Greg Shaw, a longtime friend of Fowley's and a staunch supporter of everything he did.

With an editorial remit that swung from the British Invasion to its European counterpart—American garage and early '70s sleaze; the Flaming Groovies and the punk explosion; power pop, Iggy Pop, girl groups and glam—*Who Put the Bomp* was produced for love, not money, in the days when such naivety was still considered an asset.

So when Fowley placed an ad in the fanzine seeking out female musicians to form a new band, he was targeting the kind of musical tastes that he wanted the band to epitomize. The sass of the Shangri-Las, the swagger of the Stooges, Janis Joplin's balls and Keith Richards's haircut, Robert Plant's sex appeal, and Suzi Quatro's energy. In short, he wanted a band that would sum up every dream rock 'n' roll had ever nurtured, and the fact that its members would be teenaged girls was simply the twist that stamped his imprimatur on it. Boys had been playing the game for too long.

That was why he would be so impressed by Joan Jett. Because she had the same vision playing in her head. Which meant there were two alternatives open to them. They could set up as rivals and work to beat the other to the winning post. Or they could pool their resources—Kim's connections and Jett's ambition, Fowley's determination and Jett's dedication, a man's understanding of why rock 'n' roll was such a tightly knit male preserve and a woman's demand to know why that should be the case.

Collectively, they could rewire the future of rock 'n' roll, and the most wonderful aspect of the whole affair was, they knew precisely how hyperbolic that sounded. Knew it and celebrated it. Because hyperbole, despite what so many grim-faced realists might grumble into the microphone, is what rock 'n' roll is really all about—the ability to take something that never existed before, be it a song or an image or simply a spark of an idea, and transform it into something so huge, so beautiful, and ultimately so fucking powerful that not a force on earth could resist it.

It might take time, but Rome was not built in a day. Neither was Hollywood. Nothing that is truly worthwhile ever was, which is why bands like the Velvet Underground and the Stooges, today regarded as among the most important and influential noises ever made with a guitar, could scarcely get arrested in their heyday—while a lot of the bands that did rule the roost back then merely sit in the history books and wonder why nobody ever cites them as a life-changing event.

Jett already knew about the Stooges, and the Velvet Underground as well. They were relatively recent discoveries, to be sure—the young ingénue tracking them down by tracing back through the influences that the other musicians she most enjoyed cited, which was nothing unusual. David Bowie, the biggest star in certain musical firmaments at the time, had been singing the two bands' praises since before he was even worth listening to, and now that he was having hits and an impact, he made damned sure that his record collection became everyone else's as well.

But Jett's tastes went beyond that. The first record she ever bought was Free's "All Right Now," a monster hit in 1970 and still one of the most swaggeringly defiant one-night stands you could dream of. The first major gig she attended was the three-band smash of Black Sabbath, the Blue Öyster Cult, and Black Oak Arkansas—an amphitheater-jamming, testosterone-pumping smorgasbord of Satanic riffery, militaristic leather, and Jim Dandy's manic washboard strumming. Her first musical crush was Marc Bolan, bopping out of the latest British pop convolution with a song that America insisted on titling "Bang a Gong" because its true title, "Get It On," was deemed too suggestive for delicate Stateside sensibilities.

So she was just one more suburban kid growing up listening to Alice Cooper insisting he was eighteen; Grand Funk declaring that they were an American band; and Led Zeppelin whooping, noodling, and generally freaking out halfway through the hit "Whole Lotta Love."

But unlike the majority of friends, most of whom were already firmly cemented in the social roles that young women took for granted at the time—get a boyfriend, get a husband, have some kids, and keep the house clean—Jett absorbed everything that she saw and heard around her, and knew that suburban housewifery would never be for her. Neither would any of the other options that were deemed conventional. One afternoon, Mrs. Larkin walked in on Joan and found her listening to the sound-effects passage that bisects the Zeppelin song. Loudly, she complained that whatever the girl was listening to, it wasn't music. Joan, equally loudly, disagreed. Music could be whatever you wanted it to be.

Including a terrific way of letting off steam. Jett had no real desire to learn a musical instrument at that time; she was already playing the clarinet at school, and that was sufficient. But alone in her room with the record player on full, she turned her hand to air guitar, and what did she know? That she wanted to play guitar? That she wanted to be a star? Or that she craved that excitement?

She caught the New York Dolls in DC and came away with one of her first rock 'n' roll souvenirs. "It was amazing," she told *Juice Magazine*. "I was in the front row, and I stole David Johansen's beer bottle."

It didn't matter to her that the next day at school, the other kids would simply shrug and ask, "The New York *whats?* David Jo-*who?*" She didn't like the Dolls either because they were popular (because they weren't) or even because they were good (which, very often, they weren't). She liked them because like Janis Joplin's balls and Keith Richards's haircut, Robert Plant's sex appeal and Suzi Quatro's energy, they epitomized what she wanted from rock 'n' roll. Which, in turn, epitomized what she wanted for herself.

"The main thing that attracted me about being in a band," she explained to *ZigZag*'s Mick Sinclair, "was seeing the lights and all the kids yelling and screaming and I thought 'God! You can make all those people happy at once.' It wasn't the money and limousines—I was very naive then." It was the thrill of being a thrill.

Unlike a lot of kids who are smitten by that ambition, however, Jett not only had the strength to believe that she could see it through, she also had parents who never tried to dissuade her. They might offer guidance, they might counsel caution. But if their children had their hearts set on achieving something, there was no point in standing in their way.

She told writer Jude Rogers, "I was told as a five-year-old, by my parents, that I could be anything I wanted and I took it to heart. I never thought twice about roles and like, 'oh, I'm a woman. I'm a girl so I can't do that.' I wanted to be an astronaut, an archaeologist, you know, all sorts of things before I got to school."

She wanted to be the first girl on the moon. She wanted to be the first female major-league baseball player. There was something about being the first at something, *anything*, that motivated her. It made her think, but more than that, it allowed her to live, to shrug away the shyness that was her normal suit of clothing and become something, or *someone*, else.

She got into chorus class and from there moved into drama. For a time, she dreamed of becoming an actress. And then, in the words of the Lou Reed song that she would one day be singing on stages across the world, "her life was changed by rock 'n' roll."

"You go from Donny Osmond to rock and roll," she recalled for writer Katey Rich in 2010.

> Listen to "All Right Now," "Smoke on the Water," oh my God, I want to make those sounds. This wasn't about rebelling against my family. My family and I get along great. It wasn't about rebelling against school. I love school. I was a great student. It was more about rebelling against what people tell you you can't do. I'm a good person. I'm not hurting anybody. I'm trying to make music.

She wouldn't be the first female rocker, she knew that. Grace Slick and Janis Joplin had long since beaten her to that punch. But the first *teenaged* female rocker? Why not?

"When I was eleven or twelve, I finally got the balls to say 'Mom, Dad, I want a guitar for Christmas and I don't want no *folk* guitar.' If my parents hadn't got me a guitar," she confided to journalist Mick Sinclair in 1985, "I probably would have run away."

Jett's first guitar arrived on schedule that Christmas. It was nothing fancy, a $40 Silvertone with a tiny, tinny amp, which they'd picked up from Sears. But it accompanied her everywhere, usually with a barrage of discordant twangs, yowls, and scramblings that were the first sounds any would-be guitarist learns to make.

In her room, she would try to play along with the records she loved . . . It was early 1974 by now, and the fifteen-year-old's tastes were driving through the oceans of glam. She listened to Marc Bolan and tried mimicking his voice—later, she would admit that it was T. Rex records that taught her how to scream. She played the Stooges and fell in love with the slobbering minimalism of a band that, the critics unanimously agreed, was barely more capable of playing its instruments than she was.

She spun Black Sabbath's *Paranoid* endlessly, trying to follow the slow, heavy chord progression that marks out "Iron Man," or Deep Purple's *Machine Head* and the anthemic "Smoke on the Water"—E–G–A. She nailed Free's "All Right Now." Anything that seemed slow and deliberate enough for her to wrap her fingers around the fret board and play.

Jett took guitar lessons and abandoned them after just one visit. She went to learn to play rock 'n' roll and came home with "On Top of Old Smokey" bruised into her fingertips. She bought a book instead and devoted hours to pressing her fingers into place to create one chord, then another . . . and then to slip between them effortlessly. E–G–pause–A–pause–pause . . .

When she wasn't playing or listening to music, she was reading about it. It was the heyday of the supercolor glossy rock magazine, *Circus* and *Creem* falling onto the newsstand shelves every month, with a stable of writers who created photographs from words, and photographers who made even the grayest dullard look impossibly colorful.

Creem, in particular, intrigued her. A little edgier in its language, a little bolder in its tastes, and locked away in Detroit where the best American music seemed to come from, *Creem* had its finger on the pulse of some of the greatest noises around at that time—the last living memories of the MC5 and the Stooges; Grand Funk; Ted Nugent; the rise of KISS; and from across the ocean, the best of the British glam pack as well. The crown prince of acerbic American rock critics, Lester Bangs, wrote for *Creem*; and so did Patti Smith, a New York poet who had yet to make a record but whose verse swung to the same riffs and rhythms as the greatest Stones song.

Plus, it was the only place where you could not only read about David Bowie's latest image shift but see it in day-glo effervescence too, and long after the rest of America stopped caring about T. Rex (which was about five minutes after "Bang a Gong" left the chart), *Creem* was loyally hanging onto Bolan's every pronouncement and filling its readership with the most important lesson that rock 'n' roll has to teach about itself. That at the end of the day, success is not what matters. It's the legacy that you leave—which, to raise that same hoary old ghost once again, is how the Velvet Underground could have been the most obscure group ever to walk this earth, but—as Brian Eno famously said—everyone who heard them went out and formed a band.

In America in 1974, you could have said much the same thing about Marc Bolan, and probably David Bowie as well. Bowie meant shockingly little back then, although he would soon be working to change that, by diving into disco music and having a #1 hit with the syncopated snottiness of "Fame." For now though, "Rebel Rebel" was the best shot he had, a killer riff stuck on auto-repeat, and for every radio programmer who passed it over as another slice of lumpen fag rock, there were a dozen kids who seized upon its triumphant strut of teenaged diffidence and proclaimed it the soundtrack of their lives.

Jett was one of them. "A fave of mine since the glitter days . . . and I've always loved Bowie," she reflected. Nine years later, with some downtime in the studio, she cut her own version of the song, and although it would be another two decades before she finally released it (on the rarities collection *Flashback*), still, "This was a song I almost felt compelled to do. Not to mention the killer riff!"

The problem was, you didn't get to hear much of "Rebel Rebel," or any other glam stomper, on the East Coast. In fact, you didn't get to hear much of it anywhere, but there was one place in America where every day was glam-rock day, and Jett discovered it too, in the pages of *Creem*.

It was called Rodney Bingenheimer's English Disco . . . and suddenly she was standing right outside it. In the summer of 1974, Joan's parents moved the family out to Los Angeles, two bus rides away from Sunset

Strip, but they were rides that she relished. By day, she was the outcast that the other kids in school in Brentwood threw stones at, dressed as she was in the clothes that she saw her idols wearing in the pages of *Creem*: platform boots, bell-bottom trousers, tube tops. By night, she was a part of the most exhilarating club in the city.

THREE

This Means War

Recalling her adolescence in LA for the local punk history *We Got the Neutron Bomb*, Joan spoke for an entire generation when she remarked, "A defining moment for any teen misfit is finding others like yourself. Even if the only thing you share is the feeling of not belonging anywhere else."

Chronologically, she may not have started introducing herself to people as Joan Jett just yet. But in her mind, she had already signed the deed, and moving among the people who shared her predilections, she knew she had found *her* musical home, even if the rest of the United States had never really taken to glam rock.

Born of the elfish Marc Bolan's emergence from a late '60s career of hippydom—effected by him plugging in his acoustic guitar, daubing on some makeup, and then bopping his balls off—glam ruled Britain, Europe, Japan, Australia . . . anywhere and everywhere, in fact, apart from the United States of Po-Faced Misery.

"It's too fey," whined the critics and the DJs. "Too gay, too gimmick-laden." Not for nothing did the high school jocks beat the crap out of anybody who suggested that Freddie Mercury's sexuality might have something to do with Queen being so named; not for nothing did the likes of Suzi Quatro, Alan Merrill, Sparks, the New York Dolls, Jobriath, and Brett Smiley—the United States' most authentic glam progenitors—look overseas for their biggest breaks. Merrill was a superstar in Japan and would soon conquer Britain as well, Suzi and Sparks in the UK; Jobriath claimed he'd played the Paris Opera House and had his face on the back of London buses; and the others . . . well, at least they tried.

The traffic in the other direction, however, was absolutely nothing to get excited about. It's true that the Sweet racked up a healthy string of American hits, and even developed a rabid following, but they did so with an image change that was a million miles removed from their European profile. At home, the Sweet dressed as Native Americans, gay Hitlers, and leatherboy stalkers, and all but literally bathed in makeup. In America, they were down 'n' dirty hard-rocking denim boys with a nice line in grinding riffery.

Marc Bolan and Gary Glitter scored a big hit a piece; David Bowie notched a handful more. But even Bowie's best friends noticed that the biggest of his records, 1969's folk-inflected "Space Oddity" and 1975's disco-themed "Fame," so neatly bookended his glam persona that he might as well never have released *Ziggy Stardust* and *Aladdin Sane*.

And if that was the fate of glam's international superstars, what about everyone else? Alvin Stardust, Mud, the Glitter Band, Hello—you could fill a fashion show with the bands that launched the spaceship glam into such glorious orbit, and the average or even unaverage American would not have recognized one of them.

But there were select enclaves of people who did care. The teenaged Joey Ramone, for instance. He devoured the UK music press as it dribbled three weeks late to New York, and every time he hit the city's record stores, he'd be searching for the latest records he read about in the papers, regardless of cost to either life or limb. One day he walked into a neighborhood record store and asked for a copy of Gary Glitter's first album. He was chased out of the shop by his fellow customers. "So when I heard about Rodney's, all I ever wanted to do was get out to Hollywood and see it for myself."

The young Stiv Bators:

> There was one record store in Cleveland that I used to go to, where they said they could get you anything you wanted, from anywhere in the world, so I was picking up all these records I read about in the *New Musical Express*—some of them were great, some of them were horrible, but I told everyone I liked the horrible ones as well because they were so different to anything being played in America.

And the teenaged Joan Jett. The day she discovered Rodney's was the day she discovered what rock 'n' roll was really all about. Energy, electricity, and excitement.

Rodney Bingenheimer has become enshrined in modern lore as the Mayor of Sunset Strip, but was—no less than Kim Fowley—a prime mover and shaker on the LA scene long before the cameras started rolling on the movie that confirmed that title.

A publicist with Mercury Records, Bingenheimer found himself in the thick of things at precisely the same time as glam was taking its first steps into the British consciousness; David Bowie was signed to Mercury at the time, and Bingenheimer hosted him on a promotional trip to LA in early 1971. Dig into the soundtrack of *The Mayor of Sunset Strip* and you will find a version of "All the Madmen," recorded by the future Zig at a party Rodney threw in his honor in February 1971.

A few months later, it was Bingenheimer who was playing tourist: visiting London as a guest of Bowie, listening to the radio as T. Rex and Slade commenced their dizzying rise to domestic fame, hanging together at the studio while Bowie recorded what would become his *Rise and Fall of Ziggy Stardust and the Spiders from Mars* album, and hitting the London club scene as an entire culture—or at least *couture*—sashayed out of the gay bars and into the mainstream. Boys dressed as girls, girls dressed as men, men dressed as their mothers.

A lot of so-called observers, usually people who either weren't there or whose heads were stuck so far up their own asses that they didn't want to see what was going on, look back at glam as one of those glibly manufactured musical movements that come along every few years, with no motive other than to shift a few units. In its prime and at its best, however, it was a cultural explosion as vivid and violent as any of those that it's hip to acknowledge . . . punk, grunge, whatever.

But it was one whose greatest work was done away from the spotlight, in those darkened British club corners and alleyways where lifestyle can find its feet before meeting its audience—a generation that grew up in the knowledge that homosexuality was no longer considered either a crime or an illness (it was "legalized" in Britain in 1967, even if you did still have to be twenty-one before you could actually sample it); one that was not only throwing off the mores and moralities that had shaped British culture all century, but was actually embracing the topics that polite company had hitherto ignored.

Nudity on the stage, blowjobs on the radio, transvestites in the headlines.

What was a poor boy from Los Angeles to make of it all?

Bingenheimer knew from the outset that whatever was happening on British shores could never be absorbed by America, that even something so simple and commonsense as gay rights was so busy arming itself for the oncoming political storms that nobody had the time or inclination to simply sit back and enjoy themselves. But there was more to it than that; there was also the knowledge that if society was changing, then music was changing even faster, stripping away the increasingly horse-faced peregrinations of the past five years of pretentious rock, and the porridge-like sludgery of its most egregious superstars, and getting back to the most brattish of basics.

At home, it was the age of Three Dog Night, Emerson Lake and Palmer, and Elton John. All of whom did what they did in fine, fine, form. But you couldn't dance to "Tarkus," and you couldn't fuck to "Tiny Dancer," even if popular legend did insist the song was about Elton's penis. T. Rex's "Hot Love" and "Get It On," on the other hand . . . Slade's "Get Down and Get with It" and "Coz I Luv You" and the new songs that he heard David Bowie recording—songs like "Suffragette City" and "Hang Onto Yourself," "Moonage Daydream," and "Sweet Head"—these were records that made you glad you were young, made you feel like a teenager.

In the words of another hit Bingenheimer heard during his time in London, they made you wanna leap up and down and wave your knickers in the air. And when he returned to Los Angeles in early 1972, something else that Bowie suggested to him was stuck in his brain.

Go home, open a club, and teach America what Britain is dancing to.

In October 1972, Bingenheimer and record producer Tom Ayres opened the E. (for English) Club on the site of an old peepshow theater on Sunset Boulevard. It was never intended as more than a short-lived toe in the water, but the club attracted an audience regardless. Bowie visited when he hit Los Angeles that month, and so did the touring Roxy Music, another of the bands who were riding the glam wave as it battered itself against American shores. There would be lines outside the building every night and a lot of disappointed kids being turned away when the place was full.

But Rodney wanted more. Hollywood wanted more. The E. Club was too small to really make its mark. Then, driving down the Strip one day, he spotted the Ooh Poo Pah Doo, a decent-sized club in search of new management. It became Rodney's English Disco, and its opening night was publicized by the belief that the Rolling Stones, in town to play the Forum, would be partying inside once their own show was over.

They weren't, of course. But the line of limos that the club's management placed outside the building was such a convincing ruse that the club actually ran out of alcohol, hours before closing time.

Kim Fowley, watching the action from his own sainted seat among the Gods of the Hollywood vanguard, noticed the difference between the two venues immediately. Recalling the English Disco in his *Vampire from Outer Space* autobiography, Fowley described it as "more a public-toilet version of the E. Club. The new location gave it the teenage stench it needed."

Back in the 1940s, Sunset Strip was riddled with hookers and hustlers, a fact that Fowley insisted was ideal for this new venture.

> The English Disco was exactly the same kind of decadence you'd had thirty years earlier, and in exactly the same neighborhood. You had guys saying, "I think this is a good place to get my cock sucked," not realizing that about a thousand cocks had been sucked there twenty or thirty years before, and for the same ridiculous reasons.

People dressed up to visit the Disco, even if dressing up actually meant wearing as little as possible. Girls and boys alike would spend hours getting their makeup right, even though they knew that it would be wrecked by sweat before the evening was out. And the younger the kids, the more effort they put into looking good. It was Fowley who rechristened the Disco's underage clientele Gas Chamber Nancys, for the legal nicety that declared that you could be given the death sentence if you had sex with a thirteen-year-old.

But the law did not deter too many folk.

"It was a great playpen for nymphets and older men. Everybody got fucked and sucked. There were great young bodies twisting and sweating in the half-light. People worked at it. It was like a red-light district in one club." One day, he laughed, somebody was murdered right outside the club. A girl he knew was walking past at the time, and she could hear Suzi Quatro's "Devil Gate Drive" playing inside. Fowley laughed. "She said to herself, 'This is rock and roll!'"

She was Joan Jett.

The Disco oozed style. The long, hand-carved wooden bar had, apparently, been imported to Los Angeles by a previous owner, and it dominated the room. Mirrors hung on every surface, even inside the DJ booth. Bright red carpeting gave it the feel of a down-market bordello. The audience did the rest, setting up a solid wall of glitter that kept Rodney's roaring for close to three years—years during which it made an indelible impact upon everyone who visited.

To an older generation then, the English Disco fell somewhere between a lost chapter from *Lord of the Flies* and Babylon, if it had been built by Lolita. To its regulars, it was something even more decadent than that. It was *Cabaret.*

Cabaret was Hollywood's interpretation—via Liza Minnelli and Joel Grey—of author Christopher Isherwood's memories of pre–National Socialist Berlin. But it was like nothing else Hollywood had produced in years, exquisitely erotic and subterranean sordid. It was also the hot-shit movie that season, a Technicolor rendering of the monochromatic decadence, darkness, and irrational hopefulness that tints both the movie and the original novella.

In the UK, where Isherwood was something of a national (if admittedly guilty) treasure, *Cabaret* had already rounded up its own merry band of admirers—the young and just pre–*Ziggy Stardust* David Bowie was so entranced by the original stage show that he borrowed its lighting effects for his own performance, then applied the same sense of decadent, dirty glam that enraptured Jett to his persona.

Join the dots between the music and the movie, and somewhere in the middle, something sprang out of that delicious triangle that linked the low-level cabaret singer Sally Bowles, the sexually ambiguous courtier Christopher, and the militaristic interloper Max, and drove straight into the libido of a generation.

There was something that was never spoken out loud, because it did not need to be. It was the mood of the film, the sense of life being lived on a blade of vicarious thrill seeking—damn tomorrow and live and fuck

and drink for today—that caught the imagination. It was the glamour
of the performers, the makeup and the glitter, and the undercurrent of
ambiguous sexuality that ran through the entire movie until it reached
its own dénouement, somewhere ahead of the film's actual conclusion.
The moment when an exasperated Sally confesses to Christopher that
she had fucked Max, and Christopher quietly replies, "So did I." The
secret was out of the woodshed, and every kid on the dance floor was in
on it. Thirty-plus years later, Joan Jett was asked what her all-time favorite movie was. She answered without a second thought. "*Cabaret.*"

No matter that the older kids at school echoed the critics by putting
down glam, telling its adherents that it was bubblegum at best and that
even in the UK, artists like Barry Blue and Alvin Stardust were regarded
as teenybop fodder. The music that they made, and that was spun across
the floor at Rodney's, was like nothing anyone had heard before. Echoing
Brian Eno's pronouncement on the Velvet Underground, Jett recalled, "It
hit only about a couple of hundred people in LA."

But it hit them hard.

"You'd get all these eleven- to thirteen-year-olds in the club, dancing
and being groupies. There were eleven-year-old girls in silver lamé mini-
skirts, dancing around, and all the rock stars—Barry Blue types—would
come in and get all these fifteen-year-olds. It was insane!"

And the madness continued exploding. When *Newsweek* magazine
descended on the place in January 1974, it noted incredulously,

> The dance floor is a dizzy kaleidoscope of lamé hot pants, sequined
> halters, rhinestone-studded cheeks, thrift-store anythings, and see-
> through everythings. During the breaks, fourteen-year-old girls on
> six-inch platforms teeter into the back bathrooms to grope with their
> partners of the moment. Most of the sex is as mixed as the drinks and
> the drugs the kids bring with them.

Such reportage was probably an exaggeration at best, hype at worst.
But in case it wasn't, in case Rodney's really was a depraved den of
underage sex and drunks and liquor, it was also the age of the foolproof
false ID.

LA drinking laws were no less ferocious than they are today, but if
you evicted all the underage kids from a night at Rodney's, you'd probably

have been left with an audience of one—Rodney himself. Remove the virgins from the room, on the other hand, and it was said that you'd barely notice the difference, because even if a first-time visitor was untouched by human hands when he or she entered, one trip to the bathroom would probably be the end of that.

David Bowie and his entourage, itself a spangled army of freaks and weirdoes, loved the place. "The crowd at the club ranged in age from twelve to fifteen," recalled Tony Zanetta, vice president of Bowie's management company MainMan.

> Nymphet groupies were stars in their tight little world. Some dressed like Shirley Temple; others wore dominatrix outfits or "Hollywood underwear," a knee-length shirt, nylon stockings, and garter belts. These star girls streaked their hair chartreuse and liked to lift their skirts to display their bare crotches. As they danced they mimed fellatio and cunnilingus in tribute to David's onstage act of fellatio on [Mick Ronson]'s guitar.

Some, apparently, didn't bother miming it.

A lot of these tales have been conflated by time, memory, and the natural human instinct for making something out of . . . well, not *nothing*, but certainly something a lot smaller. For most of the kids who went there, Rodney's was just a place to hang out with friends, maybe sneak an underage drink or two, or maybe not.

Theresa K., the Hollywood photographer who did as much as anyone to preserve the looming LA punk scene for immortality, was not alone among the people who stood around, convinced that their companions were downing whisky after whisky, only to sneak a taste at some point in the evening and discover that it was merely ginger ale. "There was a lot of mythmaking, even at the time," she explained. And since then, the myths have become the legend.

Not every dick got sucked, not every teen got wasted, and not every cherry got popped. But the potential was always there, simmering just beneath the surface, and the higher up Rodney's self-anointed teenaged hierarchy one climbed, above the kids from the 'burbs who were just passing through, above the regulars who simply went there to dance, above the wannabe groupies who scanned the guestlist every night, there was a hardcore clientele for whom Rodney's was everything the papers cracked it up to be, and for whom a drop of printer's ink was just one more dollop of justification for the following weekend's debaucheries.

In late 1973, the *LA Times*' Richard Cromelin discovered,

> Once inside, everybody's a star. The social rules are simple but rigid: All you want to hear is how fabulous you look, so you tell them how fabulous they look. You talk about how bored you are, coming here night after night, but that there's no place else to go. If you're not jaded there's something wrong. It's good to come in very messed up on some kind of pills every once in a while, and weekend nights usually see at least one elaborate, tearful fight or breakdown. If you're eighteen you're over the hill.

Unless you are a star. Iggy and the Stooges were living just a short way away in the Hollywood Hills, and the English Disco became their home away from home. British bands visiting the city on tour made it their first port of call. American groups, some of which had never stepped out of denim in their lives, would look in, clock how out of place they seemed, and then run to the store to glam themselves up before venturing back to Rodney's. Outside of Los Angeles—damn it, outside of the Strip—glam rock meant nothing. Enter Rodney's, however, and it was the entire universe.

"It was a place where the kids could go and you could do anything and it was really fun," Jett told the *NME*'s Chris Salewicz.

> You know, they never played that kind of music in America. It was the only place you could hear it. It was the only place you could hear all the Sweet, all the Mud, Alvin Stardust, Suzi Quatro, Gary Glitter, I mean, man, that was the only place you could hear that stuff. Even though everyone really liked it. Alvin Stardust, "My Coo Ca Choo." Wow!

And as for Suzi; talking with journalist Sandy Robertson, the Runaways' number-one UK cheerleader, Joan admitted, "She's my idol. When I first heard her in '74 I thought, 'GODDAMN! A girl playing rock 'n' roll!' Then when I went to see her I couldn't believe it!"

FOUR

California Paradise

A naturalized Canadian born in Italy, Floria Sigismondi knew she wanted to make a movie about the Runaways for as long as she knew she wanted to make movies. As one of the hottest young video directors of the 1990s, casting a vivid eye over new releases by the Tea Party, Our Lady Peace, and Harem Scarem—bands that didn't exactly make a major impact even in their prime, but who carved a niche regardless—Sigismondi finally pushed into the mainstream eye when she helmed Marilyn Manson's "Beautiful People" video in 1996. She was promptly recruited to direct David Bowie's "Little Wonder" later that same year, and when both were nominated for major video rewards, she knew she had arrived. At least in that world.

The idea for the movie, though . . . the movie wouldn't go away. It just took her a decade to make it.

The Runaways started life as a low-budget biopic, a director following her dream as opposed to the scent of box-office bucks. Of course Sigismondi wanted it to do well, but she was also well aware that there had already been one film made about the band, ex-Runaway Victoria "Vicki Blue" Tischler-Blue's *Edgeplay* documentary, and brilliant as it was, it had not sent the world scrambling for theatre tickets. And if the real thing couldn't do it—*Edgeplay* was a documentary, with four of the original band's five members on board—why should a fictionalized rendering of the same tale be any more successful?

So no, there were no high ambitions, no dreams of queues stretching around the block, and not much interest from the media either. And then Kristen Stewart signed on to play the one band member who had sat *Edgeplay* out—the one band member, too, who had ascended to the levels of stardom that Kim Fowley always said the Runaways were designed for—and suddenly, Sigismondi's little movie was not little any longer.

Stewart was box-office bounty already. Still in her teens, she set forth in the first of the *Twilight* franchise of vampire movies, so beloved of an entire generation of sweet-assed Emos who want to play bitey-neck, and when Dakota Fanning—who starred alongside her in the second of that series, *Twilight: New Moon*—came on board as well, *The Runaways'* success was confirmed before a minute of footage had been shot. And watching as the filming itself unfurled, from the framework that Fanning's character, singer Cherie Currie, had mapped out in her *Neon Angel* autobiography, you couldn't help but ask yourself why nobody had made this movie already.

Because it was pure Hollywood. Just like Kim Fowley always said it was.

It was the kids whom Kim Fowley saw nightly at Rodney's English Disco who inspired him to look away from the traditional hunting grounds of out-of-work musicians and struggling wannabes, who inspired him too to wonder why almost every worthwhile rock band of the age was predominantly male.

Almost. There was Fanny, an all-girl band that had been knocking around since the dawn of the decade, and which had chipped a degree of begrudging respect off the critical monolith with a sequence of reasonable albums and excellent live shows. There was the handful of women-fronted, male rock 'n' roll bands that carved a reasonable swathe, too, through the jungle—the late Janis Joplin, the young Grace Slick, the sensational Sonja Kristina, the stunning Jenny Haan.

But if you wanted to go beyond that, and still avoid the candy-coated sirens who sat and sang about love and loss while the balladeers queued up to hand them fresh material, Suzi Quatro was the only other rocker worth thinking about.

Born and bred in Detroit Rock City, Quatro was already leading her own band when she was snapped up by English producer Mickie Most and transported to London at the dawn of the 1970s. Paired up with songwriters Nicky Chinn and Mike Chapman, who had already guaranteed bands like the Sweet, Mud, and New World a series of solid British hit singles, Quatro was now just a handful of hits into a career that is still going strong nearly four decades later; and although she meant little in America in 1974, to the kids who did understand her, she was the hottest chick around.

"Everyone loves young cunt, even girls," Fowley wrote in 2000. "There was a lot of female action going on in 1974: female boxers, assassination attempts on Gerald Ford by Squeaky Fromme and Sarajane [sic] Moore." You could add the *Creem*-scribing Patti Smith to that equation, and the even faster-rising Patty Hearst—the heiress to the vast Hearst media empire was kidnapped that spring by the Symbionese Liberation Army. Hearst was held for ransom and then sided with her captors, joining their organization and posing for what remains one of the iconic posters of the age, the archetypal girl next door, glowering with a machine gun beneath the SLA's hydra banner. Yeah, a lot of female action. Fowley decided to hunt out some of his own.

Suzi Quatro was in Los Angeles in March 1974 to play the Roxy, staying at the Hyatt House while she was in town, and you could spot her impact the moment you walked into Rodney's. "Devilgate Drive," her fourth hit single, had just become her second #1 in the UK; and her debut album, *Suzi Quatro*, was about to be released in America.

The English Disco was hosting the record-release party, and the crush of kids that normally hit the floor was only amplified by Quatro's presence. Looking around the room, Fowley's eye must have fallen on Jett, although maybe it didn't—she wasn't the only girl in the room who had borrowed Quatro's leather and feather-cut-hair look, after all.

But she'd also been first in line outside the Roxy when the tickets for the show went on sale; and if you passed through the lobby of the Hyatt House, you'd have spotted her there as well, just sitting quietly and maybe even shyly, her hair dyed blonde and her eyes focused on the elevators. When Quatro walked through the lobby, Jett didn't even move. She just watched. And maybe dreamed.

"And then I saw her after that, at just about every show, in every lobby in every hotel," Quatro laughed.

"I wanted to be a rock star, not to be chasing rock stars for autographs or waiting around hotel lobbies for them," Jett told writers Brendan Muller and Marc Spitz. Maybe, as Rodney Bingenheimer later laughed, Jett did steal a big Suzi Quatro poster off the Disco wall. But for Jett, seeing Quatro—absorbing her style, her demeanor, her attitude—that was enough.

Besides, there were certainly a lot worse role models to be had. The first time Britain saw Suzi Quatro, she was already on television's *Top of the Pops*, five foot nothing of leather-soaked dynamite, stomping through "Can the Can" the very same weekend David Bowie was launching his latest (last) British tour, and the contradiction screamed out at everyone. "The guys in my band don't wear glitter," she snarled. "They're REAL men." It didn't take an Einstein to figure out what that made everyone else.

Quatro gripped the imagination immediately. "If You Knew Suzi Like the Tattooist Knows Suzi" was a typical music press headline, and any fears that Chinn and Chapman would not be able to deliver a song that matched Quatro's mood were vanquished on the spot.

"They saw the aggression in Suzi," Mickie Most said of Nicky Chinn and Mike Chapman's first song for the singer, while Chapman added, "It was a classic example of a record creating an artist, because 'Can the Can' certainly created Suzi. It made her a superstar everywhere in the world except America."

The basic premise of "Can the Can," and the follow-up efforts, "48 Crash," "Daytona Demon," and "Devilgate Drive," was to project Suzi as a leather-clad maneater, a role model for the girls rather than the boys. "You don't have to lie back and think of England," was the message. "But he might want to."

"Put your man in a can, honey, get him while you can," she roared in "Can the Can," and later, in "Daytona Demon," "He's a souped-up, heavy-hung, he-man." It didn't even matter that the songs were written by a pair of guys—in so effectively and unsubtly dehumanizing the male of the species, Quatro completely reversed the traditional sex-object roles. Men were nothing more than superstuds, and in an age when sexual liberation was supposedly at the forefront of everybody's mind, she steamrollered all opposition.

Fowley had already placed his own wheels in motion by the time Quatro hit town, although he was adamant that while he was well aware that the rock scene of the 1970s was crying out for somebody to follow Quatro (and indeed, Fanny)'s lead, he had no interest in playing a part in its creation. Originally he declared, "I dreaded manufacturing the ultimate female group because I always thought that the ultimate female group would manufacture themselves." He would then recognize it, he said, "and jump in there."

But time was passing. 1974 had already slipped through the hourglass, and nothing was happening. So he decided to make it happen. One night at the English Disco, Rodney Bingenheimer introduced him to Kari Krome, a fourteen-year-old who described herself as the Bernie Taupin of Heavy Metal. Taupin was Elton John's songwriting partner, the man who came up with the words that John made his own, and Fowley wasn't certain what impressed him the most: the sheer chutzpah of the girl or the possibilities that her claims laid open.

They met again at the Hollywood Palladium in February 1975, when Alice Cooper took it over for his twenty-seventh birthday party. Fowley had cowritten one song, "Escape," on Cooper's upcoming *Welcome to My Nightmare* album, but it was Krome, not Cooper, who fascinated him now, because she segued so beautifully into his own imaginings.

So he spoke of his dreams, and now it was Krome's turn to jump. Fowley became her music publisher and occasional cowriter, but he also became her mentor. Especially after Krome ran into Jett a short time afterwards and, she reported back to Fowley, overheard her too, talking about forming an all-girl rock band.

Joan already knew that Krome was a songwriter but thought she was also a musician. She suggested they form an all-girl band together, but Krome shook her head. No, she just wrote. But if Jett was serious about the band, she should speak with Kim Fowley.

An introduction quickly followed. "When I met Joan she was chewing licorice peanuts wearing a black leather jacket," Fowley laughed later. He asked her for a demo tape and when she said she didn't have one, he suggested she call him and play something on the phone. She rang the next day and "auditioned for me over the phone playing a ukulele to a Sweet record."

A few days later, Fowley hooked her up with a drummer.

Sandy Pesavento was born in Long Beach on July 10, 1959. She'd been playing drums since she was nine—before that, even—but that was when her grandfather bought her her first kit, and she'd spent the past six years becoming, as she put it, "a great drummer." She met Fowley in the parking lot outside the Rainbow Bar and Grill, a restaurant renowned as one of the Strip's hippest hangouts; she and a friend were on their way home when they saw "this guy in this weird orange suit. My girlfriend said 'that's Kim Fowley, he's made records with Alice Cooper,' so I walked up to him and said 'my name's Sandy West [an easier name for strangers to remember] and I'm a drummer.' And his eyes lit up."

Fowley took her number and, the following day, called to give her Jett's. "I'd been playing with guys all my life," West recalled, and she admitted to being surprised when Fowley first mentioned Jett. "A chick that can play guitar? I wonder how good she is?"

But she called, and because it was easier for Jett to carry a guitar to Huntington Beach than it was for West to drag her drums to Canoga Park, they arranged to meet up at Sandy's place. Plus, the Wests had indulged their daughter's passion to the limits—above the family's three-car garage an entire practice space had been set up, with a drum kit, a piano, and a Marshall amp. Kim Fowley was there as well; he arrived with Sue Thomas, another potential band member, and the first thing he had them sing was 10cc's "I'm Not in Love." Not the greatest measure of a female rock 'n' roller, but it was a start.

"I didn't know whether to throw him out or laugh at him," West's mother recalled of her first glimpse of Fowley. "When I look back, I should have tied her to the bed and said 'you can't do this.'"

It took Jett four hours to get from her home to Sandy's, lugging her $39.95 Sears guitar across three bus rides; she finally arrived, "real quiet, real meek, a little Suzi Quatro hairdo," and West was burning to begin. "Here's a fucking Marshall stack. What do you know how to play?"

"The only thing I know is Suzi Quatro. That's how I learned to play guitar."

"Well, that's cool."

West counted in, they kicked into some Quatro, and immediately all of the drummer's doubts fled. And when she turned to Fowley, she was still rabid. "This is so right on the money. This girl's got perfect timing." Fowley's eyes, she recalled, "just exploded out of his head." If there were *two* fifteen-year-old girls who could play so well together, then there had to be more.

"I got Joan and Sandy to play over the phone for a journalist called Ritchie Yorke," Fowley recalled. "I thought, if I can fool him into thinking this was [a real] band on the other end of the line, I'll go with the project. So Ritchie listens on the phone and says, 'sounds like rock 'n' roll to me.' I put the phone down and said, 'Congratulations, girls, we fooled the press. You're now a band.'"

He christened them the Runaways. It seemed to fit.

Over the next few months, Jett made the journey to Huntington Beach every weekend, jamming with West and Sue Thomas and trying their hand at writing songs. Then, as they grew more proficient, it would be Fowley who would host their sessions, at his apartment at first but further afield too. One of Fowley's friends, Ron Asheton of the Stooges, knew of a rehearsal space out in the Valley that belonged to an orchestral conductor at the NBC Studios. Taking it over, Fowley advertised as far and wide as he felt was appropriate, then sat back and watched as Jett, West, and Thomas ran everyone who answered the ad through their paces.

Ron Asheton dropped by as often as he could, not out of interest in the music, "but because it was so funny. You could tell Joan and Sandy were serious, but everybody else was a joke. I really didn't think it would take off, but you couldn't tell Kim that, so I didn't." Instead, he just gathered up a ringside seat for what, even if it turned out to be nothing else, was "the best parade of jailbait you could hope to find."

The band was not only learning to play together. They were also learning to write, elemental efforts to begin with, but as arrangements came together, much of the eventual band's repertoire had already slipped into place.

Jett's "You Drive Me Wild," the first song she ever wrote, in her bedroom at her parents' house, was an early arrival in the repertoire; so were Kari Krome's "Secrets" and a couple of Fowley/Jett cowrites, "Lovers" and "Blackmail." Fowley's own "Is It Day or Night" and covers of the Velvet

Underground's "Rock and Roll" and the Troggs' "Wild Thing"—Sandy West's vocal *piece de resistance*—rounded out the Runaways' repertoire with so much panache that almost all would survive onto the band's debut album.

Krome's "Yesterday's Kids," Fowley's "Let's Party Tonight"; the full band joined pens with Fowley to create "California Paradise"; Fowley, West, and Thomas came up with "Born to Be Bad"; Jett brought Free's "All Right Now" into contention.

Fowley introduced a new component to the team: Mark Anthony was a member of the Hollywood Stars, a band Fowley had tried to launch the previous year as the West Coast's answer to the New York Dolls. He wrote "Thunder" with Krome and "American Nights" with Fowley, and the band had a live set.

It was time, Fowley told Goldmine's Harvey Kubernik, to road-test the trio. "I bought Joan a guitar to replace her $39.95 special from Sears. Sandy had a drum kit and [Sue got] a bass from a girl from Cleveland who left it behind. I took the girls to Cherokee Studio to see how tape works." There, they had time to record five songs, kicking things off with a sensationally self-assured version of "Rock and Roll," moving on through a sensuously slow "Secrets" and the smart-ass "Yesterday's Kids" onto the swaggering "You Drive Me Wild," then wrapping up with "Thunder." And already, the band sounded a far cry indeed from the first tape he made of them, a casual mike-in-the-corner during one of their earlier rehearsals.

A few weeks later, Fowley arranged for the Runaways to host a series of open rehearsals at a room on the corner of Santa Monica and San Vincente.

Any number of would-be hopefuls drifted through both the auditions and the band. Fowley recalled "a black girl in pigtails" who lasted about a week; West remembered "this stupid girl" named Peggy Foster who was in for about a minute. But before they could expand the Runaways' membership, it first had to contract. Fowley set up another gig, this time in journalist Phast Phreddie's living room in Torrance, where they discovered, said West, that Sue Thomas suffered from appalling stage fright. She quit, but suddenly it didn't seem to matter. Phast Phreddie had heard a hot female bassist playing at a keg party in Long Beach. He passed along her name: Lita Ford. (Thomas later resurfaced, *sans* stage fright, as the Bangles' Mickie Steele.)

Sandy West recalled,

> Suddenly Lita comes up, auditions for bass. But when [the rest of the band] took a break, it was just me and her in the room, and we were talkin'. I said, "well, I been playing in live bands since I was thirteen, playing Led Zeppelin, Black Sabbath." Lita goes, "That's where I come from, that's my background." She had brought her guitar up and she played great—Black Sabbath songs note for note. We jammed, and when the rest of the band came back from break I went, "This girl's gotta be hired as lead guitarist. She's absolutely amazing."

Ford continued, "Sandy and I hit it right off, we were both listening to Deep Purple, so I went in and rattled off the guitar solo to 'Highway Star' and Sandy already knew all the drum parts. By the end of the song it was automatic bonding, and Joan stood there going 'uurgh this is great! Cool!'"

That left the bass slot still open, but not for long. One day Rodney Bingenheimer called with the news that he had discovered a new star in the parking lot of the Starwood. Her name was Jackie Fuchs.

Better known today as Jackie Fox, this latest discovery explained,

> I was dancing at the Starwood one night and Rodney was walking up to every girl there saying "Do you play an instrument?" and I said "Yeah, I play guitar," and he said "How old are you?" and I got real cocky and I said fifteen, and Rodney almost wet himself then and there. He said "Oh, oh, you've got to come with me right now to see Kim Fowley." We walked in, [and] there was this tall freak with this disaster of an apartment and a very overwhelming presence, and Rodney said "This is going to be your new [bass] guitarist."

She recalled her first rehearsal with the Runaways. The only song they all knew was Kiss's "Stutter," and they got through it well enough. "But I hated them, they hated me, and that was it. I did not get into the band."

Fowley, however, didn't seem to care. He was bored of looking for a bass player and was searching for a vocalist instead. In early December 1975, he found one.

FIVE

Cherry Bomb

Cherie Currie was another of Rodney's regulars whom everybody seemed to have noticed at one point or another, and with good reason. Born in Encino on November 30, 1959, Currie and her sister Marie used Rodney's as an excuse for going crazy. Cherie told her autobiography:

> Marie likes Bowie, but she doesn't go all out—not as much as I do. I'm dressed up as wild as can be—I've practiced at Rodney's. I am a glitter queen: satin pants, silver five-inch-high space boots, a glitter T-shirt, and make-up so bright it looks like I'm radioactive. When I'm done I admire myself in the cracked bathroom mirror. I look like an alien princess from a faraway planet. For a while—for tonight—I am no longer Cherie Currie, the sweet little Valley Girl. I am the Cherie-thing: something weird and something wild.

It was that something weird and something wild that appealed to Fowley, Currie explained. She'd heard about the Runaways through the club grapevine, how Fowley had taken three girls off the dance floor and was now whipping them into the shape of a rock 'n' roll band. Seven months had passed since Joan Jett and Sandy West rehearsed together for the first time, and word had got out that the group wasn't bad. All things considered, of course.

Still, even when Currie saw Fowley and Joan Jett bearing down on her as she sat at the bar of the Sugar Shack, sipping Coke with her sister Marie, she had no idea of what they could possibly want.

In fact, they were doing what they always seemed to be doing these days—zeroing in on any attractive girl they saw in a club and asking her if she could sing. "They went to my twin sister first and asked her if she could sing or play an instrument. My sister basically said, 'Fuck off.' Then they came up to me. I said, 'Yeah, I can sing.' Then I auditioned and it was on."

Although it very nearly wasn't. Told that she would be auditioning with a song from Suzi Quatro's *Your Mother Won't Like Me* album, but that she could pick which one, Currie spent the next few days making certain that she knew every last second of her favorite track on the record, "Fever."

"I was terrified, I sang 'Fever' until it was coming out of my ass. So Joan walks up to me [at the rehearsal space] and asks what song . . . I said 'Fever' and she turned to the others and said 'Fever'? She picked 'Fever?'" It was the only song the others had *not* rehearsed.

The audition could have ended there. But they'd already agreed amongst themselves that Currie was the best contender they'd seen so far, and they weren't going to let her slip through their fingers. Jett and Kim Fowley went off together; twenty minutes later, they were back with a new song. "Here, you can sing this instead."

"They wrote 'Cherry Bomb' in twenty minutes," an astonished Currie told *Juice* magazine.

> Done. Joan sings it to me while Kim shows Lita and Sandy the song. We did the song and then they all walked out of the room. They were gone for like fifteen minutes. I was sweating bullets, thinking there was no way I would get into this band. When they walked back in, Joan walks up to me and says, "Welcome to the Runaways!" It was the happiest day of my childhood.

The lineup was completed by Jackie Fox, the guitarist who failed the audition a few months earlier. Fowley had not forgotten her. "Jackie was the girl next door I needed . . . to balance out big-titted Lita, tomboy Joan [and] surf girl Sandy . . . It meant that guys who'd be afraid of these she-creatures could get that stewardess/nurse thing going." She was installed on bass guitar. "I went down there and learned about ten songs in half an hour, Kim went around and said do you want her in the band, Joan and Sandy said yes, Lita said no."

It was Cherie who talked Ford around. Like her bandmates, she was impatient simply to get the group up and running. Besides, "I didn't really give a damn who we got [and] she turned out to be a real gem to add to the Runaways, [because] she had a quality about her that was very different. She was into the Fredericks of Hollywood garb that she wore all the time, the guys went crazy for that."

The lineup was complete. Now it was time to begin grooming it. Fox towered over her bandmates, heightwise; Fowley decreed that the other four should wear heels, "so you'll all be the same height." He set the stage for West and Fox to battle over the leadership of the band, creating a tension that the other pair could bounce off.

"Joan was Suzi Quatro," Jackie Fox recalled. "Lita was Ritchie Blackmore. I don't know who Sandy was, probably a member of Queen." Cherie, of course, was David Bowie, "and I thought I was Gene Simmons."

What they didn't expect was how brutally those disparate components would be bound together.

Fowley's time in the military had taught him a lot—including the importance of discipline, obedience, and hard, hard work. He never dressed the part, of course, but if ever a man had absorbed everything he could from the drill sergeants who had pounded him into shape during his soldiering years, it was Fowley. And now it was the Runaways' turn to experience everything that he had gone through.

Instructed to report for duty daily, in the stinking trailer that was their new rehearsal studio, Jackie Fox shuddered, "We'd walk in and he'd be waiting for us. He'd throw a mike stand at us and say 'Come on dog cunts, play this shit.'" Or else he'd watch them struggling through a not-quite-there song, and announce that nobody was leaving the room until they had it down perfectly. "Staying up all night eating pussy, chewing Quaaludes, and listening to the New York Dolls and the Stooges with each other is fine. But not until you get this fucking song down. All right?" And then he'd count them in: "Okay, Dog shit! One two three . . ."

Choreography and a stage show were delegated to Kenny Ortega, a dance instructor who, in his midtwenties, was still a decade away from the work with Tubes, Cher, and Michael Jackson that would bring him eventual fame. Fowley's brutal heckler's drill, meanwhile, pounded every conceivable eventuality into the girls' heads, from raucous audiences with boners for brains to violent mobs intent on tearing the band limb from limb. Instructing the quintet to play through their repertoire, Fowley would then bombard them with insults, bottles, trashcans, and anything else that came to hand. Because one day, he warned them, it would happen for real, and they needed to know how to deal with it.

Sandy West and Lita Ford had both played in public before; they thought they knew the ropes. So did Jett, riding the rock 'n' roll fantasies that she'd been playing out in her mind for the past five years. They knew jackshit, Fowley told them. They wouldn't be playing for their friends anymore, or strutting their stuff before an already-adoring public. They needed to work to find those friends, and work even harder to find that public. And that meant going to play in places where the only thing that the audience—the predominantly male audience—would see would be five pretty girls on stage, at a time when that meant just one of two things. Either they were strippers or they were sluts. Or possibly both. As Fowley saw it, it was his job to teach them how to deal with those perceptions.

Everybody in the room, everyone who has heard the stories, everyone who has seen them reenacted in either *Edgeplay* or *The Runaways* agrees—you couldn't get away with treating anybody like that today. No matter what your motives were, or your intentions, or anything else. Fowley was abusive, he was foul, he was violent. But he was also correct, because that *was* how audiences would see the band, and it *was* how they would respond.

They became versed in the peculiar street slang that Fowley created, for their benefit and for that of the wider language. Half of the street slang in Hollywood, it is said, initially sprang from Fowley's fertile vocabulary—the habitual losers whom he rechristened "failure cocks," or "urine-stained failure cocks" if they deemed them to be especially doomed. He coined "pig stink" for the bullshit that he was sick of hearing, and "doing the death dance" for his own chosen vocation of taking chances whenever he could. He was doing the death dance with the Runaways, doing the dog to make it work, and if the dog meat didn't like it, then they were failure cocks too.

"He was just trying to get a charge out of us," Ford recalled, "make us show some emotion." But sometimes he went too far. "Well, I showed so much emotion that I packed up and left."

It took a frantic call from the remainder of the band to lure her back into the pack, and the reminder that they suffered just as horrifically at

Fowley's mouth as she did. They all just needed to deal with it. "You can't be great onstage unless you learn the fundamentals of rock 'n' roll boot-camp savagery," Fowley excused himself. "So that's what we did."

The Runaways were complete. And once Currie picked up her first corset from the lingerie store across the road from the Starwood, on the afternoon of their first show there, even Fowley sat back in surprise, astonished at just how quickly his scheme had come together.

Wearing that outfit, he told Currie as she modeled her purchase for the first time, "you won't just sing 'Cherry Bomb.' You will *be* the cherry bomb." And she slipped into the role so beautifully that the first time Fowley met her parents, he had them believing what he had already convinced himself of. That she was the next David Bowie.

Well, it worked for *The Rocky Horror Picture Show*.

On June 19, 1973, in a tiny sixty-three seat theater in London, a new musical opened that was to revolutionize theater for the rock 'n' roll age.

Not that that was much of a challenge. Sickly throughout the 1950s and '60s, when theater's only concessions to the energies of rock revolved around slapping a handful of ballads into any passing stage show, the infant genre's finest hours so far had been of a distinctly religious bent—*Jesus Christ Superstar, Godspell, Joseph and the Amazing Technicolor Dreamcoat*. There was the hippy love-in *Hair*, of course, but anybody looking back at the Who's "rock opera" *Tommy* and comparing the messianic subtext of that creation with the bulk of the new arrivals would have been justified for believing that rock 'n' roll had finally started to believe its own press. It was the new religion.

And then *The Rocky Horror Show* came along—with its cast of corset-clad transvestite aliens, Frankenstinian musclemen, innocent college kids, a squealing groupie, and a fabulous array of punch-above-their-weight rock 'n' roll songs—and it altered the landscape forever. Within a week of opening, *The Rocky Horror Show* had been signed up for a full-cast album, after record producer Jonathan King caught the second-night show and grabbed the rights on the spot; within a month, demand for seats every night had so outgrown the Royal Court's Theatre Upstairs that it was transferred to the Classic Cinema, on the King's Road. By the end of the year, it was selling out the three-hundred-fifty-seat King's Road Theatre. It would remain there until 1979.

Not bad for a cult play that was originally titled *They Came from Denton High*, and was the brainchild of an actor who was essentially forced out of the London production of *Jesus Christ Superstar* when he suggested that King Herod be played as Elvis Presley. The producers, on the other hand, wanted him to tapdance. Neither party would budge, and Richard O'Brien quit the play after just one performance.

He filled his suddenly vacant time by writing a rock 'n' roll musical that would allow Elvis full rein, penning songs around a plotline lifted straight from the 1950s B-movies that he loved so much, and he was still hard at work when he landed a part in a Royal Court production of playwright Sam Shepard's *The Unseen Hand*. There he met Jim Sharman, famed director of the original Australian production of *Jesus Christ Superstar*, and together they began building upon O'Brien's original vision.

Sharman's involvement brought in a host of topline theater personnel, including veteran stage producer Michael White, and a cast that included Tim Curry, Patricia Quinn, Little Nell, Julie Covington, and O'Brien himself. It was Sharman, too, who came up with a new title for the play, *The Rocky Horror Picture Show*.

Birthed at the critical and commercial peak of glam rock, *The Rocky Horror Show* was thoroughly a child of its times, but it was also a seamless addition to the already twenty-year-old history of rock. Set in that mythical era that popular culture insists existed at the tail end of the 1950s, when the younger generation was still divided between the nice kids and the bad ones (it was the bad ones who liked rock 'n' roll), it ostensibly revolved around the misadventures of clean-cut Brad and Janet, whose car gets a flat as they are driving to visit their former professor.

They make their way to the quintessentially spooky old mansion that they passed a short while back, intending simply to use the phone to summon assistance and then be on their way. Instead, a bent and sinister butler informs them, they are invited to one of his master's "events"—which turns out to be the creation of life, in the form of Rocky, a Charles Atlas–style strongman who will meet every one of the master's needs.

So far, so *Science Fiction Mystery Theater*. Where *Rocky Horror* stepped beyond anything that had been seen on stage before was in its approach to the sexuality of its cast: repressed in the shape of Brad (Christopher Malcolm) and Janet (Julie Covington); outrageously flaming in that of the master, Frank-N-Furter (Curry); unrequited in the form of the groupie Columbia (Nell); and possibly incestuous in that of the butler Riff Raff (O'Brien) and the maid Magenta (Quinn).

Add cannibalism, extraterrestrials, and a deep-seated love of old Hollywood to the blend, and essentially, what *Rocky Horror* did was take all of the streams of consciousness that were already percolating through the glam rock mainstream, from Bowie's gay space invaders to Bolan's starlet beauty, and mash them together into one single creation.

It is also notable that when the time came for *Rocky Horror* to make the shift from theater to cinema screen, all four of the mansion's primary residents journeyed with it, to ensure the most immaculate transition imaginable. By that time, Tim Curry alone had already starred in the first American production, opening at the Roxy in Los Angeles on March 21, 1974; a then unknown, but already distinctive Meat Loaf, too, joined the cast there, in the role of doomed 50s rock iconoclast Eddie.

A hit in LA, *Rocky Horror* simply curled up and died when it reached Broadway the following year; it closed after just forty-five performances, which scarcely augured well for the now imminent film version. And so it proved.

The Rocky Horror Picture Show was a commercial flop, exiting the mainstream cinemas as fast as was humanly possible, and preparing instead to live out the remainder of its sure-to-be-brief lifespan by turning up as a late-night space filler in those establishments that offered all-night movie showings.

Or so it seemed. But there was something about that movie that wouldn't say die—a sense, perhaps, that the people who disliked it were destined to hate it forever, or at least until they forgot about it. But those who liked it would *love* it; more than that, they would fall *in* love with it. And just as nobody is content to spend just one night with the object of their most ardent affection, so *Rocky Horror*'s fans were not happy to simply see it once and then move on.

They returned again and again, in increasing numbers and increasingly bizarre states of dress. It was the LA crowd, according to legend, that first started attending showings in the guise of their favorite characters, but the practice spread quickly.

By the time the *Rocky Horror* stage show made its (for now) final transfer in London, to the Comedy Theater in the heart of the city's West

End, the UK audience too was in full drag; and today, the weirdoes at either a stage revival or cinema presentation are the ones who aren't decked out in corsets or maid's outfits, '50s geek chic, or demented butler togs. *Rocky Horror* is a lifestyle, and it will never go away. As *New York Rock* put it in 2000, "For those who've never thrown rice at the midnight movie or yelled 'slut!' at a shivering celluloid Susan Sarandon, *The Rocky Horror Show* . . . has since transformed into the ultimate cult film.'"

Jim Sharman:

> I always had faith in the originality of the film and felt it would ultimately find its audience, but the early signs weren't good. The fact that it was such an unusual film and that it was devoid of conventional movie stars didn't help. The fashion of the day was for realist films and this was something else. [But] there was a certain crazy logic in the fact that the film would end up turning cinemas into theatres, which is more or less what happened.

Fifteen years old when *The Rocky Horror Picture Show* opened at the cinema, Jett was an early, and immediate, convert—along with a sizeable portion of the English Disco crowd. "I'm a fan, very much so. I'd say it was pretty instrumental in me figuring out who I was. It was a very formative time in my life."

So when Jett told her bandmates that they needed to see *The Rocky Horror Show*, they listened. And when she suggested that they go and see it again . . . and again . . . and again . . . they listened to that as well. "Me and my friends would go to see it all the time," she recalled. "We went a lot."

And Frank-N-Furter's corset was always there to grab their attention, in that same peculiar way that corsets always have when it comes to focusing people's minds. Or as Currie put it,

> I think there was a bit of friction about the corset, because I was [also] wearing garters and fishnets and I was sixteen years old. I think the girls probably didn't like the idea that it would take a whole lot of attention away, but when I wore it for the very first time on stage, the girls knew that was the selling point for the song. And it was a hell of a lot of fun.

SIX

You Don't Know What You've Got

The Runaways' first American tour kicked off in spring 1976, and Cherie Currie was terrified. She'd never sung in front of an audience in her life, a realization that dawned on her as the tour bus crossed the Arizona Desert. Suddenly she was hit by the most gut-wrenching attack of homesickness, turned to Lita Ford, and burst into tears.

"And she goes, 'I'm fucking homesick too, man, but when I come back I wanna be somebody.' And I looked at her and I went 'Yeah.' I never got homesick again."

It was not going to be an easy outing. Everything that Fowley had thrown at them in the rehearsal room came to life now, only instead of one man in a bright orange suit screaming abuse and hurling chairs, there were clubs full of people intent on doing the exact same thing. Some nights, the band could only look on in horror as the room exploded with scorn, rage, and of course, testosterone.

"People couldn't get their heads around the fact that the Runaways were serious," Randy Detroit said,

and that was Kim Fowley's fault. There was nothing to relate them to—maybe Fanny, if you wanted to really stretch things, but they went onstage dressed like a rock 'n' roll band. But Fowley dressed the Runaways like strippers, or he let them dress like strippers, I don't know which, and audiences didn't know what to do; you see a woman onstage dressed like that, the immediate reaction is, "Ah, she's a stripper, it's a sex show," and the fact that she has a guitar doesn't enter into it. So audiences reacted exactly as you'd expect them to, because how else *could* they react at that time? Fowley would say they'd never seen anything like it, but they had, just in a different environment.

Fowley agreed. He told Sandy Robertson,

There have been *women* bands, and black chicks standing up singing, but the Runaways are the first . . . When we play, we get the wankers on one side of the stage, and the guys who love guitar on the other side. I mean, a lot of people want to screw the Runaways, and they're ready to do the dog. This isn't like Keith Richards with two kids and a wife and all that bullshit, I mean these are young people. They are ready to do the dog if the right guy walks by!

Neither was it only the men in the audience who reacted so violently toward the band. Many women, too, saw the Runaways not for what history would later declare them to be—the first all-female band to play high energy rock 'n' roll—but as just one more example of the objectification of women as sex objects. In an age when the women's liberation movement was growing increasingly and ever more stridently opposed to each and every example, with the now plainly visible but markedly *un*glamorous Patti Smith dressed down as some kind of feminist ideal, the Runaways' refusal to hide their femininity behind a similarly besuited camouflage was seen as a grotesque parody of womanhood at best, and an utterly callous marketing gimmick at worst.

It mattered not that the Runaways in general, and Jett in particular, spoke out against both stereotypes at every opportunity; that they argued for people to look at the music first and then accept the packaging as simply a bit of extra fun. Nobody castigated Freddie Mercury for taking the stage in trousers so tight you could count the veins, after all. The idea that women could openly and publicly flaunt their sexuality on stage without simultaneously offering that sexuality up to all takers was one that very few observers could comprehend.

Before leaving Los Angeles, the band members' parents had been assured that they had nothing to worry about—a tutor would be provided, chaperones, everything a worried ma and pa could desire for their little girl so far from home. In fact, they had none of these. "We were completely unsupervised," Fox continued. "We were living like runaways."

The tour, the band agreed, was all about trying to survive. Fowley didn't join them on the road; tour management was handed to Scott Anderson, who in turn became Currie's boyfriend, much to the chagrin of her bandmates. Jackie Fox made no secret of the fact that the couple frequently left the rest of the band to get on as well as they could, bereft of either transport or money in the middle of nowhere.

The problems ran deeper than that, of course. Looking back three decades later, Currie recalled,

> We were all growing up, trying to deal with the transition into young womanhood. At the same time there was a whole lot of craziness going on. Our management, our booking agent—they were all feeding us drugs. The thing was, back in the seventies, if you didn't do drugs, there was something wrong with you. We were just thrown into this cyclone and did what we were told to do. We literally just had to hold on to our seats and make it from point A to point B on a daily basis.

Anderson could drill them as well as Fowley. Running through soundcheck one afternoon, Jett began playing an old Jethro Tull riff, the hoary horrors of "Aqualung," and inciting her bandmates to follow suit even as Currie was still checking her mike levels.

"Joan!" Currie asked. "Could you please stop that till we get this soundcheck done?"

Jett responded by cranking the volume up further. Currie shouted, Jett yelled, the others joined in . . . until finally Anderson weighed in at the top of *his* lungs. "Right. That's it. You have fifteen minutes to get your asses together."

They obeyed.

As the band toured on, Fowley's next move was to secure them a record deal. His first approach was to Arista, the label founded earlier in the year by former Columbia Records chief Clive Davis, and one that had already made its mark. Swallowing up the old Bell Records catalog gave the label such guaranteed hit makers as the then all-conquering Bay City Rollers and the fast-rising Barry Manilow. The arrival of the Kinks and Lou Reed brought some old-fashioned firepower to the catalog; the signing of Patti Smith proved Arista was on the cutting edge of new music too. And it was her inclusion on the label that ended any hope for the Runaways. "Why," Davis asked, "do I want to deal with an undeveloped female rock concept when I have the ultimate artist, Patti Smith, on my label?"

Mercury's Denny Rosencrantz was less inclined to overlook the band's potential. He signed the band on December 12, 1975, and when Fowley asked him why, Rosencrantz's answer made perfect sense. Years before, dropping acid in Albuquerque with Jimi Hendrix, he remembered the guitarist telling him that one day girls would be playing rock 'n' roll. "Be ready for it." That day had arrived.

The fact that Mercury Records had already housed the New York Dolls was less of a consideration. That band had long since been dropped from the roster and was, in any case, a dead issue, breaking up after their newfound manager, the Englishman Malcolm McLaren, sent them out on tour rebranded as Communists. He intended it as an ironic statement; America just thought it was stupid. The band returned to New York and shattered.

But Jett, at least, was excited to be picking up the torch that the Dolls' ignominious collapse had left for dead—there was as yet no specific musical movement that the Runaways could be tied to, but the mere fact of their existence, five kids pumping out dirty-ass rock 'n' roll, proved something. Nobody could have foreseen that within a little less than a year, that role model would be exploding out across the Western world.

Later Fowley would argue, "The lead singer found her own lingerie," and relegated his own role in the group's creation to that of a barely active bystander. He simply pointed them in the right direction, regarding imagery, intent, and—because there was no other word for it—gimmickry. But the result was worth all the pain. "Runaways were not T&A. Runaways were a sports team with musical instruments and teenaged lyrics, Wonder Woman with guitars instead of cleavage."

He prided himself too on the fact that the five were still as young as they claimed to be. In an age when rock and pop stars routinely shaved a few years off their actual birth dates in the hope of appearing more like their audiences, the Runaways were already at the lowest age admissible. In summer 1976, Jackie Fox was the youngest, born on December 20, 1959. Cherie Currie, too, was just sixteen, born on November 30, 1959; so was Sandy West, born on July 10, 1959. Jett and Lita Ford, born three days apart in September 1958, were the eldest at seventeen.

Which presented its own set of unique problems—unique for a rock 'n' roll manager, anyway. Any mother of a handful of teenaged girls would have recognized them immediately: conflicts over who wore a particular color first, who looked at who's boyfriend, whose eyes were going to get scratched out first.

Even worse were those days when all five girls would have their period simultaneously—that same mother could tell you that if you place a group of women in the same environment together for long enough, sooner or later their cycles will coincide. The resultant eruption of hormones and temper could render even Fowley speechless.

He worked to give the girls a reputation, spreading rumors because he knew they would add to the excitement, regardless of whether or not they were based in fact. Journalist Don Waller recalled a short period when Jett spent some time living in Fowley's apartment.

"She's eating pussy in my house!" Fowley complained to anybody who would listen, and it didn't matter whether she was or wasn't. The image of girls going out of control was all he wanted to see, and once the rumors of rampant lesbianism within the band had taken off, he then set about disproving them by lining up a series of photographs of the girls cuddling up to various hot male rock stars.

Lita Ford later admitted being shocked when she realized that at least some of her bandmates were sexually involved with one another. But they were also her friends, and their private relationships were their own business. They were bandmates.

A feature in the spring 1976 *Who Put the Bomp* introduced America at large to the Runaways. Wisely, Shaw turned to one of the band's own peers to state their case to the *Bomp* readership; with the Runaways—or rather, Currie—splashed across the magazine's front cover, sixteen-year-old Lisa Francher's words devoured two pages within and were deemed so authoritative that they would subsequently be reprinted on their debut album's jacket!

The white middle-class suburbs were bound to have their outbreak of teen troublemakers. That's the Runaways. Their roots are TV, hanging around and going to Hollywood on weekends because it's the only thing to do after five days of school and partying. They make you hear the frustration of teenage life, and even more, they utter bone-crunching boredom of nothing to do and nowhere to do it. The Runaways aren't just an "all-girl band" or an exercise in women's lib. They're a rock 'n' roll band. They're rock 'n' roll. They're for real.

The group were still finding their way when Fowley took them into the studio to begin work on their debut album, but their inexperience barely shows. Recorded in under two weeks, usually in first takes, *The Runaways* was "basic heavy metal, crossed with Suzi Quatro and a smattering of Stooges!" murmured *ZigZag*'s review. But their cover of "Rock and Roll" predated any other Velvet Underground cover of the age; "Blackmail" swaggered like the street anthem that Fowley insisted it was; and "Cherry Bomb," the group's first single, was soon landing regular plays on the radio, and few who heard it could resist the riff that steamrollered straight out of hard-rock heaven, the snarl in Currie's sneer-dripped voice, and a lyric that still screamed defiance even when she was purring.

The ten songs selected for the set, including nine Runaways/Fowley originals, were no more or less meaty than they needed to be—with "Cherry Bomb" inevitably kicking everything off with the loudest bang of all, and the epic "Dead End Justice" wrapping the set up with the melodrama that would swiftly develop into the highlight of the band's live set, rock theater with extra added cat fighting.

"It will eclipse anything *West Side Story* will ever do," Fowley insisted. "It's the combination of the movie *Taxi Driver*, Bogart, and Cagney. Dirty filthy rock and roll!"

Later, Jackie Fox would complain that "the songs were extremely simplistic, and most of the lyrics were really very silly." But although nobody was aware of the fact at the time, that was all that they needed to be. Across the sea in Britain, and across the country in New York City, a new musical force was building that would make a virtue of the Runaways' lack of pretentiousness and a strength from all that conventional rock criticism might have regarded as their greatest weakness. In an age when too many bands, despite all that glam rock had thrown at them, remained intent on proving their maturity, the Runaways returned rock to their juvenile basics of sex and drugs and a lot of noise; and *The Runaways* was the sound of those basics at their best.

But that didn't change the weight of the bullshit that was being piled up around them. Interviewed in one city, Jett sighed, the band members were asked whether they had ever done the things that most teenaged girls are content to do. Babysitting, for instance. Yes, they had. And how did they discipline their charges if the behavior should get out of control? Did they smack the children? Yes, if it was called for. The following day, the headline introduced a new dimension to the Runaways' reputation: they were child beaters.

Looking back on the Runaways from the safety of 2010, it was clear to each of the band members what the group represented. "No one had done what we did," Cherie Currie explained.

> No one had done it yet. I mean, Suzi Quatro was out there on her own kicking butt, and she deserves all the credit for that. And she also, I know, influenced Joan and myself and Lita and everyone. But as far as teenage girls [are concerned], fifteen, sixteen, that's young getting out there in a man's world.
>
> We were in the battlefields for a lot of years. I say a lot because it seemed like a lot, but it was only two. The legacy, I believe, for the Runaways is that if you have a dream, if you really believe that you have a calling, no matter what it is, whether it's music, no matter what it is, you stick with it. And I really think the failing would be nil. I just don't think you could fail.

That, however, is hindsight talking, the hindsight that comes from spending three decades watching what was initially regarded as another Kim Fowley gimmick, or novelty at best, transformed into one of those rare acts without whom . . .

Rock 'n' roll was changed by the Runaways. Not during their lifetimes, or even at any quantifiable moment thereafter; there is no precise point in time where the historian can say the Runaways crossed the Rubicon. For many years, in fact, they were forgotten, a mere footnote in the annals of rock and not much more in the annals of women in rock.

In 2005, the University of Pennsylvania published author Lisa L. Rhodes's *Electric Ladyland—Women and Rock Culture*, a weighty and, so far as such writings go, exhaustively authoritative study that explained how, in the words of the back-cover blurb, "female musicians, journalists, and groupies rewrote women's roles on and off the stage in the 1960s and 1970s." The Runaways receive one mention, Joan Jett another.

The group's existence has not been airbrushed from history. But for a long time, their influence was. Again, in Currie's words, "No one had done what we did." No one had taken five teenaged girls, whose musical abilities ranged from average to quite good, put them in a band and a van, and then sent them out to work exactly the same circuit as every other group out there, in the hope of being accorded the same respect and recognition. And why? Because no one else thought such an enterprise stood a snowball's chance in hell of being taken seriously.

Three-and-a-half months on the road across America hardened the Runaways beyond recognition. Early shows in the LA suburbs, headlining Wild Man Sam's to twenty people a night, were already behind them—before the end of the year, Jackie Fox would look back and say, "When the Beatles play the Cavern again, we go back to Wild Man Sam's."

"We played places where people didn't expect us to be a rock band," West continued.

> You know, like high school gymnasiums. They expected us to be playing nice, mellow Joni Mitchell–type shit. And we didn't, of course, and things like "Cotton Cunt" [a favorite title that never found a song to stick to, so it was used as a random introduction instead] really blew 'em away. Like at Esparalda High, I don't think they expected a rock band.

It was a mercurial ride then, but that, Jett insisted, was as it ought to be. She never saw the Runaways as a longterm project, the kind of band that would spend years grinding around the club circuit, paying their dues in the hope that one day they might make it. They were a teenaged smash-and-grab raid, in one window and out the next. If they weren't enormous within a year or so, they would stop.

Fowley agreed. "No one expected the Rolling Stones to last. This is the first girl band. Remember, if you support the Runaways, you support rock 'n' roll."

SEVEN

Star Star

The movie roles slipped into place, thirty-five years before there was even a movie, but *The Runaways* reinforced them regardless.

"Every movie needs a villain, and I'm a good villain," Kim Fowley laughed to Seattle's KEXP.

> And Michael Shannon plays me like a good villain. No matter who wrote the dialogue you wouldn't be jumping with joy. They got Michael, so I was fortunate. And I think Dakota is a really good actress. I think Kristin Stewart is an amazing actress. I think her performance is astounding in the movie. I think Dakota, well, she's playing Cherie the way that Cherie sees herself. As opposed to the way—she might have been. I think Kristin got Joan Jett's spirit, but I don't think Dakota got Cherie's spirit. But she got Cherie's pain and suffering. So from an Ingmar Bergman perspective, Cherie got that and Kristin got Jett's rock 'n' roll celebration.
>
> Of course, in collaboration Joan and I wrote a lot of songs, so I had a different relationship with her than I had with Cherie Currie, to whom I was Roger Vadim. And she was Brigit Bardot. With Joan Jett, I was George Martin and she was John Lennon. And that's a big difference.

Jett and Currie were both intrinsic to the movie's production—Currie as author of the autobiography that inspired it, Jett as the executive producer whose eye for detail ensured that the film would never trail off on the flights of fancy so beloved of most Hollywood productions. "I think that they were really involved in helping us as much as we wanted them to help us," Dakota Fanning told writer Scott W. Perry. "To be there and play a real person is a daunting task, especially with Cherie actually being there. Meeting her and talking to her about these experiences were more than helpful I think."

"Because there were things that we would never know," Kristen Stewart continued.

> Things that we wouldn't be able to put in the movie that would be lost that would be very important to them, just details, photos, and footage and of course Cherie's book, which is a subjective telling of one side of the story. Her book is definitely her side of it. It was nice to hear Joan's perspective of it. There's a million things that we could've done in the movie and most of them would've been wrong had they not have been there to correct us.

They realized, as so many other people had already realized—that sometimes, reality makes fantasy look like an idiot's fingerpainting.

The Runaways made their New York debut in the same September week as their album was released, opening for Television and the Talking Heads at CBGB. Both of those bands were established among the kingpins of the local scene—Patti Smith and the Ramones had both moved on now, to sign major label deals and put that bar on the Bowery behind them. But the audiences that they had nurtured, and New York's own sense of its musical invulnerability, clung on regardless, viewing CBGB not as the unhygienic hole in the wall that it was but as a biblical manger of sorts, the birthplace of the music that would rewire the decade.

The Runaways, on the other hand, discovered what the city thought about them before they'd even played a note. They arrived at the club, stepped out of the car, and one of the area's resident bums promptly threw up at Ford's feet.

Their peers, too, were less than overwhelmed by the band's pregig publicity. Joey Ramone happily admitted to finding the Runaways "a bit of a joke," although he did admit to smiling when he heard Currie describe his band's first album as "one long song."

But the two groups would hang together during the Runaways' sojourn in the city, igniting a friendship between "da bruddahs" and Jett that would not only survive the end of the Runaways but would remain strong until the end of the Ramones as well, more than two decades later. Indeed, when DeeDee and Marky Ramone's new band, the Remains, played a WLIR charity show at the Long Island Brewery Company in January 1998, Jett joined them onstage for a storming rendition of her own "Bad Reputation." "Joan's cool," DeeDee Ramone cooed.

Patti Smith, however, hated them—had in fact already made that clear when the Runaways appeared backstage at her show at the Golden Bear in Huntingdon Beach in February 1976. Smith barely glanced up at the proffered handshakes before barking, "You girls. Out."

Smith's guitarist, Ivan Kral, had already witnessed the Runaways in action, at the Starwood. Kral has never forgotten walking into the backstage area, just as Kim Fowley emerged with Robert Plant by his side. The following night, onstage with Smith, he made a point of wearing his newly obtained Runaways T-shirt. But Patti didn't want to know.

"She was being real rude to us for no reason," Currie condemned. "I guess she was seeing us as female competition."

English journalist Chris Salewicz caught the fallout. Currie kicked off the conversation. "'She was such a *lurrghhh*! I mean, she was so disgusting with those saggy—"

"Tits," Jett helped out.

"Tits," nodded Currie.

The Runaways paid for their harsh words, however. Or they thought they might, anyway. Currie: "When we played CBGB, there were these four chicks all dressed like Patti Smith. We thought we were in for trouble."

In fact, the Runaways were themselves rebelling against much of the publicity that they had received so far, a media blitz that was more likewise obsessed with tits than talent. Mercury's own efforts at pushing *The Runaways* had driven the album no higher than a less-than-stellar #194 on the US chart, and the possibility that more people were being turned off than on by the continued insistence on marketing the band as jailbait first, a musical sensation second, was becoming ever more avid in the band's thoughts.

Dark and dangerous, closeted in her perennial leather jacket, Jett resolutely refused to play the game, forever glancing disdainfully over as Cherie donned her latest corset or Jackie flipped one strap on her shirt. But the others found their limits in the end, and when a photographer for the French magazine *Oui* suggested that all five unbutton past the point of no return, they finally put their foot down. The Runaways had shown all the flesh they were going to reveal. From now on, let the music stand naked.

It was more than capable of doing so; in musical terms, judged purely on the strength of that debut album, the Runaways had an awful lot going for them. When word crept out that Fowley had asked former Silverhead bassist Nigel Harrison to deputize for Fox in the studio, a few knowing sneers were naturally snorted.

A few more eyebrows raised when it became known that guitarist Steve Hunter, veteran of Lou Reed's latest band, had dropped by the studio to assist with the arrangements for "Rock and Roll"—a song that he had, on Reed's *Rock and Roll Animal* tour, helped to redefine.

But such commentaries only overlooked the fact that Currie, Jett, Ford, and West were all present and correct, and that the band's self-titled LP was quite possibly the most exhilarating rock disc of the post-Ramones year. "I didn't break things down to fingernail polish or cup size. I wanted noise, I wanted slime, I wanted golden garbage," Fowley swore. "I succeeded. And so did they."

Ben Edmonds, reviewing the album in *Phonograph Record* magazine, nailed its value.

> [The Runaways] score their heaviest points on attitude. It's cute at first to think about sixteen-year-old girls strutting around the stage like rock and roll badasses, but it becomes much more when you realize that they *mean it*. And I'll take a band with genuine commitment to rock and roll, how ever limited their means of expressing it might be, over milquetoast "professionals" with no commitment to anything but union scale, any day.

From the outset, Kim Fowley believed that the Runaways' greatest chance of making a splash was to conquer the UK. So much smaller than the United States, but just as influential in terms of rock culture, it was Britain that had salvaged both the Stooges and the Velvets from the dustbins into which the American media had consigned them—Britain that regarded rock's history as something to be learned from and absorbed, as opposed to simply an unrelated sequence of events that unfolded without any ostensible acknowledgement of what had happened before. The Runaways, Fowley knew, were a vital part of rock history, year zero for whatever future convolutions might be destined to emerge from around them. Britain, he believed, would recognize that.

The Runaways' first slice of UK press came in July 1976, with visiting journalist Chris Salewicz salivating over their show at the Corral, in Topanga Canyon. "There's not a number over four minutes. Every song they play grinds Classic Rock and Roll Construction into your nerve-ends . . . aggression and energy pouring out of the speakers and, most of all, the Runaways are drowning the audience in their utter, unrelenting beautiful arrogance."

He compared the group to the Small Faces and, painting the Runaways into what was surely their best-anointed haven, asked "why the hell *shouldn't* five teenage girls from the Orange County suburbs of Southeast LA take as a reference point the best of what comes out of London rock pubs around 9 pm on a Thursday night?"

Compare that to their American reception—the journalists who simply shrugged the band's existence aside or attended their shows with their preconceptions already in place. To many of them, it mattered not how proficient, or energetic, the band might be. The fact is, they were *girls*. Literally *girls*. And *girls* cannot *rock*.

The band's first British tour was set to begin in early September 1976. Capital Radio, London's number-one local station, picked up on "Cherry Bomb" almost as soon as it was released that same month, while further-sighted observers were already nudging the band into what the media had decreed was the next big thing to tear up the British music scene: punk rock.

In fairness, and with absolutely no hindsight whatsoever, punk itself had still to truly be defined as anything more than a vague grab bag of moods and motives; that early fall of 1976, after all, none of the newly formed British punk bands had even released a record. Most of them hadn't been heard outside of London itself. Punk was a movement waiting to happen, and it was left to the musical polarities of the visiting Ramones and Patti Smith to fly the flag in the United Kingdom.

Now the Runaways were coming over to offer up a West Coast take on the burgeoning phenomenon, and at precisely the right time for maximum media exposure.

The Runaways' first British tour—three months after the Ramones visited the country for the first time, and just two weeks after the 100 Club Punk Festival confirmed that there really was an audience for this new musical noise—caught the tabloid media in full howl.

A flying glass at the 100 Club Festival had blinded a girl in one eye. With the unimpeachable logic with which the media can associate anything with anything if there's a story to be told about the connection, punk rock suddenly became indistinguishable from mindless violence—rampant nihilism—and of course, because the average tabloid reader ultimately cares for nothing else, obscenity and filth. A few weeks down the road, one of the British gutter papers would hear rumors of a new all-girl band called the Slits, and there would be no end to the tremors that set in motion. For now, there were the Runaways for them to get their teeth into.

An all-girl rock group? An all-*teenaged*-girl rock group? One of whom wears a corset and not much else? *Phwoooaaarrr*!

With the Runaways being billed as California girls yanked straight out of an X-rated Beach Boys single, the vast majority of the people buying tickets for the group's first tour had not even heard a note they played. It was the pictures and the posters—and the promise of one night of pure, unalloyed bad-girl delinquency—that drew them in, and the Runaways' own groans of despairing protest were already being lost beneath the keening clamor of stampeding hormones.

Flying in at the end of September 1976, the Runaways played just a couple of shows, in Glasgow and Birmingham, then made their way to the continent to stoke up more media attention. Measuring their impact in terms of press coverage, however, they landed far more publicity when the officious manager of London's White Horse Hotel called the cops on them after noticing the loss of a hairdryer from one of the rooms.

In fact, the law had already caught up with them in Dover, where they were waiting for a ferry to take the band to the continent. It was road manager Anderson's walkie talkie that first aroused the authorities' suspicions—in Britain at that time, only the law and emergency services tended to carry such items in public. Anderson explained his need for the device, and in the course of their conversation, the Runaways' ages— or more accurately, the fact that they were *under*-age—was revealed, and now immigration weighed in. "We'd like to check their passports before you can leave to cross the Channel."

So they checked the passports, and then they checked the luggage. Where they found a collection of London hotel keys.

Currie picked up the tale for *Backfire* in 2000.

> Robert Plant, I think, told us to start collecting those little skeleton keys. He had shadowboxes of his hotel keys, like souvenirs, and they clock all the places you've been—these cities 'cause it's kind of hard to remember, "Was I there?" "Yeah." Well, we started collecting those keys. There was this detective guy, like the guy in *The Pink Panther*, Peter Sellers, but a very mean, evil twin of Peter Sellers, who basically looked at us and hated us for no reason . . . As soon as he finds the keys in Joan's bag he goes, "What are these?" And he dumps 'em all out and it's all the hotel room keys, and he goes, "Book her."

The group were caged for nineteen hours—four of the band in one cell but Jett in one of her own, down the hall. According to West, "We all sang songs as loud as we could 'cause it was a big cement room, you know? Jett was down the hall in this little tiny cell, crying and screaming the whole night."

Finally released, they continued on to Europe for a handful of promotional appearances, and then it was back to London for two nights at the Roundhouse, before another week sent them zigzagging between clubs and universities until it was time to return to Los Angeles. And everywhere they went, the same journalists waited with the same questions, and the same fans howled out the same suggestions.

"Get 'em off!"

"Show us yer tits!"

"*Gissakiss!*"

There were moments when these Brits made even an American college frat crowd sound gentlemanly.

"Although they play a more respected music, the Runaways can be compared to the Bay City Rollers," wrote *Melody Maker*'s Harry Doherty. "For, like the Rollers, their main asset is most definitely their promiscuity. The fact that the Runaways actually can boogie a bit is a welcome surprise to their audiences, and because they do play fairly well—when they're not expected to—their talent and potential is wildly exaggerated."

The group dealt swiftly with accusations that the entire Runaways project was simply a post-Monkees manufacturing job, pieced together by Fowley as an all-girl answer to the Ramones. The Sex Pistols—cobbled into place by an ambitious haberdasher named Malcolm McLaren—were scarcely the most organic construction either. But there was one question that none of the group were truly able to answer, although it was coming up more and more. "Are you punk rockers?"

Maybe they were. They were the right age after all. They had the right reference points too—the British punk crowd, too, grew up on glam rock.

But the key elements were that they were kids—which gave them a different attitude to adults—and girls, which gave them a different attitude to boys. "Did you know that the drummer in Spirit is fifty?" Joan marveled.

She could have added any number of other chastisements, including some that kicked punk rock just as hard in the balls. Vibrators' frontman Knox was reliably forecast to be in his early thirties. So were at least two of the Stranglers. The Clash's Joe Strummer was in his mid-twenties; Patti Smith was almost thirty. If punk really was the music of youth, then the definition of "youth" had taken some very strange turns in recent years.

Unfortunately, a lot of people still found it easier just to stare and shout. Journalist Mick Farren caught the Runaways' Glasgow opener, and the audience response that he observed set the tone for the remainder of the tour. "Rock and roll may drive these guys a little addled, but rock and roll with tits (not only tits, but scarcely post-pubescent Californian tits) renders them ultimately ape."

From the other side of the stage, Lita Ford was equally stunned. "There were so many guys, just a sea of guys, all dressed in black leather and denim going 'hwaaah, come on, baby.' And I'd get nervous."

It didn't show though. Originally the Runaways were booked in for just one London show at the Roundhouse. It sold out so quickly that a second was added.

The support act, Suburban Stud, came and went. Not a great band, but not a bad one either. The Birmingham Quartet were still trying to pull their sound in line with the noises they were hearing everywhere else and hoping nobody remembered that until very recently, they still had a saxophone in their lineups. Punks did not have saxophones.

Neither, as the Runaways took the stage, did the audience seem that fussed about what musical category they ought to be filed away within. From the self-mythologizing throb of "Cherry Bomb"; through the best of the album and a filthy-grind "Wild Thing"; and onto the dying kick in the head of the superstaged "Dead End Justice," Alice Cooper sent to juvie for crimes against *Little Orphan Annie*, the Runaways were phenomenal. And when you looked around the assembled hordes hustling into the backstage party, sundry members of the Pistols and the Clash seemed to be having as good a time as anyone. They didn't care whether the girls were punks or not. Or maybe they just fancied their chances as well.

"They rock with the best," wrote journalist Jonh Ingham later,

> a tight, hard hitting combo that don't apologize about their gender. As one who's wanted for years to lust after female rockers the way girls fancy Rod or Mick or etc., but who doesn't get aroused by such winsome displays of demure feminine virtue as Joni Mitchell or Linda Ronstadt, it was a very nice feeling to find myself wanting to screw at least three of those tough young ladies dominating the stage.

He was not the only one. When the band played Liverpool, the crowd burst through the safety barriers, and the Runaways were hastily rushed offstage. In Leeds, Jackie Fox looked out at the audience and was astonished to see just one female face in the crowd. And everywhere, the band was drenched in spit, the punk movement's greatest tribute to the bands they liked. "The more spit you got, the better you were," Ford told Marc Spitz. "We had loogies hanging over us by the end of each set. It was awesome—'man, look at that loogie on your neck. That's cool!'"

"There were some people that were receptive," Jett told writer Steve Olson. "A lot of people thought that it was cute, and kind of funny, but there were definitely bands that had a problem with us."

One band that instinctively recognized the Runaways as outsiders, for they shared that status themselves, was Motörhead, the dense metallic trio led by Lemmy, but who were still a couple of years away from any kind of commercial or critical acclaim. In late 1976, they too were regarded as a curio by the hypercritical UK music press, and audiences followed suit. As the Runaways prepared to take the stage for their first London show, Lemmy loaned Jett his bullet belt. He took it back afterwards, much to her disappointment, but the gesture was meaningful all the same. It let her know that in his mind, the Runaways belonged.

The British visit had one more treat in store, however. The Runaways were in London, bunkered down in their hotel rooms, and Jett was flicking through the channels on the television—all three of them—when she caught what looked like a music show: a half-hour teatime escapade hosted by a band called the Arrows.

She'd heard of them already; two Americans and a Brit, the Arrows were another of the bands rounded up by hit-making Mickie Most and set loose on the libidos of the country's teenaged pop fans. "A Touch Too Much," their first big smash back in 1974, had been one of the records that got the English Disco dance floor moving, but Arrows had faded from earshot since then, and even in England, most people had forgotten them by the time their television series rolled around. Two TV series, in fact—a year apart and fourteen weeks apiece—and every episode filled with every hot should-have-been-a-hit that the host band could throw at the crowd.

Tonight they were saying goodbye with a number that had already been established as their statement of intent, even if it had never seen more glory than the B-side of one of their later flop singles, "Broken Down Heart." Self-composed by band members Alan Merrill and Jake Hooker, "I Love Rock 'n' Roll" was glam rock *in excelsis*, a stomping rocker scratched straight out of their own New York childhoods, the joys of jamming dimes into a jukebox and celebrating the greatest music ever made. And relaxing in her hotel room in central London, Joan Jett was squealing with excitement. In her daydreams, all songs sounded as good as this. In her private dreams, so did hers . . .

EIGHT

I Love Playing with Fire

Punk rock arrived in Los Angeles late in 1976, around the same time as the Runaways returned home from England. You could almost say that they brought it with them, in the form of five eyewitness accounts that spoke more for the sheer energy and purpose of the music than any imported newspaper cutting ever could.

The music moved in slowly, of course, as though it was unsure as to how it would be received in the land of the Eagles and Linda Ronstadt. But maybe that was the point; it was *because* LA was so tightly bound up with the so-called West Coast sound of country rock and the last gasps of hippy that there was a gap into which an alternative could squeeze— and an alternative that was about as far away from the Hotel California as it was possible to go.

Punk rock took even the most slapdash values of previous generations and ripped them all to shreds. It bred a new, swaggering dissidence, and a demented diffidence to the so-called California lifestyle. Most cultural revolutions are searching for something to fight for. This one simply wanted to fight.

Home from Europe in mid-October 1976, the Runaways set to work immediately on their next album, already titled *Queens of Noise*.

It was not an easy album to make—not as easy as their debut, anyway. Last time around, the band had operated in a virtual bubble; they were unknown beyond a few friends and the handfuls who'd caught them playing live, and simply being in the studio for the first time in their lives concentrated their minds deliciously. Plus, they were in and out so fast that there really wasn't time to do more than bang down the numbers as Kim Fowley called the shots, and hope they'd done enough to keep him happy.

This time around, there were distractions: friends dropping round, fans hanging around, parties to attend . . . all the social paraphernalia that is attached to a rising star was theirs, and it was difficult sometimes to concentrate on the job at hand.

The material wasn't as strong, either. *The Runaways* had more or less exhausted the best songs in their repertoire—only Jett's "I Love Playing with Fire" and the Three F (Fowley/Ford/Fox)'s self-explanatory "Neon Angels (On the Road to Ruin)" really stood out from the record; and whereas the first album had been loaded with the glam chops that inspired so much of it, *Queens of Noise* looked towards louder, heavier pastures—Kiss and Aerosmith received hearty nods, particularly once Lita Ford kicked into overdrive.

Kim Fowley produced in tandem with Earle Mankey—a founding member of Californian oddballs Sparks—and his influence on the proceedings was strong. According to one observer, he was even able to suppress some of Fowley's wilder schemes, to ensure a more even sonic playing field.

But although it was a great rock album, that's all it was. There was little of the teenaged passion that fueled the first record, and little too of the spiky punk ethos that pumped through *The Runaways*' veins. Even Jett's "Take It or Leave It" rode a riff that could have been lifted from KISS's *Destroyer*, while the closing epic "Johnny Guitar," a Ford/Fowley creation, lurched along on a quaalude riff that simply went . . . on . . . far . . . too . . . long . . .

There were other tensions—noticeable not only on the finished record, where Currie sang lead on just half the songs, but also raw in the studio, as the band tried to buck against what Jett dismissed as "that whole 'Cherry Bomb With The Corset' thing": the all-pervading imagery that was preventing anybody from taking the Runaways seriously. Anybody, that is, who might actually appreciate what they were doing as musicians and songwriters.

The sessions were wild. Drink and drugs were rife in the band now, while Currie had fallen pregnant, which led to further divisions and diversions. Midway through the sessions, she needed to take time away for an abortion; she returned to the studio after two days in the hospital to discover that the song she had earmarked for her own grandstanding performance had already been recorded, with Jett taking the lead. "Queens of Noise" was penned by another of Kim Fowley's "discoveries," Billy Bizeau, the keyboard player with the LA Band the Quick, and was written specifically for Currie. "And that really hurt because that was a song that I had brought to the band," Currie recalled. "That started some pretty ill feelings between me and Joan."

There were distractions, too. The Runaways were well accustomed to having a small audience of fans, hangers-on, groupies—to be truthful, the group were never sure how to describe their most loyal stalkers. But two guys in particular were especially dedicated. Paul Beahm and George Ruthenberg were always around; Kim Fowley even labeled them "baby brothers," and when the pair spoke of the band that they were intending to form, Jett in particular offered all the encouragement she could. She was rewarded, both musically and historically, by their eventual emergence—as first, the Revlon Spam Queens, and then, the Germs, perhaps *the* number one Los Angeles punk band. And as the Germs rose, so did a scene that could call them its own.

The English Disco had closed its doors by now, fading out with glam rock around the same time as the Runaways began to fading in. It wasn't quite a ceremonial changing of the guard, but there was certainly a serendipity to that, and Rodney Bingenheimer, at least, knew it.

He headed out to Pasadena to host a radio show, *Rodney on the ROQ*, with the express intention of airing a constant barrage of "new" music, from New York and London, Australia, and France. Not all of it was good, not all of it was inspiring. But the Damned and the Vibrators, the Ramones and the Saints, Little Bob Story and the Hammersmith Gorillas were the first shots in a musical barrage that would provide the soundtrack to the next twelve months of Hollywood action.

The clubs heeded the beat. The Starwood and the Whisky opened their doors to embrace every newcomer, and fresh bands arose to take advantage of the offer. Without even trying, the Runaways were a part of the ensuing transformation, with Jett's apartment swiftly becoming one of the key after- (and before-) hours hangouts. Just across the street from the Whisky a Go Go, four blocks from the Roxy and a stone's throw, too, from the legendary Licorice Pizza record store, 969 San Vicente was what photographer Theresa K. calls the "do drop in" place for friends who were going to, or coming from, a show.

"Joan's parties were pretty notorious," Sandy West smiled, although Theresa K. reflects,

> In retrospect, I think they're only called notorious because adult things were being experienced by teenagers and teens who were only chronologically adults at the time. There was drugs and drinking— underage. Does that make it notorious? Instead of doing it in the basement of your parents' homes, this was happening in an apartment where an eighteen-year-old lived with another eighteen-year-old [Jett's friend Lisa Curland]. Notorious, I guess, because it was like Peter Pan on drugs and booze . . . no parents to supervise or even dodge!

Flick through the index of any book on LA punk; the names writ large in there were the names that made things happen, and they did that by making sure that nothing stayed static. Whether it was a new drug, a new dance, or a new sexual position, they would be on it like flies around feces, and when they'd sucked it dry they'd move on to something else. Some would go on to be musicians, some would become writers, some artists or photographers, and one or two, the really dedicated ones, would wind up dead before they'd even had much life. But they crammed a lot of living into it anyway, a bunch of emancipated kids doing whatever they wanted, with nobody around to tell them "no."

Los Angeles caught its first up-close and personal glimpse of British punk in spring 1977, with the arrival in town of the Damned. One of the first of the British punk groups to form, and certainly the first to release both a single and an LP, they had now become the first to visit the United States, and of course they made their own way straight to Party Central.

Plans for a tour with Television fell through after Tom Verlaine's angular New Yorkers refused point blank to share a bill with something so gratuitously uncouth. The Damned funded their own activities instead— gigs in Boston, New York, and Los Angeles—and that, apparently, was where they picked up enough experiences and anecdotes to fill a book.

"We fucked our way across America," drummer Rat Scabies proudly announced in *Zig Zag* magazine. "Fucked ourselves stupid. The only time I got out of bed was to do the gig or have some photos taken." American groupies, he insisted, are "great . . . and they've all got cars, too, so you can get to the gig without the expense of taxis." He told tales of rampant groupies and the girl backstage at the Starwood who distributed blowjobs to nine different men while her boyfriend held her hand; of penetrating the same girl with Captain Sensible's bass; of the abandoned nature of American groupies, so different, he declared, to the women they met in England; and so on and so forth. And then there was Joan Jett.

"Yeah," Rat smiled. "I fucked her."

No he didn't. In fact, the closest he got to any Runaway was when Sandy West decked him backstage at the Starwood. She walked into the room and found him "yelling at Joan . . . and wanting to punch her and shit, so I moved in fast and smacked him one upside the head. Hard. Cold-cocked him. Calmed that motherfucker's ass right down."

"I turned him down several times," Jett reflected, also in *ZigZag*, "which destroyed his ego, so he had to say that he fucked me, which he didn't. I mean, goddam, with a name like Rat Scabies who's gonna take him anyway?"

Take him? Or take him out? "We were gonna kick his ass," Jett revealed. "We had plans." By the time they caught up with him however, during their second visit to the United Kingdom, the Damned had slipped so far from fame that "now, he's not even worth it."

In fact, it very quickly became known that you didn't fuck with the Runaways. One night at Jett's apartment, some guy started messing with them. Jackie Fox told *Mojo*, "We gave [him] a popsicle that was 10 percent lemonade and 90 percent pee. We were smoking a joint and licking our popsicles when he goes, 'This tastes like shit.' Without missing a beat Joan said, 'You're gettin' close.'"

NINE

Why Can't We Be Happy?

Queens of Noise was complete, and listened to in the cold light of day, it achieved everything that the five musicians wanted it to—an album that elevated the Runaways above the teenaged jailbait stakes and revealed them as authentic contenders. Unfortunately, they reckoned without Mercury Records still having their heads in the same juvenile fantasyland as a lot of the general public. "We thought they'd like it too," Jett sniffed . . . but they didn't. Compared to the lavish advertising campaigns that surrounded *The Runaways*, *Queens of Noise* would barely be noticed as it hit the marketplace at home or abroad. It would marginally improve on its predecessor's chart placing—it reached #172.

That was nothing to celebrate, but on the road around the United States through the spring, the Runaways were at the peak of their powers. "We are the best that's come outta LA in years!" Jett boasted to the English newspaper *Sounds*. "Definitely. We kick ass to Steven [Tyler], we kick ass to any other LA bands that play the Whiskey. We can sell out four nights straight and there's still lines around the block. The Starwood, when we played there, they turned away over a thousand people a night."

The rest of the country turned out to pay attention too, and occasionally got more than it bargained for. Headlining Boston's absurdly hot and sweaty Rat in April, Jett astonished the packed club by stripping down to her bra as the set progressed—"a Maidenform bra," laughed one witness. "Afterwards, we couldn't decide if she was making some really strange feminist statement, or if that was just what she happened to be wearing. But even the guys in the audience didn't find it particularly sexy!"

Another night, Iggy Pop dropped by to see the band play—his latest tour, his first since engineering his comeback with *The Idiot*, was washing up in many of the same cities as the Runaways' own. Jett told journalist Sandy Robertson, Iggy "was so wasted that he took about five minutes to shake their hands, after which he went to the bathroom and promptly fell over."

Hostility continued to abound, of course. "These bitches suck," snarled *Creem* critic Rick Johnson in the magazine's April 1977 edition. "The whole hype reeks of that age-old rock 'n' roll maxim—girls are just sissies, after all."

But the Runaways could give as good as they got. The moment the tour bus rolled into Detroit, they were pounding on the *Creem* office doors, demanding to be handed Johnson's head on a plate. They calmed down a little when they discovered that he was a freelance contributor who didn't even live in Michigan, let alone Detroit . . . but only a little. Instead, Jett sat down at the office typewriter and hammered out her response.

"Since you seem to know that girls are sissies, come see us sometime. We'll kick your fuckin' ass in."

Japan beckoned. Less than a decade had elapsed since the country first opened up to Western rock 'n' roll. Its first American superstar, in fact, was the same Alan Merrill who cowrote "I Love Rock 'n' Roll," the song that Jett fell head over heels with in her London hotel the previous fall. His Tokyo-based band, Vodka Collins, singlehandedly inducted the country into the glam-rock life in the early 1970s, and since then, the country had gone rock 'n' roll crazy. The Rollers were bigger there than anyplace else; eventually, Cheap Trick would rise up to take their place. But in between times, it was the Runaways who were capturing the nation's attention, as the band discovered when they touched down at Tokyo Airport. Nobody had even thought to warn them ahead of time.

"We were huge," Jett marveled.

Like the Beatles. It was all very unexpected. Nobody told us that we were well thought of there. We went through a lot of shit in America and a lot of shit in England, too. We had no idea what to expect. We were probably expecting the same sort of receptions we were getting elsewhere. But when we got to Japan, it was literally like we were the Beatles.

The difference was their following was primarily *female*, a reaction to the lowly status that women suffered in the country at that time. In America and Europe, Jett explained, their audience was primarily males "yelling, 'take off your clothes!' In Japan, where women are really thought of as second-class citizens, thousands of girls were chasing us down the street."

Even stranger, all these girls seemed to want was for their favorite Runaway to brush her hair, with a brush provided by the fan. They would wait patiently while their request was met, and then excitedly scoop out the loose hair from between the bristles. It was more polite—and a lot less painful—than pulling out chunks of it by hand!

They had a full itinerary, dominated by more photo opportunities and television performances than they had ever imagined could be shoe-horned into a single week, and including a special appearance at Suzi Quatro's wedding reception. Quatro and her longtime partner, guitarist Len Tuckey, had married the previous year in England, but decided to repeat the ceremony in traditional Japanese style during their own Far Eastern tour the following year. The Runaways hardly grabbed the lime-light for themselves, but they certainly shared it.

They recorded a live album, the sensibly titled *Live in Japan*, its dozen tracks split between the debut album and the just released *Queens of Noise*, and everywhere, they were bombarded with gifts. Lita Ford remembered having to buy extra suitcases to carry all the presents that she was given by fans. Other unprecedented luxuries included being given their own private hotel rooms for the first time in their careers. But it was in Japan that the cracks that began to form during the *Queens of Noise* sessions began to widen.

Every morning, the band would receive copies of every magazine that carried a mention of their name, including one that seemed devoted to Cherie Currie alone—posing in what she acknowledged to be "some pretty risqué" outfits. None of her bandmates had even known about the session, let alone attended it.

Currie, understandably, justified it by pointing out that first, she was the visual icon of the band in many people's eyes, but more importantly,

Fowley had organized the shoot in the first place. "But when the mag came out they went ballistic. I remember Lita walking up to me, throwing it at me and saying 'you bitch.'"

Fowley himself was nowhere to be found.

No matter how luxuriously they were being treated, the business end of things was as chaotic as ever. Nothing had been taken care of, unless the promoters had seen to it themselves. Fowley, once again, had absented himself from the proceedings, and whoever was meant to be looking after things simply didn't reach the band's expectations. And Fox was undergoing a crisis of her own, beginning with the money worries that she alone seemed to be aware of—such as the fact that the band members were still as broke as they ever had been. Kim Fowley, on the other hand, seemed to be doing all right out of the whole operation.

She was sick of him, sick of his excuses, sick of having to cover songs written by artists whose songwriting rights he published—Billy Bizeau, author of the new album's title track, was one of Fowley's protégés, and it didn't matter that "Queens of Noise" was a great song. It was the fact that the Runaways weren't even asked if they wanted to record it that rankled. The rage that it provoked between Currie and Jett was simply the icing on an increasingly unpleasant cake.

Then there was the business about management. Fowley had them so locked into his own clutches—sensibly, of course, because he needed to watch his own back—that there was noplace else to turn. So when Kiss manager Bill Aucoin let it be known that he was interested in adding the Runaways to his stable, he also made it very clear that they would need to dispose of Fowley first. He was not, he told them, going to fork out however much it would cost to run the band and then as much again to get Fowley out of the picture.

She was fighting with Currie too. All this was on Fox's mind as the Runaways toured the States in the spring of 1977, and it was still there when they arrived in Japan to find everything as disorganized as it had been on their first American tour. Now as they came offstage following a show, Fox was being told that her bass, a 1960s white Gibson T-Bird, had gotten broken when it fell off the already wobbly guitar stand that she'd been demanding they replace all tour long. And that, she averred, "was the last straw."

When that guitar neck snapped, so did Jackie Fox.

She returned to her hotel room, smashed a bottle against the wall, snatched up some glass, and began hacking at her arms. She wasn't trying to kill herself, she and her banmates were adamant about that. "Any idiot knows how to kill themself if they want to," Jett told journalist Sandy Robertson, when he asked about the rumors that Fox had attempted suicide. "I walked in and she was sitting there with her arm cut and I told her she was a jerk!"

She clearly couldn't play, however. Back at the hotel, Fox began packing for her return to the States—everybody agreed that was what she needed. As for the following day's show, at the Sixth Tokyo Music Festival, appearing alongside the Freshmen Four, Marilyn McCoo and Billy Davis Jr., and Filipino superstar Didith Reyes, Jett announced that she would play bass for the evening. Fox was sent home and Jett made her bass-playing debut in front of one of the largest audiences of her life.

Back in California, Kim Fowley too felt as close to giving up as he ever had. Instead he chose to diversify his interests. Arguments with the Runaways were coming more and more frequently, and usually ended with one party or the other swearing that they would never be speaking again. It was during one of these eventually patched-up hiatuses that Fowley conceived Venus and the Razorblade, another all-girl band; his concept this time was to create America's next sweetheart—a new Fleetwood Mac or Abba, for instance—only sharpened by a pure punk edge.

Like the Runaways, the Razorblades enjoyed a brutal apprenticeship. Fowley once claimed, albeit with some exaggeration, that the Runaways played sixty-seven gigs before they were allowed to play in Hollywood, because no one took them seriously. Venus and the Razorblades were doomed to a similar fate, only this time, it wasn't so easy escaping from it. Island Records turned them down, and while Atlantic apparently did make an offer, through the auspices of producer Bob Ezrin, this time it was the band that turned them down. They didn't feel ready to take that next step.

The Runaways grabbed—or were given—a couple of their songs: "Alright You Guys" and "I Wanna Be Where the Boys Are" were both in the band's live set by the time they got to Japan. Cheech and Chong's latest movie featured an all-girl band, Juice, performing another Razorblades number, "Some Like It Hot," and a new LA rock band, laboring under the unlikely name of Van Halen, were playing their "Young and Wild."

Everything seemed to be leaning toward a serious Razorblades break-through. But despite Fowley's lingering enthusiasm for the project (and his ability to extol their achievements to encyclopedic proportions), the group was destined never to make the kind of splash that Fowley envisioned—although they were certainly good enough. The album they cut that summer, *Songs from the Sunshine State*, remains a cult camp classic; their singles were stunning, their live show amazing. The Dead Boys covered their "Big City"—they were, it seems, the name to drop in the most discriminating of musical circles.

Which may be why there was talk, briefly, that Razorblades bassist Danielle Fay might be joining the Runaways to replace the errant Jackie Fox—who made it clear, once her bandmates arrived home, that she had no intention of rejoining the band. But Faye was ultimately passed over in favor of the impressively named Victoria Tischler-Blue, a bassist whom Fowley promptly described as "seventeen years old [with] a tattoo on her left hand. She came to the audition wearing a black leather jacket and carrying an import of *Suzi Quatro's Greatest Hits* or something, and plays in a style that is very compatible. She's a shy girl, a quiet one, but she looks like she could be Lita Ford's cousin."

"I remember walking through the courtyard . . . to the audition," Tischler-Blue recalled, "I pulled open the door, they're all sitting there, and then Lita goes 'oh god, she *does* look like me.'" The newcomer was not in for an easy time however. As Ford herself remarked, "she came into the band at a really hard time when the girls were tired and fucked up and pissed off, then here comes Vicki. 'I'm a fresh young bass player and I'm really happy to be in the band.'"

What Vicki Blue—as Jett quickly renamed the newcomer—didn't realize, and nobody had thought to tell her as she readied herself for her audition, was that the Runaways were still in disarray, this time as Cherie Currie began looking toward her own future. "I was miserable. The band members didn't like each other, and Kim was playing one member against the other."

Again, the problems built up slowly, and the remainder of the band knew that they weren't always in Currie's control. She had never wanted to take such a great slice of the limelight, Jett admitted. Even that solo photographic flight, they all acknowledged in the cold light of day, had been out of her hands; like the rest of them, she simply did what she was told to do when it came to promoting the band, and there were so many photo sessions piling up that it was difficult to keep them all straight.

At the same time, however, it rankled that she didn't do anything to stop herself from being projected as somehow separate from her bandmates. She acceded to the private photo sessions, she didn't object when one photographer after another placed her in the center of the band lineup. And as time passed, "she thought she was a goddamn queen." Or so it seemed to her bandmates.

"She wanted to be Cherie Currie and her back-up band," Jett told Sandy Robertson. "If she had her way, the four of us would be sitting here with masks over our faces so you couldn't tell who the fuck we were."

There were multiple grounds for divorce, then, all piling up around the already fractured unity of the band. When the end finally came, however, it was another photo session that provided the flashpoint. Currie needed to leave the shoot at a specific time to pick up her sister, and had made it very clear beforehand that her schedule was tight. She had two hours in which to pose for photographs, and then she would have to leave.

Two hours that she and the rest of the band spent waiting for Lita Ford to turn up. Finally she walked in just as Currie was preparing to walk out, and nothing could persuade the singer to stay.

The photographer was furious; his camera went flying across the room to shatter on the floor, and Lita lost it as well. Currie was in her dressing room when Ford burst in, kicking the door off its hinges and standing steaming in the shattered doorway.

"You have to choose," she announced, pointing a finger at Currie. Cherie was spending as much time with sister Marie as she ever had. "Choose between the Runaways and your family." She, Jett, Vicki Blue, and Sandy West had already made their decision. "We've chosen the band."

Currie sniffed. "Forget it man, I choose my family." She picked up her bag and walked out. "Bye."

A few days later, Kim Fowley called her. "Are you really quitting?"

"Sorry, yeah."

TEN

Bombs Away

The weekly British music paper *Sounds* broke the news of the changes to the band's European following in early September 1977. "The new line up of the Runaways is: Joan Jett/Lita Ford/Sandy West/Vicky Blue." With Jett handling lead vocals, the group had already been in and out of the studio, recording what would become their next album, *Waiting for the Night*, and Kim Fowley was as effusive as ever, waxing lyrical at every chance he got.

"*Waiting for the Night* is ideal for fighting, rioting, burning, trashing, looting, screwing, and pogoing. The single is 'Schooldays/Wasted.' 'Wasted' is about the joys of . . . death, throwing up, herpes, banditry, bleeding in the streets . . . 'Wait For Me' is about the great fuck that may get away. 'Schooldays' is about indoctrination."

The Runaways, too, threw their two cents' worth into the mill. One song, its author Lita Ford proudly declared, was called "The Trashcan Murders," and concerned a killer who was then loose in LA, a brute who stabbed his male victims, cut them up, and then stashed their remains in trashcans. Jett's "Schooldays," meanwhile, simply slammed through the downfall of organized education and proved such an anthem that thirty years later, it wasn't simply back in Jett's live set, it was also being rerecorded for her latest greatest-hits collection.

For all his hyperbole, however, Fowley would not handle the entire album. He and Earle Mankey had just completed work producing AOR songstress Helen Reddy's *Ear Candy* album and suddenly found himself with two singles on the massively influential KHJ radio Top 10. Offers for further work were suddenly pouring in and, with them, more money than the Runaways could ever have dreamed of generating. Fowley made his apologies and got to work.

Vicki Blue later said the early days of the four-piece lineup were the only moment of camaraderie she ever felt with her bandmates, with a new album percolating and a new future, apparently, stretching out before them. Those horizons became even brighter after the group finally made the decision to break with Kim Fowley and pledge their troth instead to Toby Mamis, of the AEM (American Entertainment Management) management concern.

The band already knew him—by reputation if nothing else—as Suzi Quatro's American publicist in 1974; it was Mamis who penned the liner notes to her first American album:

This record combines the brutal, hardnosed rock and roll that Detroit has always been known for with the tight, rhythmic, almost sophisticated rock and roll that has been coming out of London in recent years. In some ways, it is an ideal assimilation of these influences, allowing Suzi Quatro to become the first lady of rock and roll in a relatively short period of time.

Now he was working with Blondie, the New York garage-pop band that was just breaking through in Europe with its self-titled album—and whose ranks had recently been swollen by the arrival of Nigel Harrison, bassist on the Runaways' debut album. "X Offender" and "Rip Her to Shreds" were hit singles; singer Debbie Harry was the pinup girl of the age; and though the band's marketing sometimes seemed only marginally less sexual than the Runaways' own, there was a sense that Blondie were at least in control of it. If the Runaways could get a similar handle on their own public image, there was no telling how far they could climb.

Unfortunately, *Waiting for the Night* was no *Blondie*, as Mercury made very clear the moment the tapes were delivered. Having seen so many other supposedly punk rock acts turn toward power pop once the records started selling, Mercury assumed that the Runaways would follow suit. Instead, they had grown even harder edged, and the label had no interest whatsoever in it.

The Japanese live album had already passed them by, released in Japan only (where it promptly went gold) and available elsewhere as an expensive import alone. Now *Waiting for the Night* was to be allowed to wither as well. It was hard to believe that just a year earlier, the Runaways had been regarded as one of the label's number-one priorities. This time around, there would scarcely even be any advertising, let alone promotion. The label would just release the record and hope the Runaways' own reputation did the rest. Needless to say, it didn't.

Privately, however, Jett seemed to share at least some of Mercury's misgivings about the album. Cherie Currie's departure, while it smoothed away some of the personal differences that ripped at the Runaways, also deprived Jett of her chief ally in the fight to keep the band on an even musical footing, a hybrid of their shared love of glam, plus Ford and West's base metal instincts.

She was aware, too, that the deeper into hard rock the band moved, the further they were removing themselves from what she, Jett, viewed as the Runaways' core audience—the disaffected kids who were elsewhere responding so vehemently to punk rock. Across the Runaways' debut album, the group delved deliciously into the root cause and effect of the punk movement—the endless gray future that older generations had splayed out in front of the late '70s teenagers. Instead, they had been left behind. Neither *Queens of Noise* nor *Waiting for the Night* had anything in common with the punk scene.

The Germs were off and running now, and so were a host of other acts: X, the Weirdoes, the Bags, the Screamers—so many of them now were rising up in their wake. But only Joan Jett was out at their shows at every opportunity, sometimes shrieking encouragement, other times watching with an almost maternal eye, knowing that after the gig someone or other would stop to ask what she thought.

The Runaways returned to Europe in October 1977 for a British tour that this time would see them headline the Hammersmith Odeon, a three-thousand seater that was almost as far from the Roundhouse, where they'd played the year before, as it was possible to go.

Certainly the Runaways' audience thought so. A growing number of homegrown bands were already playing similar venues—the Clash were as established a theater group as any prepunk dinosaur. But still Jett would not forget the day that she and Lita Ford were making their way down Kensington High Street, when a fan approached them to draw them into a conversation that highlighted just how disconnected from her own musical roots and dreams she had suddenly become. The kid, a typical London punk, initiated the conversation. "You in the Runaways?"

"Yeah."

And the floodgates opened. How come the Runaways didn't dress like their fans did? How come they were playing the Hammersmith Odeon rather than touring the clubs? How come they'd sold out?

Jett tried to answer back, to explain that the band had spent two years playing the clubs and that it didn't matter how big or small a venue was, so long as the group was able to fill it with noise and excitement. Especially excitement. And in many ways, she was right.

But the larger the venue, the harder a band has to work to generate that atmosphere, and the harder an audience has to work to experience it. Punk rock, for all its later glory and success—the Jam closed out their career playing London's massive Wembley Arena; the Clash ended theirs at Shea Stadium—was the sound of the tiniest bolt-hole of all, a jam-packed room oozing sweat from the walls, and band and audience so close they could cuddle. The Runaways may have *deserved* to play the Odeon—or at least, the tour promoter thought so. But they didn't need it, any more than they needed any of the other venues they were offered on that tour.

Nevertheless, the tour was a success because the Runaways were so tightly oiled a touring band now that nothing that happened on- or off-stage could faze them. Not the Y-fronts that still made sporadic flights between audience and stage, not the deftly choreographed chants of "tits out for the lads" that still floated out of the crowd, not even the banks of empty seats that glared back from the stalls to suggest that maybe that kid in Kensington had been right all along and they should have been playing smaller venues.

With London Punks 999 trailing behind them as support, the Runaways' tour hit major theaters in two weeks' worth of cities and generally fell upon considerably more fertile soil than the last time around. With three albums under their belt now (four if you counted the live one, available from a handful of import stores), the Runaways had done more than enough to shake off the old image of jailbait . . . well, almost. "Joan Jett is gorgeous," drooled *Sounds'* Phil Sutcliffe following the band's Newcastle

City Hall show. "Vicki Blue is delectable. Lita Ford is the American Pie smile backed by the American Dream ass. And Sandy West is mine!"

True, Sutcliffe observed, there were some people who would never learn. Nine numbers into the set, "a section of the audience [was] still . . . so unaffected by the music that they organized a chant of 'Get them off.'" For them, "It's not about music/love: it's a wank."

But the show was a victory all the same, and audiences didn't even seem to mind when they realized that "Cherry Bomb" was no longer a part of the repertoire. "I'm sorry, we didn't bring our corsets," Jett apologized slyly. Once past the reek of testosterone rising from the stalls, the band no longer needed them.

On October 25, 1977, the Runaways appeared on BBC television's long-running *Old Grey Whistle Test* rock show, becoming the first even nominal flash of new-wave sensibility to gatecrash a show that had hitherto steadfastly ignored the embrace of punk rock in favor of a continued diet of singer-songwriters, prog heads, and art rockers. They were rewarded, following wild performances of "Wasted" and "Schooldays," by host Bob Harris's offhand drollery about lipstick and rock 'n' roll, and elevation to the select ranks of other acts that Harris had dismissed with just a bearded tut: Roxy Music, the New York Dolls, Sparks, Patti Smith. Another halt, in Bremen, brought the band onto the set of German television's long-running *Musik Laden*.

But the big deal for Jett was finally being set free on the streets of London to absorb the punk ethos that they had otherwise caught only in passing or by proxy. She caught the Clash on the road as they headed out in support of their debut album.

> There were two thousand kids all jumping up in the air at the same time, which we had never experienced or even thought about in America. This was when they still called it pogo-ing. It was so overwhelming. It was just incredible. It was so powerful. It felt really good to see that and come back to the States and try to just carry that on.

Jett spent more time with Gaye Advert, bassist with the Adverts and, in a land that was obsessed with conferring such titles upon its heroines, the punk pinup of the age. The two women were similar in both appearance and build, and Gaye laughs at the memory of one being blamed for the other's indiscretions as they raised hell around the capital's clubs.

"We first met at a Blondie do, guess it was an aftershow. I remember photographers there taking pictures of us together, and when the three of us left, Tim [Adverts vocalist T. V. Smith] muttering something like 'oh god, now there's two of them,' and climbing up a lamppost."

Jett and Sandy were both regular visitors to Adverts' one-room apartment in Hammersmith, stopping off at the shop on the corner "and rummaging excitedly through the sweets, to the shopkeeper's amusement. Joan got me to carve my name on her arm and she decorated my shirt." Another time, the pair turned up accompanied by Sex Pistols Steve Jones and Paul Cook. "There was a fair bit of alcohol, I remember Joan was nearly unconscious, I was rousing her whenever her drink threatened to tip over!"

"We never saw them live," Advert mourned. "They put us on the guest list when they played at the Lyceum [the following year], but when we got there, the bouncer told us we [the Adverts] were banned, along with, I think, the Pistols and the Clash." A number of London venues still barred punk rockers from darkening their doorways, long after there were any newspaper headlines to be garnered from such prohibitions. "Joan came out and found us afterwards, and when we told her they wouldn't let us in, she threw her drink at the bouncer on the door."

Time spent with the Sex Pistols, as they lived out the last couple of months of their existence, would also prove memorable, and might have been even more so. A rumor was circulating that Johnny Rotten was among the contenders to take the Personality of the Year Award at American TV host Don Kirshner's Annual Rock Awards. Rotten himself had no intention of attending the ceremony, and asked Jett if she would go in his stead and, if he won, accept the award and then read a speech deriding the show. Sadly, the award went elsewhere.

Back in the US, the new year saw the Runaways launched onto a three-month tour with the Ramones. "That tour was crazy," Joey Ramone recalled, "and the Runaways hated it. They were a good band, but we had very different audiences by then, even in America, and it wasn't a good mix personally, either." Jett, he said, was the only band member who made more than a token effort to socialize with the headliners: "She had a lot to say about music that I didn't think the others would even have thought about," Ramone continued. "So we did a lot of talking."

Joey, more than any of his own band, was a self-confessed music nut, seldom happier than when he was sitting around with a like-minded soul to rabbit on about the bands he loved, the records he'd bought, the gigs he'd seen. Jett could match him memory for memory.

She needed the distraction. The tour took the Runaways through some of the worst weather in recent memory—snowstorms that piled up around their van, as heavily as the Quarter Pounder wrappers piled up inside. By the time the tour was over, Blue laughed, she could no longer listen to the Ramones. Or eat McDonalds. She was also suffering from seizures, the legacy of a childhood horse-riding accident, which added to the sheer surrealism of the tour, not only for Blue but for her bandmates too.

It was while they toured that they discovered that Mercury Records had dropped them. But the band slammed on. On January 27, 1978, they opened for the Ramones at the Santa Monica Civic Center, their biggest ever show in the United States, and a solid triumph even in the face of the loyal support that the Ramones always drew. Indeed, at a time when dah bruddahs' nonstop diet of one-two-three-four-buzzsaw was growing just a tiny bit samey, the Runaways were putting on a show that blistered in variety and intensity, as Joey Ramone reflected.

> I remember that tour. They'd really turned into something great, little Joan was a far more convincing rock 'n' roll frontman than [Cherie Currie], she kinda reminded me of what would happen if Nils Lofgren and Keith Richards had a baby, someone who looked like they could really live dangerously, but knew when to pull back as well. I liked her.

British journalist Sylvie Simmons, watching from the Santa Monica stalls, agreed. Having noted that much of the crowd was still in the foyer when the band took the stage, "Fine, solid playing brought the audience trickling back in to listen and leer, and the final numbers of the short set—the tough and raunchy 'I Wanna Be Where the Boys Are,' featuring a dynamic Lita shoe-horned into her costume, and Joan Jett's gritty, tough vocals on 'Playing With Fire'—were greeted with much applause."

New material was breaking through alongside the old; the Runaways were firing on all cylinders as they crisscrossed the country—but to what end? A new record deal was as far away as ever, and the days when the likes of Bill Aucoin made come-sign-with-me eyes in their direction were long past.

Audiences were shifting. Suddenly, *Flipside* magazine was confronting Jett with the growing conviction that the group was appealing more and more to lesbians, to the exclusion even of the horny male fuckers who used to hang on their every bead of perspiration.

Jett laughed. "I heard something about that. 'Runaways dyke audience.' And some people going 'Hey Sandy, what a fox!' But I don't think that's the majority of our audience, though I don't care if they're anybody. I don't give a shit if they're transsexual or bisexual, gay. I don't care, just so long as they like it and enjoy it."

As for her own private pleasures, because where else could any interviewer lead after a question (or answer) like that, Jett merely smiled.

> Well, if they're private, they're gonna stay that way . . . I buy every dirty magazine in the world. I like to read them. I do. You know how wives go "Why are you reading that?" "Well, honey, the articles are good." Well, it's true, a lot of the magazines have really good articles. I always buy *Hustler* 'cause they're tasteless. *Oui.*

You check out the girls?
"Well, what the hell are you supposed to do, close your eyes?"

ELEVEN

I Need Someone

The band was falling apart. Not necessarily personally—every member of the group, past and present, had pointed out that the individuals were rarely all the best of friends. But each of the alliances that they did form with one another—Jett and Jackie, Cherie and Sandy, Lita and Jett, around and around in the way that teenagers in every walk of life are wont—were nevertheless the building blocks upon which the ultimate unity of the Runaways was forged.

Musically, however, they were definitely splintering, and the savage failure of *Waiting for the Night* broadcast those divisions to the world. While Jett was growing ever more dedicated to the ethics and energy of punk rock, Lita and Sandy were leaning ever further toward the love of metal that was their bond when they first met.

Jamming together when Jett wasn't around, they lay down a heavy barrage of riffery and rock shapes that echoed their personal musical fascinations and left them all but dreading Jett's arrival in the studio, to try and reshape their endeavors into something fast and spiky.

"From the summer of '78 it was growing apparent that me 'n' Lita were growing apart," Jett told *ZigZag*'s Kris Needs. "The way she wanted to go musically and the way I wanted to go. We were always such good friends and you can't just say 'fuck you.' We could see it coming, but nobody wanted to scream because we never fought. We weren't a fighting band, but it went slowly so far and I could see it was gonna happen." Months before she actually spoke aloud her final words to the band, Jett knew that the day was fast approaching when she would have to say "I quit." Because "if I didn't quit they'd probably have said 'We fire you.' It wasn't working."

For now, they inched on, with a new LP at the top of their agenda. Assuming that they could find anybody to release it—or even record it.

Any number of suggested producers either turned the band down or were turned down by the band. Suzi Quatro's mentor Mike Chapman, about to enter the studio with Blondie, was one of the names who passed them over—so was Kenny Laguna, the 1960s pop veteran who was enjoying a remarkable renaissance of fortune with the likes of the Greg Kihn Band and a finickily entertaining British rock band called Bethnal. Phil Wainman, who oversaw so many great singles by the Sweet, the Sensational Alex Harvey Band, and the Bay City Rollers, was recruited but withdrew shortly before the sessions began. Finally, Toby Mamis hired John Alcock, a production veteran whose 1970s had included stints with John Entwistle, Thin Lizzy, the Sharks, Keith Relf, and more, and in September 1978, the Runaways set to work on what they already knew would be their final album.

The band was more or less functioning as a three-piece now. Vicki Blue's health problems, dramatic on the Ramones tour, had now become serious enough to sideline her throughout much of the recording. Lita Ford took over bass duties, in addition to her lead guitar playing, and the musical links she had always enjoyed with Sandy West went into overdrive.

Alcott's own musical tastes were certainly favoring West and Ford's contributions to the album. While Jett turned in one classic, "Takeover," alongside the two weakest songs she had ever written, "My Body and Me" and "Little Lost Girl," the guitarist yowled and soloed over the too-long "I'm a Million." Cover versions included a mediocre march through the Beatles' "Eight Days a Week" and a positively lackluster take on Slade's "Mama Weer All Crazee Now," and if the record had any saving graces at all, it was Sandy West's "Right Now" and a single song that seemed to remember the thing about the band that Jett loved the best: its capacity to step out of line.

"Black Leather" was scarcely the greatest song that ex–Sex Pistol Steve Jones had ever dipped his pen into, but it was a solid punk-fringed rocker, compulsively riffing and electrifyingly screamed, and Jett strutted her way through its (admittedly pedestrian) lyric with a lot more style than the song deserved. "The pop was going," West explained, and the hard rock was coming in.

Most of the band's studio time seemed to be spent on getting the right sound and textures for drums, lead guitar, and bass. Jett's vocals often felt like an afterthought, something laid down because the audience expected it, not because the instrumentation required it. There was no time, she was told, to layer any harmonies, no need to double-track her singing to make it sound stronger. She was left feeling cheated; worse than that, she was left feeling marginalized.

And Now . . . the Runaways would not see release for close to another year, by which time the Runaways were a dead issue. That's how long it took before the small but brilliantly ambitious London label called Cherry Red picked them up, allying the Runaways alongside the even further-sighted signing of San Francisco's Dead Kennedys and Detroit's Destroy all Monsters in a catalog that, to this day, remains one of the most eclectically brilliant of all British outlets.

Label founder Ian McNair recalled,

> I'd seen . . . the Runaways play . . . at The Roundhouse. They were great! When I heard that Phonogram in England didn't want to release their new album, I tracked down their manager in New York and offered him a small advance for the record. I was a little nervous at first. Were a band who were used to the financial benefits of a major record company going to be happy with the minimal resources of Cherry Red? I needn't have worried. Toby Mamis . . . was just pleased to get the album out.

At the time, however, the band's failure to find a new major label deal was just one more nail in the band's coffin—as was the album itself. *And Now . . . the Runaways* emerged as a very determined set, but it was scarcely crucial listening, while the gigs that followed the recording sessions were little more than last rites. Vicki Blue had bowed out now—she was pictured on the album cover but would play no further part in the Runaways' life. In her stead, the group turned to Laurie McAllister, the twenty-one-year-old bassist who lived downstairs from Duane Hitch-ings, the session musician who added keyboards to the album.

Those final months were rough. In the six months since the Run-aways returned from their spring 1978 trip to Europe, the band's sole live show was at what Jett called some dumb celebrity thing in Century City. Novelist Harold Robbins's wife had thrown a party for him, "and they wanted a band to play, and Toby, our manager, got us the gig."

She outlined the evening to *Flipside*. "You name it, Zsa Zsa Gabor, they were all there, Jacqueline Bisset—all these huge fuckers were there and they were plugging their ears and by the end of the set, they were all walking out"—just as Sex Pistol Steve Jones walked on, to join the Run-aways in a raw retake of "Black Leather." "It was really great, really fun," Jett concluded. "There was a review of the party in the *LA Times*, but it only talked about us."

The words didn't help. Nothing could, not even the offer to make a movie about the band. Thirty years before the cameras rolled on *The Run-aways*, writer/director Alan Sacks's *We're All Crazy Now* would tell the story of the Runaways, and shooting was set to begin in August 1979, out in the California desert. And all the Runaways had to do was stay together long enough to make it.

They couldn't.

On December 31, 1978, the Runaways played their final show in San Francisco. Two months later Cherry Red released another new LP, *Flaming Schoolgirls*, and it was only when you peeled away the shrink-wrap that you discovered that it could have been their first album too. Half studio, half live, it drew a bunch of recordings from the earliest days of the group, including what must rank among the most grisly covers of the Beatles' "Strawberry Fields Forever" ever inflicted on the listening world. It was a sorry epitaph.

For it *was* their epitaph. The band did not break up immediately after that San Francisco show, although Laurie McAllister did quit, complain-ing that she only joined because she thought the band was still under Kim Fowley's aegis and didn't find out the truth until too late. Now she *was* working with Fowley himself, while Jett, West, and Ford cancelled the tour they'd set up for the New Year and sat back to consider their options.

For now, that meant a stint of session work for Ford and West, playing alongside a local hopeful named Alan Ross. They had not seen Jett since that final Runaways gig, and while Jett continued adamant that the Runaways had *not* split up, there was a sense of finality about the band's silence, and Jett knew it. Which is why, as West and Ford got on with the Alan Ross project, she told Toby Mamis to find her something else to do. "There ain't much call for a rhythm guitarist session musician."

The problem with the Runaways was that they had no ultimate direction. Forever torn between the glam contingent, the metal mob, and Kim Fowley's own eccentricities, the group never truly grasped the elements that made the original concept so appealing—teenagers playing teenaged music, teenaged girls playing the music that teenaged girls like.

The industry gets it wrong every time. Girls, the tastemakers insist, like sweet and cuddly pop idols. In the late 1970s, the likes of Leif Garrett and John Travolta were the role models; a few years earlier, it was David Cassidy and Donny Osmond. It was the boys who liked the hard-riffing, foot-stomping, fist-waving rock 'n' roll. So a group of girls playing music for boys—of course they were labeled little more than sex machines, because surely, that was all they set out to be.

Two years later, that attitude was still prevalent. Punk rock had opened some eyes, of course. Particularly in the UK, the women were giving as good as the guys, and while not quite steamrollering over the old preconceptions, they were at least denting them. Patti Smith, the Slits, Penetration's Pauline Murray, the Banshees' Siouxsie Sioux, X-Ray Spex's Poly Styrene—all had thrown the gender stereotypes into the garbage and forged ahead with the music they wanted to make.

Gaye Advert let the world know that women loved the Stooges. Asked by one UK music paper to name her five favorite LPs, she simply reeled off the Iggy Pop discography instead. The old beliefs still persisted, and there was a steady stream of singing sisters who maintained the pretence with pretty-frocked poise. But the idea that women could rock as well, and that those who did weren't simply Quatro-esque oddities, was no longer so strange . . . so alien . . . so open to abasement.

Right now, the media had still to decide where the Runaways fit into this new scheme of things. The Cherry-Bombs-with-Corsets designation that Jett would disdainfully spit out at audiences on the band's first post-Cherie tour was still foremost in a lot of minds, but that, Jett knew, was a consequence more of certain members' dress sense than any failing on the musical side. The Runaways may never have been KISS (at least, not after Bill Aucoin lost interest), but they weren't only out for kisses either.

Take that attitude, strip away the burlesque grind, shower on the music that Jett was still intent on making and that the Runaways had barely scratched the surface of. Jett had already taken her first steps alone, announcing her independence within days of the final Runaways' show by leaping onstage when the Dead Boys came to town, to jam through their signature hit "Sonic Reducer."

Dead Boys vocalist Stiv Bators was especially close to Jett. The first time the Dead Boys visited Los Angeles to play the Starwood on November 13, 1977, he led his bandmates to her San Vicente apartment to jam and party; photographer Theresa K. recalls,

> For Stiv, Joan was a very close friend and confidante. We frequently hung out together. Nothing wild and crazy—just normal friends hanging out—listening to records, gossiping, and having a few drinks. We *did*, however, take a lot of photos together—a few of which ended up in *Creem*, as we were all fans and took pictures made especially for *Creem*.
>
> Taking the photos did conjure up what people would call 'hijinx,' as we took the most ridiculous photos we could . . . such as Stiv ironing Joan's hair . . . Stiv and his girlfriend sitting with Joan in her bed . . .

reclining beneath the huge Sex Pistols poster that hung on the wall above her pillow, amid the jumble of books, records, and bedclothes that filled the room. A couple of years later, the very mention of Jett's name prompted a shit-eating grin from Bators. She was, he said, probably the coolest woman he'd ever met in rock 'n' roll.

It was Bators, too, who introduced Jett to the subject matter that would permeate "Takeover," the finest track on the entire last Runaways album. An avowed conspiracy nut, a subscriber to the infamous Dr. Peter Beter's cassette-tape digests of the manifold shadowy powers that were apparently poised to take over the world (if it had not already done so),

Bators's influence was all over the song's saga of dastardly Kremlin-fired mischief, and Jett's own justification for the song's paranoia. "You can't put *anything* past them."

The friendship wasn't all fun and games, however. Or at least, it didn't always end that way. One night, Jett told the *NME*'s Adrian Thrills,

> I got drunk with Stiv . . . and this girl I know. We went to this hotel room then onto some apartment and I had this bottle of Tequila that nobody wanted, so I drank the whole pint myself. Apparently I fell over and smashed my face on this elevator, and Stiv and this chick had to try and get me into a cab to take me to hospital, while I was trying to punch them out.

The resultant scar would stretch from her forehead to her chin.

Bators was also plotting a solo album, a follow-up to his just-completed *Disconnected* set—a concept album this time, titled *Allies*. A host of punkoid illuminati would be accompanying him, including the Heartbreakers' Jerry Nolan, Sex Pistols' Steve Jones and Paul Cook, and of course Jett, and a few of the songs were already demoed. *Allies* never materialized, as Bators instead linked up with the rump of Sham 69 and formed a whole new band, the Wanderers. But, he insisted, it would have been amazing.

PART TWO

I Love Rock 'N' Roll

TWELVE

Doing All Right with the Boys

Young, dark, and smoldering; painfully good looking and talented too, the Arrows were the sort of band that every marketing department hopes it will one day be handed, but which only a very fortunate few ever get.

And even those that do aren't always certain what to do with them. The Arrows formed in London in 1974 and scored their first hit, "A Touch Too Much," with the ink still barely dry on their record contract. A follow-up chased it to further chart glory—and then nothing. And not because they had nothing worthy of releasing in the aftermath, either. It was record-label chief Mickie Most who set up the roadblocks. He viewed the Arrows from the outset as simply another pretty-boy combo that would do what they were told, and then got in a strop when he discovered that they wouldn't.

Before moving to London in 1974, the Arrows' frontman Alan Merrill had been a star in Japan with Vodka Collins, writing most of their material and leading them to several shades of Far-Eastern glory. Naturally, he assumed that he would continue writing the songs he sang in his next band.

Most, however, had not arrived at the pinnacles he now occupied by allowing his artists to dictate such matters. He had his own teams of songwriters that he preferred to trust, and so the heart of Arrows' repertoire would be composed either by Nicky Chinn and Mike Chapman, the writers behind the Sweet, Mud, and Suzi Quatro; or Bill Martin and

Phil Coulter, the team that had already tasted glory with the Bay City Rollers.

"I Love Rock 'n' Roll," one of the first songs that the Arrows brought to Most's table, was buried away on a B-side. A little later, it did make it out as an A-side, but Most's label, RAK, had already stopped promoting Arrows' records by that time, to punish them for daring to seek out independent management. Soon, RAK would stop releasing them as well, while holding tight to the contract to ensure that the band couldn't go anywhere else.

By the time television producer Muriel Young snapped the Arrows up to host a weekly series of teatime pop shows beginning in March 1976, the group was essentially up shit creek. Every Wednesday for fourteen weeks—and then for another fourteen when the series was renewed six months later—eight or nine million kids tuned religiously in to watch *The Arrows*. And there wasn't a single new record on the shelves for them to buy.

But there were a few old ones, which was just as well.

"'I Love Rock 'n' Roll'" was a knee-jerk response to the Rolling Stones' "It's Only Rock 'n' Roll," explained Merrill. The title track (and hit single) from the Stones' latest album arrived in spring 1974, at a time when Mick Jagger was hanging out in aristocratic circles far beyond the club and pubgoers with whom he'd once socialized, and Merrill continued, "I almost felt like 'It's Only Rock and Roll' was an apology to those jet-set princes and princesses that he was hanging around with. That was my interpretation as a young man: it's *only* rock 'n' roll, and I like it. *Like.* Well, I loved it, so okay—I love rock 'n' roll. And then, where do you go with that?"

> You have to write a three-chord song with a lick that people remember, and it has to build. So I had the chorus, which to me sounded like a hit. And I thought, I'll do something really unusual. I'll write it that this is a song separate from the verse. So the actual chorus is something that's coming out of a jukebox, and the two kids in the disco who are flirting are hearing this song that's a hit. It felt like the *Twilight Zone.* A hit within a hit. A fictional hit coming out of the chorus with the kids singing it as their favorite song in the verse of the song.

That was what Jett heard as well, that September 1976 evening in a London hotel. "I Love Rock 'n' Roll" closed *The Arrows* show that evening, playing out as the final credits rolled, and Jett fell head over heels for it. She picked up a copy of the single while she was still in London, and it sounded as good on the record player when she got it home as it had on the television in the White Hart Hotel. She thought about covering it with the Runaways as well, and they even worked up a version for their October 1977 British tour. But when her bandmates resisted—for they weren't half as keen on it—she decided not to force the issue. There was something about the record that demanded something special.

Alan Merrill felt the same way about the Runaways. With their debut album newly released in the UK, the Runaways were hosting a record release party, which is where the Arrows' drummer, Paul Varley, caught them. He turned up at Merrill's flat immediately afterwards.

Merrill recalled,

> Paul and his girlfriend walked into my flat, pissed, and tossed the Runaways album into the wall in a spiral. It hit the wall, and fell to the floor. I had high ceilings, so it was a given to me that the vinyl was probably broken. Paul explained that what they had just seen was a "chick band" and that they were dreadful . . . but, after they left I looked at the album and it was still intact. Not a single crack in it.
>
> I put [the Runaways album] on, and I got instantly interested. I liked the song "Cherry Bomb," and as I listened I looked at the album cover. I had a peculiar sense of *deja-vu*. I thought, *I am going to marry one of these girls.* The image from the photo was so strong to me. After all, they were my ideal girlfriends, all of them. Any one of them. A girl I could have sex with and play guitar with afterwards, maybe even someone to write songs with. It was my ultimate dream girl. I was an American in London. These were American girls who played rock music. I could have more than one passion with one girl! Music and lust!

The feeling was mutual. Three years later, Jett was still playing "I Love Rock 'n' Roll" in her head and looking for an opportunity to record it. When the Runaways broke up, she knew its time had come. She picked up the phone and dialed Sex Pistols Steve Jones and Paul Cook.

The Runaways were still officially on hiatus, although it was looking increasingly like the break would become a break-*up*. There was talk of auditioning a new bass player, but the trio could never seem to find the time. And Jett was bored.

"I was in LA wondering what I was gonna do with my life, so I gave [Jones and Cook] a call and said, 'You wanna cut a couple of sides with me and produce?'" Toby Mamis had apparently agreed a solo deal for Jett with Phonogram, parent company of the Runaways' old home at Mercury, even though Jett was aware that "Sandy and Lita will be upset when they find out I'm . . . doing this."

But she put it to the back of her mind. Cook and Jones said yes, and behind the scenes, another pair of eyes glanced in Jett's direction. It was only later that Malcolm McLaren, Cook and Jones's manager throughout the Sex Pistols adventure, admitted that he should have been paying more attention.

The one-time manager of the New York Dolls; the so-called Svengali behind the Pistols; and a passing ship through the lives of Adam Ant, Bow Wow Wow, and Madame Butterfly did not make many mistakes—at least, not that he admitted to. And he didn't make a mistake with Joan Jett either. In fact, he didn't do anything; and that, he said, is where he went wrong.

> All the time that she was in London, first with the Runaways and then with Steve and Paul, I was watching her and thinking that she had an amazing career ahead of her. Regardless of who she was working with, or who was looking after her. She was smart, she was good looking, but what was most important was, she was one of the boys. I'm sure there were plenty of young men, and young women as well, who fantasized over her in sexual terms, but if you looked around at the other women in music at that time, Debbie Harry and Kate Bush and the Welsh one who thought she was Rod Stewart [Bonnie Tyler], your fantasies began and ended in the bedroom.
>
> With Joan, they went everywhere else. You could see yourself playing football with her, lending her your Led Zeppelin albums to listen to, borrowing her T-shirt. And there had never been a woman in rock like that before, a woman who you'd want to do everything with. That is why Joan Jett made it, because unlike every . . . other

. . . woman . . . in . . . rock, she was someone you'd want to hang out with.

Jones and Cook certainly thought so. The fifteen months since the Sex Pistols split up, at the end of a murderous American tour, had seen the pair fall into a semi-twilight existence of session work and hanging out. They recorded, it seemed, with whomever asked them to, and it was their good fortune that the majority of their suitors—ex-Doll Johnny Thunders and Thin Lizzy's Phil Lynott among them—were names that they could be proud of recording with.

The Pistols, after all, were never built for the long haul. Too volatile, said their apologists; too nightmarish, said their foes; and too bad, said their admirers—the people who understood that beneath the tabloid headlines that sprang up every place the Pistols walked, there was indeed a musical evolution taking place: it was one that flowered across just a quartet of singles and a hit-and-miss LP but which, within that paltry haul, set the stage for everything that would pass as punk for the next three decades and beyond.

So they broke up and headed in so many different directions—singer Johnny Rotten, reverting to his given name John Lydon, to the industrial funk dub convolutions of Public Image Ltd.; bassist Sid Vicious to a Rykers Island cell and death; and Cook and Jones to the land of whatever opportunity knocked next. Which is when Jett called them up.

Malcolm McLaren looked back and wondered "what if" . . . What if he had persuaded her to remain in London, rather than head back to Hollywood? What if he had landed her the kind of record deal that he had proven time and again he was capable of negotiating, rather than watching her go off with the first lightweight Euro-consortium that offered her a one-off deal? And what if the musicians who pushed her towards these new frontiers had been those who had already visited the future themselves? "The Sex Pistols changed the world," McLaren continued. "But so did Joan Jett, and one day, people will see that for themselves."

In March 1979, Jett booked into Chapel Studios in Wimbledon, Southwest London, a neat little outfit set up inside a disused religious chapel, but one that could produce a truly savage sound if one were required.

The session, Jett said later, "was very easy. I found them [Cook and Jones] to be extremely professional and really into what they were doing.

They were very concerned about making a good record and we had a lot of fun. We were laughing the whole time. It was really, really great to work with them."

It was also very fast—so fast that not even Alan Merrill realized that two Pistols and a Runaway (plus pianist Jeff Bannister and sax-man Mike Eaves) were recording his song that day. He too was in the studio at that time, preparing the final mix of the debut album by his latest band Runner.

> We were in the vocal harmony stage of the recordings. Overdubs. Billy Lyall from Pilot was there adding some keyboards on our stuff. Alexis Korner dropped by to encourage us, with his son Damien engineering. I saw Joan and was too shy (without first having a drink) and had far too big a crush on her to say hello, even though I wanted to.
>
> So, instead I took a Rickenbacker twelve string into the studio hallway on our breaks and was playing Byrds/Stones/Kinks songs, hoping Joan would come over and start up a conversation. She didn't.
>
> She was cool, LA style. Walked by a few times, saying nothing, looking straight ahead. I knew Jonesy, but he was never with Jett at the same time in the hallway and I was too "cool/shy" to ask him to introduce us.
>
> I knew they were working on material, but I didn't know she was cutting "I Love Rock 'n' Roll." I was in the area, and I was completely unaware that the first seeds of the song's revival were being sewn in the next room. It doesn't get much stranger than that.

In truth, the version of "I Love Rock 'n' Roll" that was recorded at that session was not the one that Jett still heard in her head. Cook and Jones of course brought all their old Pistolian grandeur to the proceedings, and Jett's vocal was awash with teenaged spunk. In fact, it was difficult to say *what* was wrong with the recording. But even Ariola, the German-based label that would be signing Jett to her first solo record deal, were happy to bury it away on the B-side of one of the other songs she cut with Cook and Jones at the same session, "You Don't Own Me."

Alan Merrill shrugged the song's disappearance away. It came out, it sank without trace, and that was the end of that. Or so he assumed. "What are the odds of someone recutting a song? Very slim." But Malcolm McLaren was less forgiving. "Well, they were deaf, weren't they?" he condemned years later.

> Like all Germans. I couldn't believe it, a record that sounded that good, and they lost it, and maybe that's when I should have stepped in, told Joan to stop wasting time in Los Angeles, set her up in London and built a new band around her. And it would have worked as well, because instead I built one around Annabelle [Lu-Win, schoolgirl singer with Bow Wow Wow], and if you want to know how these things go around in circles, who produced Bow Wow Wow's biggest hit? Kenny Laguna. And who produced Joan Jett's biggest hit? Kenny Laguna. So maybe everything happened as it needed to anyway, and that's why I never regretted a thing.

THIRTEEN

Love Is All Around

Kenny Laguna was old school American rock 'n' roll, without ever actually appearing old himself.

A decade or so Joan Jett's senior, Kenneth Benjamin Laguna was just twelve years old when he grasped his entrance into something approaching the music business, playing keyboards behind an array of visiting pop hit-makers as they turned out to play the New York City high school hop circuit for the WMCA Good Guys—the deejay team that is credited (or in some circles, blamed) for creating Top 40 radio as we know it.

Across the late 1950s and early '60s, alongside DJs Joe O'Brien, Harry Harrison, Don Davis, and Jim Harriott, Laguna worked with some of the greatest legends of the East Coast airwaves. But it was Jack Spector he especially loved working with, and who supported him back in turn. Partly, Laguna explained, because he knew every one of the Top 40 hits that the hop audience would require the band to play, but mostly because he only asked twenty dollars a day to play. By the time he graduated high school, Laguna already had a musical resume as long as his arm, and his move from being a pick-up musician for passing road shows to an integral part of the studio setup was as smooth as any transition could be.

He was an ideas man first and foremost, hitting waves as they prepared to break on the shores of popular culture and seeing what sort of splash he could make. It wasn't the most profitable way of making a living; Laguna grew up in an age when managers and entrepreneurs regarded musicians as something only less marginal than a necessary evil, fobbing them off with contracts that would make a blind man blanch today, and financial agreements that essentially agreed there would be no finances. Not for the performers anyway.

But simply being a part of the music industry, collecting a weekly pay-check for doing something they loved—that was all a lot of kids wanted, and Laguna was no exception. Besides, those session fees added up, even when they were union rates at best. At one point in the late 1960s, Laguna later reckoned, he was making $2,000 a week, which wasn't bad at a time when the average wage in America was little more than three times that *a year*.

Not all of his concepts worked. Laguna's first recordings, with bands like the Nighthawks and the Viscaynes, were as obscure when they were released, in the mid-1960s, as they are today. And when the Kama Sutra label allowed him to cut a solo single in 1966, "Do You Know What I Think?" went nowhere either.

But he was a part of the Kasenatz-Katz bubblegum manufactory when the Ohio Express cut the fluffy pop classic "Yummy Yummy Yummy"; he was part of the team that relaunched Tony Orlando on the road that would lead to megahit makers Dawn; and he was astounded when one of their instrumental B-sides, a harp instrumental titled "Grooving with Mr. Bloe," became a #1 hit in the UK, after the BBC started playing the wrong side by accident.

Laguna worked with Darlene Love and Bill Medley, and wrote a song about Muhammad Ali. He recorded the soundtrack to Andy Warhol's *Lonesome Cowboys* movie, and he formed a five part a capella band called Moose and the Pelicans, which could have been huge had their frontman, Bobby Bloom, not gone off and had a solo hit with "Montego Bay."

He toured with Tommy James and the Shondells, and by the time Laguna relocated to California in 1972, he'd either written, played, or sung on more than *fifty* Top 40 hits. Which means that Jett was just one of the millions of teenagers who had spent her entire adolescence listening to him.

Neither did he stop there. In London in 1973, Laguna worked with Dave Edmunds and David Essex on the hot movie soundtrack *Stardust*, and there's a little piece of wry synchronicity there for readers of the Run-aways' spring 1976 *Who Put the Bomp* magazine to hand; Dave Edmunds shared that same issue, and so did the Shangri-Las, the immortal '60s sirens whom the young Laguna played with when they hit the New York–area live circuit.

Three years later, back in the UK, Laguna's friend Bill Curbishley, manager of the Who, invited him to take a look at the Steve Gibbons Band, a hard-rocking Birmingham R&B band that seemed doomed to trail around the club circuit forever. Laguna was impressed and agreed to work with the group. Together they created *Rollin' On*, the landmark album from which spun "Tulane," a tumultuous slice of seething wax that slashed through the UK chart during the summer of 1977.

The following year, Laguna was back in the Who camp, producing the *Dangerous Times* debut for Pete Townshend's latest protégés Bethnal, and wringing from them the finest version of "Baba O'Reilly" this side of the Who's own *Who's Next* original. And now he was back in the studio in London with Advertising, one of the best of all the pretty power-pop bands that were being flung at the marketplace in the aftermath of punk. Their "Lipstick" single remains a fabulous dash of flashy pop, and Laguna found the time to round up another fab slab of prime British power pop as well, the ever-dazzling New Hearts.

It was Tony Mamis who first suggested that the Runaways get together with Laguna while they were searching for a producer for the band's final album. Laguna turned it down. Having just produced the *8.5* album for Earthquake and overseen the Modern Lovers' *Live* LP, he was about to start work on their Beserkley labelmate Greg Kihn's new set. The Runaways went elsewhere, and so did Laguna. "To me," he explained to writer David Snowden, "anything that's really gimmicky is hard to deal with and that was [the Runaways'] reputation."

Mamis was not giving up, however. Laguna may have been playing hard to get where the Runaways were concerned, but Mamis knew that once he actually met Jett and talked to her, there was nothing that could not be accomplished. So he called again.

The end of the Runaways had not spelled the end of the *We're All Crazy Now* movie project. Jett was still contracted to appear in it, and was still required to create its soundtrack as well. Something close to an album's worth of songs needed to be laid down in three days. Was Laguna interested?

Once again, he wasn't. It was his wife, Meryl, who suggested that he at least take a look at what Jett had to offer. She had read enough to know that Jett had something special, something that Laguna would find appealing, and finally the producer agreed. In May 1979, they set up a meeting at the Hyatt Hotel on Sunset Boulevard, and just as his wife had predicted, Laguna was sold.

Jett arrived for the meeting, he told *Spin* magazine, "with a baseball cap on, ripped-up T-shirt and jeans, and looking pretty screwed up. Overweight. Like she'd been drinking."

Which she had. The Runaways had finally confirmed their dissolution now. Back in March, talking to the UK music press, Jett admitted that "no one knows what we wanna do right now. Everybody's tempers are flaring, we're fighting a lot, there's a lot of tension." She insisted that she would not be the one to call time on the Runaways, that everything depended upon how "the other girls feel." But when she returned to LA from London in April, it was clear that the band was over and it was time to move on.

"I felt like everybody in LA, whenever I was walking round the streets, was saying 'haha, Joan Jett. The Runaways finally broke up.' I felt like those people who hated us were really having a laugh." So she got drunk, and stayed there. "I was not in very good shape at all, in any sense of the word."

But Laguna was convinced. He had never met a girl like this before, and knew he never would again. He told her, "Joan, I'm gonna help you get a record deal."

Laguna did not intend to do it all on his own, of course. His address book was almost as fat as his track record, but he didn't even have to open it to know who else should be brought aboard the unfolding fantasy; and when Laguna sat down with Jett for the first time at the Hyatt, he did not do so alone. Ritchie Cordell was alongside him.

It was Cordell who produced and/or wrote many of the records that Laguna played on, first for the Roulette label—that string of hits by Tommy James and the Shondells—and then for Kasenatz Katz; the 1910 Fruitgum Company's "Indian Giver" and Crazy Elephant's "Gimme Gimme Good Loving" were both Cordell classics.

Of all his creations, however, the Shondells remain the most significant, and not only because they looked (and sounded) so great. Their first hit, "Hanky Panky," was written by the forever-winning team of Jeff Barry and Ellie Greenwich, and it was only the first shot. Because the Shondells followed up with "I Think We're Alone Now," then followed *that* with "Mony Mony." Tommy James and the Shondells were set to dominate American pop like no band before or even since, and Ritchie Cordell was going to rule alongside them.

Of course it didn't work out quite like that. Although he flowered dramatically, Cordell's reign was short; by the end of the 1960s, Cordell later admitted, "I was suffering from serious burnout. There was drugs, there was shit coming down, there was all this stuff going on around the only thing I wanted to do, which was write songs and produce records. So I stepped back and just watched."

Watched while glam rock, a music that was at least the bastard child of his beloved bubblegum, soared across Europe and Japan. Once or twice, he admitted, he thought of returning, finding—or better still, inventing—a band that could take on and triumph over any of the movement's masters. But there were too many other people working the same template: Mike Leander and Gary Glitter; Chas Chandler and Slade; Bill Martin, Phil Coulter and the Bay City Rollers; and most significant of them all, Nicky Chinn and Mike Chapman, with their deft manipulation of the UK charts, week in and week out.

But in many ways too, it was the Chapman half of that duo who did finally nudge Cordell back into action at the end of the decade. Having turned down the Runaways, Chapman had taken on the job of producing Blondie, and overnight he transformed them from a medium-achieving garage band with a sharp eye for updated Shangri-Las motions into a veritable behemoth. Their third LP *Parallel Lines*, the single "Heart of Glass"—these were destined to become the biggest records of the year, maybe even the decade. Shortly before his death from pancreatic cancer on April 13, 2004, Cordell recalled, "I decided to find my own Debbie Harry. Instead, Joan Jett found me."

He was as smitten by her as Kenny Laguna was, and it was impossible for Jett not to be caught up in the duo's enthusiasm. "They can appreciate where I'm at," she told *ZigZag*, "and I can appreciate the fact that they had many hits. They being able to hear what can be a hit can only help if I write songs with them. They can show me how to write a hit song but I can still get across what I want to because I've got a lot to do with it. It's a good combination."

The game plan was simple. Songs first. Jett was constantly writing, and so were Laguna and Cordell; in fact, they had started work on four new songs on the plane to Los Angeles. "When we got together, we worked real quick and didn't allow ourselves to get hung up on details," Laguna explained to Jett's *Bad Reputation Nation* fan club magazine. "That was a good chemistry and everything was pretty direct. Inspiration only takes a moment and it was great vibes."

Booking into Fidelity Recorders in Studio City in early August 1979, Jett, Laguna, and Cordell cut a bevy of new songs: "You Don't Know What You've Got," "I'll Never Get Away," " Tell Me," "I Want You," "Jezebel," "Too Bad on Your Birthday," "I'd Rather Be Hectic," "You Can't Get Me"—suddenly there was all this great music pouring out, and Jett could scarcely pick up her guitar without another idea bursting forth.

Old songs were revised. "One of Them" was a number she wrote during the last days of the Runaways. With a revised, Laguna-led lyric, it became "Love Is Pain." Another newcomer was "Bad Reputation," written, said Joan, because that was what she seemed to have developed. She and Laguna lost count of the number of times they would hear her mentioned, and then followed up with the words "I hear she's got a bad reputation." So they wrote a song about it.

They grabbed some favorite old covers. "You Don't Own Me" was lying neglected on an old LP by Lesley Gore. The Isley Brothers' "Shout" was a chest beater that no audience could resist, "Hanky Panky" was reprised from Ritchie Cordell's bubblegum cabinet, and there was even a blast from Kenny Laguna's past. "Make Believe" dated from his days alongside Tony Orlando in a short-lived band called Wind. A couple of Gary Glitter hits, "Do You Wanna Touch Me" and "Doing All Right with the Boys," slipped into the repertoire, and the Arrows were still there as well. It was, as they say, one helluva package.

Now all they had to do was find somebody who wanted to open it.

Laguna had been in the studio for just two days with Jett when he decided he wanted to continue working with her, once the session was complete. The chemistry between the two had been immediate, he continued; the entire project was due to last just three or four days. But in that time, they bonded; knew that they had found a musical soulmate.

She reminded him, he said, of Darlene Love, the one-time Phil Spector cohort with whom Laguna had worked at the end of the 1960s—it was Darlene who voiced his Muhammad Ali tribute. Now Jett was singing "You Don't Know What You Got," and as she swung into the "ooooh baby" chorus, Laguna melted. She was, he said, the artist he had spent his entire life waiting for.

There was just one problem. Jett refused to sing without her guitar alongside her, and Laguna was convinced that she would do a better job if she sang first, then dubbed the guitar on afterwards.

Jett was having none of it. "If my guitar isn't on the original track, then there ain't going to be no song."

Laguna was stunned. He told Musicpix.net:

I thought—"shit," y'know? Because I came in there with this natural prejudice about looking at this little girl in a baseball cap and thinking she can't play guitar, but it turns out she played guitar better than anyone on the tape.

Joan is pure and she has an amazing sense of the kind of music that she likes . . . She doesn't even try to bother, or try to understand the music that she doesn't like. But she's really into the music that she likes. She's always happy when she's listening to music that she likes. And really annoying music, mostly for her, is really pretentious. That's why her perspective is so good because she's a fan. She never stops being a fan . . . being about to hear other people's music. It's really a good thing.

He told *Bad Reputation Nation*:

Joan is very hardcore. If I'm left alone, the album's going to sound like a Beach Boys or Tommy James record; if Joan's left alone, it's going to sound like a super hardcore punk record. In between we get this punk-pop thing happening . . . I come from a rock and roll pop background. My bubble gum background fell into the late '70s new wave and what they called punk. I did a lot of Beserkley records and had hits with Jonathan Richman, and I worked with Greg Kihn when he started to have hits. For some reason, that bubblegum background fit into what the punks were doing, and I was able to be a part of that. So in a way, Joan and I sort of connected there.

But, he laughed, "It wasn't meant to become [a] permanent thing.

Jett-Lag Productions, the punningly brilliant combination of their own names in one 50/50 arrangement, was set up almost immediately. For Jett, it was an opportunity to actually forge forward in tandem with someone who believed in her; for Laguna, it was enough simply to have someone he believed *in*.

In the meantime, Jett had a movie to make.

The very different setting of high school drama notwithstanding, Jett had never acted before—unless, of course, one considered her nightly transformation from her normal shy self into the she-cat Joan Jett. But she had been noticed by Hollywood all the same—or at least by its television cousin.

In 1977, *Happy Days*—actors Henry Winkler and Ron Howard's prime-time sitcom-recounting of the golden age of fifties rock 'n' roll— was going into its fourth season, and the show's producers were looking for a tough little rocker chick to play the leather-clad sister of Pinky Tuscadero, one of Fonzie's ex-girlfriends, across seven episodes.

Casting through the available talent, and with one eye certainly on the show's already established musical quotient, the scouts settled upon three possibilities. Jett was one of them, Debbie Harry was another, and Suzi Quatro was the third. Quatro got the job. "They said Debbie was too old," Jett laughed to *ZigZag*, "and I was too tough looking. Can you believe I out-toughed Suzi Quatro? Can you believe that when I was fifteen, I could have thought I'd out-tough Suzi Quatro?!?"

Now all she was being asked to do was play an approximation of her natural self.

Predicting by a full thirty years the scenarios that director Floria Sigismondi would layer into *her* Runaways movie, *We're All Crazy Now* focused on the background and the antics of an all-teen, all-girl rock band as it tried to make its way through the masculine jungles of rock 'n' roll.

But it did so on a tiny budget, and with a script that rarely aspired to anything more than a below B-movie tag—an artifice that might have worked well in the hands of Roger Corman, as he proved when he shot the Ramones through the joys of *Rock 'n' Roll High School*, but which left *We're All Crazy* looking cheap and nasty.

Today regarded among Hollywood's elite, Alan Sacks was best known at the end of the 1970s for his television work—in particular, the season's worth of *Welcome Back Kotter* that he oversaw between 1975 and 1976. *We're All Crazy Now*, titled for the Slade cover that misfired on the final Runaways album (but which was always a riot in concert) was to be his debut as a big-screen director, albeit on a less than star-studded budget. The Runaways alone among his cast had any kind of name, and the departure of the rest of the band could have scuppered the project altogether.

But writer Barney Girard, of *Twilight Zone* acclaim, reworked the script to focus on Jett alone, and on schedule in August, the crew assembled to begin filming.

Jett was not enthusiastic. Even though she was impressively armed with five of the new songs she'd penned with Kenny Laguna and Ritchie Cordell, including the movie's putative title track, she readily admitted that there were a lot of things that she'd rather be doing than sitting around in a trailer in the California desert waiting for the director to call her.

"My life was breaking up," she admitted in a major *NME* interview in 1982. "I was doing that movie out of desperation. Basically it was some money and something to do; it kept my name alive while I figured out how to continue." At least, that was the intention. The desert is an inhospitable environment at the best of times though. Filming there at the height of summer just makes it worse. And a layer of smog that the experts were describing as the worst to hit the state in two decades added the finishing touch to a cruelly grueling operation.

"It got to be too much," Jett shuddered. "A lot of people got sick." But she got sicker, coming down with a fever that simply wouldn't let up. Finally she was rushed back to Los Angeles and deposited in the hospital, there to be informed that she had picked up a virus.

Nothing to worry about, so nobody did. Spend three days in bed, she was calmly advised, and you'll be all right. So she returned home, but rest did nothing to alleviate her symptoms; in fact, they only worsened. By the following day, she was unable to breathe.

Finally she was taken to hospital in LA where she was diagnosed with pneumonia, which in turn had developed into a heart infection—a rare condition, but a potentially fatal one. Left unchecked, or simply mis-treated, the infection would set about forming abscesses, not only in her heart, but also in other organs and even her brain. Add severe hemoptysis (coughing up blood) to her state and it was hardly surprising, as she later put it, that "I was really sick. It was terrible. I almost went *phut*."

Ultimately she remained in hospital for six weeks, and it was the realization of just how close she came to dying, her friends around the old Hollywood punk scene are convinced, that turned Jett's entire life around. Once she had been content to play her guitar and love rock 'n' roll, living it in as much of its stereotypical glory as she possibly could.

She still was. But now she was in control. The movie was abandoned when she fell ill, and with it any need for her to bow down to anyone else's demands. With Laguna and Cordell promising to back her instincts to the hilt, she would never allow herself to swallow bullshit again.

FOURTEEN

Let's Do It

It was the end of October 1979 before Jett was finally declared fit enough to be discharged from the hospital, and on the 24th, she flew to New York, intending to spend four days doing absolutely nothing. But downtime has a strange habit of becoming quite the opposite, and she wound up spending four days without sleep, bouncing around the city with friends and acquaintances, just shaking off the detritus of a month and a half enforced rest. By the time she flew back to Los Angeles, she had been on the go for almost ninety-six hours.

Days later, the first album by the Germs was released. And so much had happened to Jett over the past three months that she could have been forgiven if she'd forgotten even recording it.

Two years had passed since the Germs took their first steps out of the rehearsal room—or at least, the room within which they crashed and thrashed through a succession of barely formed yowlings, working to create some kind of order from the anarchic thrashings that four utterly untrained, would-be musicians are wont to make. Two years, during which the Germs in general and vocalist Darby Crash in particular, had succeeded in leaving a scar on every surface they touched.

He and guitarist Pat Smear were unrepentant Runaways fans. "We thought the Ramones were throwbacks to the long-haired denim '70s thing," Smear later remarked. "Paul [Beahm, Crash's real name] and I were much more into the Runaways."

It wasn't necessarily a case of hero worship. Rather, the pair picked up on the same punk ethos that had inspired myriad British bands to form in the wake of catching the early Sex Pistols in concert, and ran with it. "We thought if they could do it," Smear explained, "there was no reason why we couldn't, too."

The Runaways were in the studio cutting *Queens of Noise* when Crash and Smear, familiar faces already from the tightly knit Hollywood club scene, turned up one day in late 1976 to announce they'd decided to form a band of their own. "They'd seen us play gigs in Hollywood and they got inspired," Jett recalled. "Darby liked the tough girl thing. The rebel aspect. He got a real kick out of that. We were flattered."

The Germs came together fast. In the band's first-ever interview, with *Slash* magazine, Smear explained, "We went into a record store and some lady said she wanted to be a manager, so we said we'd start a group. We walked down to University High School [Kim Fowley's old alma mater] and picked up three girls, and we called it Sophistifuck and the Revlon Spam Queens, and then all three girls quit."

Flyers demanding "two untalented girls" to form a new group began appearing around town, to be answered by the immortally named Lorna Doom [Terry Ryan as was] and Dottie Danger . . . Belinda Carlisle to be. But Dottie contracted mononucleosis and fell out of circulation, so Donna Rhia (Becky Barton), recruited because she had a credit card and was happy to use it, replaced her.

According to legend, Crash was so nervous before the Germs' first gig, opening for the Weirdoes at the Orpheum in the spring of '77, that he smothered his body in red licorice whips, then stood beneath the hot lights and melted. Even worse, the band had rehearsed just two songs, so they played them over and over, bludgeoning the audience with sheer volume and repetition, until the plugs were finally pulled on them.

He gathered confidence quickly, however, developing a persona that—at its best—could make the legend of Iggy Pop look like Bobby Goldsboro in the self-destruction stakes. Crash's lyrics were already in place; now his bandmates needed to develop a framework within which to balance them, and they did it. The Germs' music echoed Crash's chaos; indeed, through their earliest days, the band went out without any formal music at all—it was enough simply to be up onstage and making as much noise as they could. One night, it is said, Crash stuck his microphone into a jar of peanut butter until the soundman pulled the plugs on the racket (although one wonders how noisy peanut butter can be); other nights, the group would simply encourage the audience to throw things at them, for the fun of throwing things back at them. Jett rarely missed a chance to see them, and the Germs repaid her with undying loyalty—even when they were putting the Runaways down.

"I think they're a bad joke, but I like Joan," Crash told the fanzine *Slash*.

"I think they're a *good* joke," responded Smear.

A single, the turbulent (some say tuneless) brevity of "Forming," saw the Germs make their first vinyl mark on the local scene; a series of increasingly self-immolating gigs established them as legends. By early 1979 they were ready to go for the full-length LP. The Slash label, formed around the success of the fanzine, signed them up in March 1979; in return, they were handed three late-July weeks at Quad Tech studio on Sixth and Western, a $6,000 budget, and free rein in deciding who would oversee the recordings.

"We wanted a big-name producer," Pat Smear recalled. "Darby was set on Mark Lindsay from Paul Revere and the Raiders for some reason, but he was too expensive. We thought, 'who's our most famous friend?' and we came up with Joan."

She agreed. "The Germs were great. Since I had seen the Germs live so many times, I knew that there were great songs. I thought we had the potential to just really make a classic record, and I think we did . . . the record captures the energy really well."

Slash label head Bob Biggs was in charge of making certain everybody was in the studio on time. "I had a big international truck," he told Darby Crash's biographers. "Typically, I'd go over to Joan's house first, and there'd be naked girls all over the place doing each other. Then I'd pick up Pat at his house over in West LA. We'd get to the studio, and Joan would pass out at the console, and I'd have to wake her up and get her going."

"She slept on the couch!" Crash teased on. "Listen to 'Shut Down' and you can hear where she's asleep on the couch." But that was just one day out of the twenty or so that the band was working, as Jett later explained.

> We were really on the ball most of the time, not drinking and trying not to party while we were doing the record. There was one day I was drunk, and I probably did pass out; that was the day we recorded "Shut Down" live in the studio, and Darby made that joke about me being passed out or whatever. But that was just one song and one day. I had a lot of fun doing that album, and I really took it seriously.

The recording itself was "really straightforward."

For her first solo flight behind the recording console, Jett relied a lot on engineer Paul Burnette . . . Other observers later described Burnette as the uncredited coproducer. But, Jett continued,

> there wasn't the time or the budget or the technology for it to be anything other than the way it came out. Sure I doubled tracks here and there, and had them do things they'd never done before. I had Darby doing harmonies. Darby took it pretty seriously. Did what I asked him to do. They were trying to get something done, and they were very serious about it.
>
> It was fun because those people were my friends and I had a good time. But they were really wild, and it was just an accomplishment to get them all in the same room at the same time. Now that I think about it, that I even got them to record thirteen songs on tape is incredible. Somebody wrote in a review someplace that the album really captured what the Germs were like, so I was proud of that.

The Germs may have long before have earned the reputation for being "the world's most volatile band," and then done everything in their power to retain it. But recording *GI* (*Germs Incognito*, revealed Crash), they were as disciplined as they needed to be. And Jett is right. The album *is* a classic.

Slash was describing it as "[an] awesome monument to . . . genuine insanity" before the Quad Tech Studios had even quit echoing to the noise, and by the time *GI* actually hit the streets, the *LA Times* was comparing it to the Doors' *LA Woman* . . . or more accurately, describing it as the city's "most remarkable . . . studio achievement" since *at least* that album. *At least.*

Six months later, the Germs broke up.

The group had been growing increasingly more chaotic in the months since *GI* was released. At a time when conventional media wisdom suggested they would build on the grand response meted out to their album, the Germs swung the other way entirely.

Crash was smacked out most of the time, offstage and on. The best remembered image from Penelope Spheeris's *The Decline and Fall of Western Civilization* movie, a cinema vérité account of the Hollywood punk scene, captures Crash in what was becoming an all-too-familiar role, crashed out on the edge of Zombieville; and when it became apparent to him that the world at large was never going to regard punk rock as anything more than a cult of abject sickies and weirdoes, he seemed determined to become the sickest and weirdest of the lot.

Even more painful, however, was the realization that everything that the Germs had pioneered (and they did pioneer a lot, with a style and rage that utterly preempted what would become the hardcore scene of the early 1980s) was now being lifted wholesale by a host of newly formed bands, all going balls-out to out-Darby Darby himself, all introducing their own twisted interpretations of what the punk lifestyle should evolve into. Which, in turn, sent Crash in search of even greater extremes, simply to keep himself at the head of the pack. The Germs finally collapsed in absolute disarray, and Crash headed for London for a vacation. Only to find himself back in Los Angeles.

"We went halfway across the world to get there," his friend Amber recalled, "and when we get there it turned out the bands playing were all from LA!"

X were visiting for the first time; Belinda Carlisle's Go-Gos were there to cement their deal with Miles Copeland's IRS label; and Jett was there as well, promoting the much-delayed but finally consummated release of "You Don't Own Me."

Jett, Laguna, and Cordell first returned to London in December 1979, to record sufficient material to fill her debut solo album. Bill Curbishley had offered Laguna the freedom of the Who's Ramport Studios, in the South London corner of Battersea; record now, pay later, was the deal, and Laguna, who'd been wondering how he and Jett were going to finance anything, leapt at the opportunity. They would begin work immediately.

Chunks of the record were already in place—they needed to be, simply to keep the eventual studio bill down low. The songs that Jett recorded with Steve Jones and Paul Cook were already earmarked—so were the fruits of the August sessions in Studio City. Now, armed with a clutch of new songs, they essentially sent out an open invitation to the city's young musicians to drop by the studio and see what they could offer.

A host of musicians came and went—some to play, some to hang out. At the same time as he was overseeing Jett's album, Laguna was working with another of the Beserkley label family, Sean Tyla. It only made sense to use some of the same musicians on both sessions—Tyla, drummer Paul Simmons, and guitarists Buzz Chanter and Martyn Watson, then repaying them by calling Jett in to sing some backing vocals on Tyla's LP.

She was on hand too, to sing along with another Laguna production, the "Summer Fun" single by the surfing-crazy Barracudas: a little piece of California sunshine wrapped up in the British rain. (A year or so later, Barracudas drummer Nicky Turner would be teaming up with Jett's old friend Stiv Bators in a new band, the Lords of the New Church.)

Mick Eve from the mid-'70s pub rockers Ace and Jeff Bannister of Bronco showed up, along with the cream of the late 1970s London club underground: Lea Hart and Jeff Peters of the Roll-Ups, a raucous pub band cut firmly in the mould of the Small Faces, were also along for the ride, and it was no musical coincidence that Hart himself would soon be resurfacing in a glam-shaped band, former Bay City Roller Ian Mitchell's superstar-spangled La Rox.

Jett told writer Danny Solazzi,

> When we did the album, Kenny used an English band that he had worked with a lot to do the basic tracks. [Then], towards the end of the album, Blondie was in town and I was talking to Clem Burke and Frank Infante, and asked, "If you get a chance, why don't you come down to the studio and play on a song?"
>
> They came down twenty minutes before they had to do a sound check, and we had no song to do. Kenny said, "Why don't we do 'Wooly Bully?'" We learned it right on the spot and it came out so well that we put it on the album. It was just a spur of the moment thing.

Infante and Burke would also play on a version of the studio owners' own "Call Me Lightning," one of those unjustly overlooked songs from the

Who's pre-*Tommy* era that so effortlessly kick the ass of the sound-and-vision impaired pinball player.

Hammered down in near-record time, the album hung fire for another couple of months before one final session in March 1980, laying down a new version of "Bad Reputation." It was complete, and now it was time to move on, to shake off the need to recruit so many session players and get the show on the road as well. "What I'm aiming for is my own band," Jett mused. She had some interesting ideas for the new outfit as well. For starters, "I'd like not to sing all the time, so I can fuck off and play instead of being glued to the microphone. I just wanna go nuts."

She was also adamant that this would not be the Runaways Revisited. She was not going to put together another all-girl group. "I want guys in the band—I just love the Runaways too much to do another girl band. It was fuckin' great, that's for sure." And she remained determined to ensure that they were never forgotten. When the Runaways toured Britain in fall 1976, there was not another female group worth mentioning to be found. Three years later, the Slits, the Dolly Mixtures, and the Raincoats headed up a litany that may not *all* have been inspired by the Runaways' example, but who certainly owed a little of their acceptance to the Americans' pioneer spirit.

"I think so many people overlooked it who shouldn't have," Jett told writer Kris Needs. "Some people got an immediate impression and they just had this criticism in their minds. Honestly, you gotta mark us down as the first all-girl rock 'n' roll band. The first one with spirit."

What history would call "the legacy of the Runaways" is an issue that has pursued Jett throughout her career—all the more so after it started to become apparent precisely how far-reaching that legacy was and more and more people became willing to step forward and offer their own interpretations.

To Jett herself, however, "it's about following your dreams and that girls can play rock 'n' roll. It's sexual. It's sexual music." At the press day marking the opening of *The Runaways* movie, she asked the assembled hordes to

> think of Led Zeppelin, think of Robert Plant standing there with his shirt open and standing there with the mike down here. Think of the

[Rolling Stones'] *Sticky Fingers* album cover with just the zipper there. Think about how sexual that music is, why they wouldn't let people listen to Chuck Berry because they were afraid he'd steal their sixteen-year-old daughters, why they showed Elvis from the waist up. I mean, it's sexual.

And so, when girls now say "I want to do this, I want to own it," it's different than pop music which is kind of like "You can do what you want with me." Rock 'n' roll is assertive and people are threatened by that. I thought people were going to be blown away by The Runaways. So, I think the legacy is—I know it sounds cliché—but it's just to follow your dreams and don't let other people dictate your path, because if you're going to make mistakes and if you're going to have triumphs, make them your own. And it doesn't work out the way you want, you gave it a shot. You won't live with going, "What if I had only tried? What if I had only tried?" You won't get that ulcer and maybe you'll have some great stories too.

FIFTEEN

You Don't Own Me

Jett pieced her first band together early in 1980. It was a shoestring operation—ads in the LA press were headlined simply, "Joan Jett is looking for three good men" and called for players who could resist posing and boasting and grabbing the limelight.

Around those criteria, and a series of auditions at SIR Studios in Los Angeles, a group coalesced. Her friend John Doe, guitarist with the mighty X, sat in on the audition process, holding down the bass as other players came through, and then suggesting one of his own friends, Lorna Doom's fifteen-year-old boyfriend Gary Ryan, for the gig. Ryan was crashing on Doe's couch at the time and playing with the band Rik L. Rik. It turned out he was also a Runaways fan, one of the kids who'd been visible at every local gig, and Jett recognized him the moment he walked in to the studio. She had her bassist.

She had her guitarist as well; Eric Amble, too, played with Rik L. Rik, and came along on Ryan's recommendation. A drummer friend of Kenny Laguna's, Thommy Price, threw himself into some of the group's early rehearsals; he was Laguna's own first choice for the lineup and he might have joined as well. But he had just accepted an offer from another band, Mink DeVille, and decided to go with that instead. He would keep in touch with Laguna though, and years later, he would become a Blackheart after all.

In his stead, Jett turned to another of Gary Ryan's friends, Danny "Furious" O'Brien. In rehearsal one day, Jett happened to mention that it would be great to have an Avenger in the band . . . San Francisco's most potent answer to the Los Angeles punk underground, the Avengers are probably best remembered today as the opening act at the Sex Pistols' final concert. At the time, they were one of California's brightest punk hopes, and the news that they had broken up was still fresh as the auditions carried on.

Furious and Ryan had worked together before, the rhythm section in a scratch band that Furious called the Fuck Band; "So I went down to Hollywood and got the gig," recalled the drummer.

It was not the happiest setup, it seemed. It was clear from the outset that guitarist Amble was less than overjoyed with Furious's then ongoing romance with hard drugs; the drummer had recently discovered heroin, and he admitted to the *Summer of Hate* punkzine, "My mind was definitely *not* on being a pop star! I spent most of my three months in Hollywood fucking rich teenage punk 'groupies' and shooting dope with Darby Crash, who lived across the street with his 'girlfriend' Michael."

But there was a chemistry between the four—one that sparked the moment they plugged in—and the first rehearsals left everybody feeling good about the future. Tryout gigs at the Golden Bear and the Whiskey confirmed their optimism. And so the group hit the road, piling into a van together and playing where- and whenever they could.

Crowds were small to begin with—resistant, perhaps, to witnessing what a lot of people perceived could only be the dying days of a former cheesecake idol. Only Cherie Currie so far had endeavored to prove that there was life beyond the Runaways, with her Kim Fowley–produced *Beauty Is Only Skin Deep* solo album, and it had done next to nothing. Neither was her latest venture, a duo with sister Marie, shaping up to be anything more than average.

Jackie Fox was busy on the other side of the industry fence, embarking on a career that has included promotions, agenting, and entertainment law. Sandy West had all but retired, working as an enforcer for sundry local drug barons; and Lita Ford was biding her time, talking about making a comeback sometime but not yet ready to put her promises into action.

Only Jett was actually out there and playing, which meant only Jett was receiving a harsh reminder of just what life is like at the shitty end of the rock 'n' roll stick: waiting backstage for hours while the promoter ran through every excuse he could muster for not paying the band their full fee; trying to find the cheapest food in town because all the spare cash had just been spent on new guitar strings; and for the three boys, hanging around in motel parking lots, waiting for the desk staff to look away so they could all crush into the single room that had been reserved for Jett alone and actually catch a good night's sleep.

It was Furious who started calling the band the Blackhearts, a name that the others quickly seized upon. "We looked for a name that you could put like a graffiti on a wall," Jett told German radio in 1994. "You just write *Blackhearts* with a black magic marker and say that your band was there. Since then I've actually learned that *Blackhearts* has a meaning. In Jamaica, a black-hearted person is a loner. I found that very interesting."

Furious was unhappy however. The band's repertoire was based, of course, on the material that filled Jett's album, padded out with whichever cover versions came to mind. "I really didn't like the music Joan was playing nor did I like her management. In fact, aside from Gary and Joan herself, I didn't like anything about being in this band."

He was already thinking about quitting when word came through that they were leaving for England in May to play a few shows around the release of *Joan Jett*. And that was an opportunity that Furious was not going to pass up, even if the UK quickly proved no more welcoming than the US.

Here as there, the band played wherever they could, for whatever they could get—although Ariola Records was at least willing to spring for the star's accommodations. Highlights of the outing, however, were hard to spot, although the band did headline a show at the London Marquee on May 27. They were also shoehorned onto the bill for a festival in the Netherlands with Motörhead, using the headliners' equipment to cut costs even further.

Which is where Darby Crash showed up and immediately landed himself in trouble. Joan recalled:

> Darby scaled this huge fence and got up on the twelve-foot-high stage; he used to get kind of crazy a lot, and I guess he just wanted to jump around on the stage or something. Well, the security guys and some of the guys from Motörhead grabbed him and were going to beat the shit out of him; I had to stop [playing] and tell them, "No you can't do

that, that's my friend." They just wanted to pummel this guy cause they thought he was harassing me.

"They didn't understand it at all," Crash continued. "The band tried to explain, 'well, people do this in LA all the time,' but no, they freaked. They didn't know what was happening."

It could all have been an exhilarating experience then, but Furious remained unhappy, and that naturally translated itself to the remainder of the band. The slightest thing, it seemed, could enrage him, although the drummer remains adamant that he was right to be pissed off. The night of the festival, for example.

> Joan stayed in Amsterdam and the band stayed in a terrible motel in a town called Apeldorn. Such fucking shit! Joan was . . . how should I say, a complete asshole for treating her band so badly, and I have no regrets for quitting, although I have no ill feelings towards her. We had some good times together. We'd pick up girls together.

Finding himself feeling far more at home in London than he had ever expected, he announced he was quitting the band, and following a three-week Dutch tour, he did.

There were times when Kenny Laguna felt like following him. He had never intended taking over Jett's management; he envisioned working with her only in the creative department, producing the records that she would make, and concentrating all of his attentions on the sonic end of things. But a falling out with Toby Mamis left her bereft and apparently rudderless, and Laguna knew what he had to do.

"I didn't want to see her lose herself," he told *Trouser Press*'s Jim Green, "so I figured I'd just try to help her survive until she could get other management. That I was stuck being responsible for her career would keep me up all night. I kept telling people, 'I'm not her manager, I'm her producer.'"

But he kept on doing what he needed to do, with his wife becoming more and more like a co-manager alongside him, until they reached the Netherlands, and Laguna suddenly found himself being detained in a Dutch hospital for two days, suffering from a migraine headache brought on wholly by the job of being Joan Jett's manager.

I was ready to jump off a building. Everybody wanted money. You can't do anything without money, and nobody wanted to pay us. On the road, the band rented a motor home, which they all slept in, except for Joanie—unless they drove all night between gigs to save on her hotel room. They were living— including Joan—on ten dollars a day. That was it.

He never did quit though. As a kid, he'd been as thrilled as any other by the story—in print or on film—of *Cinderella*. He never thought that he'd find himself living it.

Returning to the United States, Jett made her final break with the Los Angeles scene that had nurtured her—her final break too with the lifestyle that had at least contributed to her health breakdown the previous fall. She moved across the country to Long Island, close to Laguna and close too to New York City, the nerve center of the music industry. Gary Ryan and Eric Amble followed her, and there they set about replacing the departed Furious.

"I had to move to New York," she told *Juice* magazine, "because when you're a band with no money in LA, how many places can you go and still get home that night? There's Riverside and Orange County and San Diego. But how many places can you play and still get home without spending money for a hotel?"

New York, on the other hand, offered a world of destinations, all within a few hours' drive—Connecticut, New Jersey, Delaware, Maryland, Pennsylvania, Long Island, Upstate. It was an ideal location to base herself from and the ideal market to concentrate on: playing every club that would take her, building a name and an audience from the grassroots up. It was a chance to start anew.

Auditions quickly turned up a new drummer; Lee Crystal arrived from the Boyfriends and former New York Doll Syl Sylvain's band, and barely was he installed behind the kit than the Blackhearts went straight back on the road, kicking off with an appearance at the New York Ritz. Jett was suffering from a broken toe ("probably from doing sports," she remembered), and her doctor had recommended she not play the gig. But they couldn't afford to cancel the show, and Jett wouldn't have permitted it if they could have. She simply didn't want to give in.

The show was part of a multivenue festival being arranged by IRS Records' chief Miles Copeland, as the foundation for what he seemed to believe would become the new wave's own version of the Woodstock movie, *Uurgh! A Music War*. The summer 1980 filming would bring in bands from across the US and UK, and was filmed as far apart as well: Wall of Voodoo, Skafish, Oingo Boingo, the Fleshtones, the Go-Gos, the Cramps.

Many of the acts, both British and American, were ones that Copeland already had an interest in through his network of labels—a roll call that included the movie's obvious headliners, a dreadful cod-reggae band called the Police.

Jett and the Blackhearts would appear midway through the film, plowing through a supremely defiant "Bad Reputation." (Another track from the same show, a pounding "Do You Wanna Touch Me," would later be included on Jett's *Fetish* compilation.)

It was a blazing performance, its fire completely belying the band's own most pertinent question: just how self-fulfilling that title was going to become before they finally turned the corner? Because, Copeland's movie notwithstanding, there was not a record company, or record company man, in America that was even prepared to stand in the same room as the Blackhearts' music, let alone agree to unleash it upon the general public.

No matter that it was drawn from almost a year's worth of recording sessions with what amounted to three different bands, *Joan Jett* sounded sensational. Ariola was certainly gagging to give it a European release and had already earmarked "Make Believe" as a follow-up single to "You Don't Own Me." "Jezebel" would follow, shortly after the *Uurgh!* performance was filmed in July 1980. Three great singles, machinegunning onto the UK market and each one looking across the ocean, just daring someone to take a chance on them.

Nobody would.

Live, audiences constantly beseeched the merchandising table—which usually *was* a table, a borrowed trestle or card table laid out with buttons and photographs—for some kind of aural souvenir of the show. Every night, Laguna made a point of taking their names and addresses, promising to let them know when the record would be out; other times, kids would simply offer to send the money to him and have him mail the record back to them. He took their names and addresses as well, and every morning there'd be another few pages of scrawled contact information for him to ponder over, wondering how it was that every kid they played to wanted a Joan Jett album to play, and not a single record label in the country felt like giving them one.

He tried everything he could think of; by the end of the summer, Laguna was actually offering to hand over the album master tapes for next to nothing, just as long as the label would press them up and get them out to the people who wanted them. There were no takers. He upped the ante a little more. "Look, manufacture the fuckin' record, collect, *then* pay me at the end of the month." They still passed. "They thought she didn't have enough class for their label," Laguna sighed.

"*Nobody* wanted it," Jett agreed. And why? She could think of just one reason. "It was Runaways backlash." That band may have been behind her, but a lot of American industry men still remembered them, still recalled the disbelief and disgust with which they heard, or were told, or simply assumed, that the madman Kim Fowley had manufactured a pop group from a bunch of teenybop popsies. And now here was one of those popsies trying to get a deal. No chance, sister. America did not want to know.

Even Laguna's friends, throwing their all behind his endeavors, couldn't break through the wall of . . . you couldn't even call it apathy. It was hostility: stubborn, blinkered, and unbending hostility.

Steve Leber, of the Leber/Krebs management company (which handled KISS and Aerosmith, among others), had long ago granted Laguna use of a spare desk and telephone in the office. Now he sat in as Laguna's managerial assistant. It made no difference. The Howard Bloom Agency, one of the largest and most prestigious in the country, came on board, pulling in live shows in ever larger and more impressive venues. And the labels still weren't interested. "When that happens," Jett shuddered, "you *know* you're in trouble! We were rejected by every company you could name."

Later, Jett laughed, the likes of Clive Davis at Arista would be demanding to know how their people missed out on signing Joan Jett and the Blackhearts when they could have had them for nothing. He'd forgotten, apparently, that he personally rejected her himself. Other A&R men, and names higher up the corporate rung as well, blamed Kenny Laguna for not having played them the most obvious hit on the record. They'd forgotten that they had probably told him to turn the tape off before they reached it.

Finally, Laguna decided it was time that he and Jett took matters into their own hands.

Endless trips around the record companies had drawn nothing but endless refusals. Laguna told the *New Musical Express*, "It was one of those things where the music was right for the kids and right for the radio guys, but it wasn't right for the industry. So we had to go round kicking everybody's asses, because suddenly we were selling out two- to five-thousand-seater stadiums, and no one was taking Joan Jett seriously."

He had, he said,

> letters of rejection from every major record company there is. CBS in America said she couldn't sing. I couldn't believe it, I was looking at them totally astonished, pointing to this garbage and that garbage and wanting to know why the fuck they were signing it. What's wrong with Joan Jett, what's wrong with Kenny Laguna? I couldn't understand these people. We were going to give it to them free, no advance just market the record and pay us a monthly salary, I said, and they *still* wouldn't do it.

There was just one solution.

Rounding up whatever money he could lay his hands on—including the fund he had set aside for his daughter Carianne's college education, and a loan from one of his former bandmates, Marty Sanders of Jay and the Americans—Laguna set out to locate the cheapest record-pressing plant that he could, followed by the cheapest printer. A few weeks later, he took delivery of a couple of thousand copies of the *Joan Jett* album, resplendent on their own Blackheart Records label; loaded them into the trunk of the car; and as Jett headed out on the road once again, piled the discs up on the merchandising table and sold them direct to the fans.

Then, once the first pressing was exhausted, he sent out for a fresh batch. Only this time, he ordered up more copies, and there were some to spare for other purposes as well, such as handing them out to a newly hired team of record pluggers who were sent off state by state to push the album to American radio.

"This is when you could still have regional hits," Jett told writer Kevin Kelly in 2010.

> When you could still call into radio stations and they'd play your requests. You would have like, you know, Northeast hits, or something would be a hit in the Southeast. But anyway, the fans had power, so word would spread. And so we played a lot in the Northeast and the records kept selling and so finally we created Blackheart Records. It was out of the trunk of Kenny's caddy.

Dan Neer at New York's WNEW-FM was one of the first DJs to fall for *Joan Jett*'s charms; John DeBella at Long Island's WLIR-FM followed—the first bricks in what Laguna was soon calling Jett's own Blackheart network and the first steps towards cementing an almost personal relationship with the stations that best supported her.

One day, for example, Jett got wind of the fact that DeBella had been heard badmouthing her look, even as he aired her music. She called up to put him in his place; DeBella responded by putting her call on the air, live to however many million listeners—who were in turn privy to hearing Jett announce that she was on her way to the station, where she would debag DeBella in midbroadcast. She did, as well, and although radio probably isn't the most suitable medium in which to witness one public personality forcibly removing the pants of another, the ensuing broadcast kept Long Island glued to the station regardless.

A spot of airplay here, a spot more there. Market by market, inch by inch, tracks from *Joan Jett* began to scratch their way up the local airplay charts. And every time another cut was aired, it seemed, the station switchboard would light up. So the jocks would keep playing them, and then, as the airplay figures came into the office, the Howard Bloom Agency would take over, booking whatever sized show they thought each city could support . . . which encouraged radio to play the record some more, which brought more people out to see the show.

Without an ounce of record company interest, Jett wasn't simply selling out gigs that fall of 1980; she was locking the latecomers out of the venues.

And still, there wasn't a label that would touch her.

Laguna shrugged. He had reached the point where all he had to do was call a label and he'd be turned down. "We had guys saying, 'If it's Joan Jett, we don't even want to listen'; letters from famous A&R men about how her voice isn't up to the standards of their label. Everybody passed on her, most of them three or four times."

There was just one set of ears that had faith. Or at least, that didn't close down the moment Joan Jett's name was mentioned. They belonged to Neil Bogart, and when Captain Superduper finally gets around to erecting the Bubblegum Hall of Fame, it will be shaped like Neil Bogart's brain.

Joan Jett, *left*, and Lita Ford in LA, January 1976—the opening band New Order has no relation to the eighties dance-poppers. (Michael Ochs Archive)

Joan's apartment was the number-one after- (and before-) hours hangout for the Hollywood punk crowd . . . as one look at Billy Idol's expression confirms. (Theresa Kereakes)

Stiv Bators and girlfriend Cynthia pay a visit to Joan's typical teenage bedroom. (Theresa Kereakes)

Hair by Stiv Bators. (Theresa Kereakes)

With Dee Dee Ramone, bad meets bad! (Donna Santisi)

Clockwise from top left: Lita Ford, Cherrie Currie, Sandy West, Joan Jett, and Jackie Fox, 1976. Most American bands in London for the first time have their pictures taken by a well-known sight. The Runaways upstaged the lot of them. (Chris Walter/WireImage)

Joan shows the boys how it's done. (Donna Santisi)

Joan Jett, and Debbie Harry of Blondie—probably not consoling one another about missing out on *Happy Days*. (Donna Santisi)

Riot grrrl action—Joan guesting with Bikini Kill at Irving Plaza, New York, July 2004. (Ebet Roberts/Redferns)

I love the '80s. Joan at her iconic best. (Getty Images)

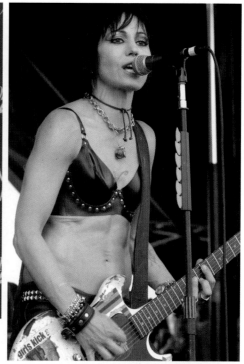

New Look Joan at the 2000 New York Awards at Irving Plaza, December 2000. (Ron Galella/WireImage)

Killing it at the Vans Warped Tour, 2006. (Chris Gordon/Getty Images)

Los Angeles premiere of *The Runaways*—Director Floria Sigismondi, with Kristen Stewart, Dakota Fanning, and Joan, 2010. (Jeff Vespa/WireImage)

Rockin' down under with the Blackhearts, New Year's Eve 2010, at the Falls Music and Arts Festival in Lorne, Australia. Thirty-plus years after the Runaways, as hard as ever. (Zak Kaczmarek/WireImage)

SIXTEEN

My Generation

Ritchie Cordell and Kenny Laguna were the children of the bubblegum era. Neil Bogart was its architect. But he was a lot more than that as well.

Armed with just a smattering of long-forgotten Midwest pop stardom in the guise of Neil Scott, he rose to become vice president of Cameo Records, one half of Cameo Parkway, and scored a major hit with "96 Tears" by the grinding Question Mark and the Mysterions (the song gave Cameo their first ever number one), and while neither Cameo nor the Mysterions were ever to repeat that one great success, Bogart was suddenly established as a man with a finger on the pulse.

It was Bogart who united the bubblegum songwriters Kasenatz and Katz, but when he formed the Buddah label, he wasn't only scoring hits with the Lemon Pipers and Melanie, he also became the first American record company man to give Genesis a chance. He picked up the fledgling Bob Seger, grooming him for his later success, and had Iggy Pop not split for Chicago and left his teenaged band, the Prime Movers, for dead, he too is said to have been high on Bogart's wish list.

And then he launched Casablanca Records, and through the second half of the 1970s, Bogart ruled the world. KISS and Donna Summer were certainly the biggest acts in their respective ponds, and Casablanca had them both. The label picked up the Village People, and they became enormous as well. And when Casablanca finally collapsed beneath the weight of its own success at the end of the 1970s, Bogart simply established a new label, Boardwalk Entertainment, lined up Ringo Starr and the Ohio Players as the enterprise's front line acts, and it was business as usual.

According to Kenny Laguna, it was Bogart's lawyer who first suggested he listen to Joan Jett—and that says a lot for the early 1980s music industry, that the attorneys had a better grip on what was happening out there than the record companies. But it didn't matter. Bogart passed away two years later, just thirty-nine years old, but his faith in Jett had already been vindicated.

No other record company on the planet would touch her. But Bogart not only wanted to sign Joan Jett; he was also happy to go along with their insistence that she and Laguna, Jett-Lagg Productions, would retain complete control over everything from the songs she recorded to the sleeves they were wrapped in. Boardwalk's primary responsibility was to make sure that she received everything she needed to keep making them.

Still, the pair did allow Bogart some input. It was he who suggested that they remix *Joan Jett* for its rerelease, and he who insisted that it be retitled *Bad Reputation*. His instincts were correct, too. *Bad Reputation* just missed the Top 50. Her second album, *I Love Rock 'n' Roll*, just missed the #1 slot.

Even as Laguna and Bogart pieced together the deal that would finally lift *Joan Jett* out of the trunk of his Cadillac, life continued tumultuous, a blur of live performances and noses to the grindstone. They were in and out of the studio quickly, making some sonic tweaks to *Joan Jett* before Boardwalk relaunched it. And as it inched into contention, so the Blackhearts became as tight and well drilled as any band could be, honed into shape by gig after gig, and now hungry to prove themselves in the studio.

Journalist Roy Trakin caught the band's performance at Los Angeles' Rock Lounge in May 1981 and was already noting that Jett's "trademark" look had spawned a legion of lookalikes, and that despite her having yet to score a hit record. That, however, would come. Few artists can carve such an identifiable niche into the hearts of their audience—particularly a primarily teenaged crowd, old enough to know what it likes and young enough not to care what their elders may think of it—without being poised on the brink of some kind of major breakthrough.

Trakin continued,

On stage, Jett's muscular backup band provides the backbone for her own little-girl-lost vulnerability crossed with a proud post-liberation celebration of sexual independence. The band's hard-edged heavy metal machismo is undercut by its female leader's combination of innocent bravado and hard-earned experience . . . She drags the theme of female freedom-of-choice implied by the original fully into the modern world providing young women with a strong, yet not unfeminine, role model with which to identify.

Rolling Stone continued with a similar analogy in its April 1981 review of the reissued *Joan Jett/Bad Reputation*, singling out "You Don't Own Me" as "an anthem . . . lachrymose teenage kitsch turned epic," and while "the LP works better as gesture than as music," still it was clear that Jett was flying directly into that corner of the teenaged market that demands something more from its artists than mere lip service to an ideal. It *demands* the ideal as well—the spirit that made "My Generation" such a fabulous Who record and *Tommy* such an overblown conceit, which suggests the Sex Pistols should have broken up after "Anarchy in the UK" and that Patti Smith could have retired after cutting "Hey Joe." Rock 'n' roll comes in a lot of guises, but the spirit of the music is simple. It's about kicking whichever ass gets in your way, and continuing to kick until the road is clear.

Jett had the field more or less to herself as well. The explosion of feminine rockers that had shaped the UK as it moved into the 1980s had yet to translate into anything more than a minor cult in America, while the Americans that *were* considered contenders were already turning their backs on the basics that had made them worth listening to in the first place.

Patti Smith had retired, Blondie were certainly on their last legs, and Chrissie Hynde's Pretenders were already turning out ballads and boredom. The unknown Madonna was still doing whatever it was that Madonnas did before they discovered the public's g (for "gullible")-spot, and while Pat Benatar was certainly up and moving, four-hits-old and flash as you like, there was something peculiarly sexless about the erstwhile Patricia Andrzejewski . . . including the fact that she was pushing thirty and overdressing like Barbie was going out of fashion.

The boys thought she was hot, and some girls thought she was cool. But she was cool in the same way that your best friend's mum might have been cool if she didn't keep stealing your boob tube and legwarmers. Besides, Benatar left nothing to the imagination. Jett, seven years younger, was *all* imagination, and that was the role model that teenaged *female* America had been waiting for. Because she was the only one who was actually being herself.

"Joan Jett is unique and something special," Kenny Laguna told British journalist Gavin Martin.

> If you look at Chrissie Hynde's make-up and hairdo—she's acknowledged this, because she's a gentleman—you'll see she took a lot of her role from Joanie, as did Pat Benatar. Joanie was out there sweating her guts out, and taking the abuse because she was a chick with a guitar. They call things like Foreigner, Styx, and REO Speedwagon rock 'n' roll but is it? I don't think so.

"I don't think of it as an image," Jett continued. "It's just me. I used to get really mad, [because] the first thing that hit with most people was sex. But people don't give me too much shit anymore. If they do, I blow up at them or Kenny does it if he's around."

She talked about sport, how she fell in love with the Green Bay Packers after seeing them on the cover of *Sports Illustrated*, back when she was six or seven. She laughed about her love for the Baltimore Orioles, the fact that she dedicated the reissued *Bad Reputation* to the team, and she recalled a visit to the dressing room where, she happily announced, "I saw a naked Oriole."

This wasn't a passing phase either. In 1987, as the Orioles got off to one of the most horrific starts imaginable, a run of twenty-one consecutive defeats, the fans adopted Jett's "I Hate Myself for Loving You" as a very appropriate theme song. Two years later in 1989, Jett was invited to perform the national anthem on the opening day of the new season, and on September 6, 1995, she would perform it again, on the night that Orioles shortstop Cal Ripken Jr. broke Lou Gehrig's fifty-two-year-old record of 2,130 consecutive games. "It was an incredible honor to do that in front of all of Baltimore and the world," Jett said during a 1996 online interview on the Prodigy Service. "Cal Ripken is the kind of hero that we need now."

But she wasn't being a tomboy, or muscling in on a male preserve, when she spoke of, or demonstrated, her love of baseball. She was being herself.

1981 was a queer year in rock 'n' roll terms. The Rolling Stones, the traditional barometer of such things, were still cranking it out, and all the little Rolling Stones who had ever formed in their wake and around their image were still cranking away as well. But even the best of their efforts seemed somehow soulless, as though the six-year-old observation that had provoked Alan Merrill into writing "I Love Rock 'n' Roll" had become even more halfhearted than it used to be: "It's only rock 'n' roll and I guess it's okay."

Maybe it was battle fatigue. There can only be so many times, and for so many years, that an artist can wake up in the morning knowing that there's another crowd of kids waiting out there, all of them primed to wave pretzels in the air and shout "Way to go," and all you, the performer, need to do is come up with a riff that sounds like it's raucous. Certainly there was a lot more artifice than art about the Stones' latest single, the behemothic bluster of "Start Me Up," and the knowledge that we'd be hearing a lot more of that same pallid posturing as the year went on was scarcely the most appetizing premonition for the average fan.

So people looked elsewhere for fresh kicks, and what did they find? The 1980s launched fewer lasting superstars than any preceding decade (although more than any succeeding one) and created more so-called one- or two-hit wonders than the '50, '60s, and '70s combined. Particularly in the years that followed the birth, and rapid absorption, of MTV into the mechanics of the music industry, it really did seem that all you needed to score a hit was a pretty face, an unusual haircut, and a song that packed more quirk per minute than any of its immediate competitors.

Britain, the home of so much that had once pointed music in fresh directions, was torn between a warmed-up version of Jamaican ska shot through with a singularly self-referential study of local sociology; and a science laboratory full of electronic instrumentation, laced with dance beats and the icicle bleep of synthesizers. And because they all made catchy videos, MTV made them stars.

That wasn't all. Filling in the gaps around the British invaders, there arose several battalions of American contenders, equally adept at twisting knobs and surfing synthesizers until a rock song wasn't a song any more. It was a succession of test tones, bleeping, and burping out something approximating a dance beat, while a not-always-particularly attractive face postured behind it.

Tommy Tutone, the Romantics, even the Cars (who at least strung together a few grisly hits)—not one of these groups even threatened to enjoy any kind of true Top 40 longevity; all rose instead on the shoulders of a supercatchy song, an even more maniacal chorus, and a video to die for. And as MTV lapped them up, the general public swallowed them down.

Thirty years on, it is difficult to recall a time when MTV was such a power in the land as it was when it first started broadcasting; the channel's declining emphasis on music video has been so pronounced that one scarcely credits a time when you simply switched on the television and received wall-to-wall rock and pop for twenty-four hours a day. But it was, and seated in front of the family television, the ear-to-ear wallpaper that spewed out of the set created passing superstars from a host of pasty talents.

But you couldn't sweat to Depeche Mode, any more than you'd want to raise your cigarette lighter to the sky when J. Geils got round to playing "Centerfold." Because it didn't matter how dramatic the production technique may have been, or how eye catching the accompanying video may have been; at the end of the day, the music was gutless.

And that was the realization that Jett was waiting for: the knowledge that there will always be an audience for music that steps beyond the norm and faces the future from a brand new landscape, and another for records that place style above substance. The belief that at the end of the day, the only noise that really moves you is the noise that begins in your belly and spreads out from there, with the seismic rumble of a bass guitar, the rhythmic kick of a well-miked drum kit, and the frenzied adrenalin of an electric guitar, laid down with the minimum of flash and technology and laid out with the panache of a set of knuckle dusters.

That was the sound of the Blackhearts in concert. That was the sound that Joan had always heard in her head.

Nightly—and setting the stage for all the years since then—"Bad Reputation" kicked the live show off, a straightforward declaration of independence that didn't care a hoot for sexuality or gender. I'm me, I'm now, and that's all.

"Be Straight," "Bits and Pieces," "Wait for Me"—the band was as adamant to have a great time playing as the audience was to go mad. Why not throw Eddie Cochran's "Summertime Blues" into the mix? Up there with "My Generation" and very little since then, "Summertime Blues" said more for how it felt to be a kid than just about any other song you could name. You can't use the car because you didn't work late. I'd like to help you son, but you're too young to vote.

Most of the Blackhearts *could* vote now, and had been able to for two or three years. But in that age before the club scene started coming down so hard on the idea of under-eighteens having fun, and banned anyone without a fake ID from even dreaming of catching a band live in concert, a lot of their audience was still awaiting that pleasure, which meant that it didn't matter what they thought about the world they lived in; nobody gave a fuck. Joan Jett was different. She *did* give a fuck.

Nightly, twenty songs in little more than an hour left audiences reeling, sweaty, and howling; and with "I Love Rock 'n' Roll" firmly entrenched in the middle of the set, it was amazing how many kids were howling for it, even though it was just one more song on an album full of the things. If anybody watching had any doubts that the Blackhearts had the biggest record of the next year up their sleeves, the response to it in concert would have killed them dead.

There again, you could have said that about a lot of the set.

Back in the mid-1970s, when Gary Glitter toured the UK and Europe, watching journalists would come away reeling, astonished at the sheer devotion that Glitter not only inspired but also choreographed.

"It's scary, man," shivered the *New Musical Express* in 1974: "It's almost like Hitler, everybody has their arms raised yelling 'Hey!' Everybody in the whole place is yelling 'Hey!'" A decade later, with Glitter reborn (thanks in no part to Jett reminding everybody how great his old records were), *ZigZag* magazine was shuddering likewise: "With the most disparate audience imaginable, completely united in one common cause, the chants sounded like the Nuremburg Rallies, the sing-alongs like the Welsh Male Voice Choir."

Not quite smack halfway through that span, the average Joan Jett gig slipped seamlessly into the very same mood. "Do you Wanna Touch Me" was sandwiched between the first album's recounting of Steve Jones's "Black Leather," amped up far beyond even the Runaways' version, and the Rolling Stones' "Star Star" . . . the ode to groupiedom that an outraged world once refused to permit them to title "Star Fucker." And every night, it incited bars, clubs, theaters, stadiums full of Americans, kids who had probably never heard of Glitter and thought Glam was the woman their grandfather married, would be on their feet, fists in the air, punching the sky and bellowing their lungs out . . . yeah, oh yeah . . . and when Jett sang the chorus line, *yeah!*

Described by one UK music paper as "a Yogi Bear li-lo disguised as David Bowie," Gary Glitter himself was always the unlikeliest of pop stars, and at his peak, his strongest point was always his knowledge of precisely why he was where he was. It wasn't ego, it wasn't artistic fulfillment. It was outrage, the knowledge (as the *NME* once indelicately put it) that a rock star growing fat was committing a revolutionary act.

Even at the beginning, in 1972, Glitter's live show was a battering ram at the twin gates of Taste and Decency, his imminent descent into grotesque buffoonery prevented only by the sheer absurdity of the whole occasion. He transcended simple tackiness and got away with it.

No gesture was too hammy: whether he was thrusting his pelvis forward and bellowing "Do you wanna touch me there"; or shedding real tears, overcome at the intensity of his reception, turning on the houselights to see how beautiful the audience really were; or throwing roses to the crowd at the end of the show, he was superpop personified.

Jett toned down the vaudeville aspects that were so essential to the Glitter experience, transferred Gary's bludgeoning physicality for teenaged tigress rawness. But she ascended to Glitter's throne regardless, taking songs that meant the world to the glitterkids of her own days at Rodney's, and making them available and accessible to a nation that had had no awareness of them before.

Neither was Glitter her only role model. Live, her version of the Isleys' "Shout" might have owed far more to its epochal appearance in National Lampoon's *Animal House* movie, a massive hit three years before, than it ever did to any other version of the oft-covered stomp-along that she may have heard. But how many kids went to see that film, then spent the rest of their days wishing that their college had been like that? For five minutes toward the end of the evening, Joan Jett could have declared a toga party, and there'd have been a roomful of Romans splayed out on the dance floor before her.

And so on. Other bands played programmed sets and sounded real slick and neat. The Blackhearts played rock 'n' roll, and if you didn't like it, then they weren't playing it for you.

Or for anybody else. Boardwalk Records leaned in, suggesting that the Joan Jett image was maybe a little too tough for mainstream consumption. *Bad Reputation* rode in on a sassy leather-clad cover shot, as befit its title. Fair enough. Next time around, could she tone down the aggression, at least for a photo shoot; could she maybe dress herself a little more like the girl next door?

Could she? Hell. One daring soul even suggested that she pose lying on a couch in leopardskin. So she told them what to do with their couch. And their leopard skin.

SEVENTEEN

Crimson and Clover

Sessions for what would become Jett's second solo album got underway at New York City's Soundworks Studio in late spring 1981, again under aegis of Laguna and Cordell. And the sessions were a joy. Seated excitedly alongside engineer Glen Kolotkin, with whom Laguna had first worked during his years at Beserkley Records, they watched as Jett and her Black-hearts nailed take after take of the songs they'd selected for the album.

There was a stunning cover of one of the first singles that Jett ever bought—"Crimson and Clover" would have sparkled even if Ritchie Cordell hadn't written it and Kenny Laguna hadn't played on it, although Jett was surprised at just how much everybody loved her version of it. She'd only started playing it to tease Kenny Laguna during soundchecks.

She latched onto the Dave Clark Five's "Bits And Pieces," ripped from a childhood spent watching the British Invasion and nailed down by one of the most insistent drumbeats in history. When the Blackhearts performed it live, you could feel the older venues physically shaking as the entire audience seized upon that rhythm and hammered it out with feet and hands. In the studio, the recording needles were still twitching from the echo, and Jett recalled, "It was my idea [to record it] because I always loved that song. It was fun to sing. We were in Washington DC, doing a soundcheck, just messing around and we did the song. After we were done, all the security people just freaked out applauding."

Digging through Laguna's record collection one day, Jett found a copy of the Halo's "Nag," a doo-wop delight from the early 1960s. She made it her own, because she knew exactly what the song was saying: the fact that there is *always* someone hanging around trying to tell you what to do. On the road, the Blackhearts took to dedicating the song to their road manager, but really, it could have been about anyone.

The old Runaways' live favorite "You're Too Possessive" was revisited, and she sat down with Laguna for "Victim of Circumstance," written about her teenaged Hollywood days, making her way to and from the English Disco with the cops watching every teen in the hope of catching him or her doing something wrong.

There was even a raw romp through "Little Drummer Boy," punked up and poised to become the biggest Christmas hit-record ever. Jett happily admitted that she took the idea from her Anglophiliac leanings—it was a British pop tradition for the biggest bands to release one-off Christmas singles, and they usually scored a monster hit with them—Slade's "Merry Xmas Everybody," Mud's "Lonely This Christmas," and Showaddywaddy's "Hey Mr. Christmas" all fell into this glorious tradition. Now Jett was joining that select band. She had long been thinking of recording a Christmas song, "and 'Little Drummer Boy' just seemed to fit."

Neil Bogart certainly thought so, as he overruled Jett and Laguna's decision to make "Crimson and Clover" their next 45 and pushed out the festive frenzy in its stead. The album was already scheduled for a December 1981 release; nobody doubted that radio would flock to the seasonal closer, and when the holidays were over, the next pressing of the LP would simply drop the track and replace it with "Woe Is Me."

It was Bogart, too, who suggested they record the old garage growler "Louie Louie" and slam on "Summertime Blues" as well; indeed, he was so adamant that the Eddie Cochran oldie be cut, insisting that it would make a killer followup to the "Bad Reputation" single, that nobody could understand why it wasn't scheduled as the Blackhearts' next single.

But somewhere down the line, Bogart either forgot or he changed his mind. Instead the tapes just sat on the shelf, until Laguna took matters into his own hands and sent the tapes out to a handful of radio stations. The record went Top 10 at AOR, and Laguna still laughs as he remembers Bogart's response when he discovered there was a song out on his label that he didn't know about.

So far, so great. But documenting the sessions for *Mix* magazine's Blair Jackson, engineer Kolotkin recalled, "We recorded all these songs that were pretty good, but I didn't hear any hits. I kept saying, 'What are we going to do for a hit?' So Kenny Laguna said, 'We have one song that could be a hit, but I don't know if we're going to record it, because Roy Thomas Baker wants to record it.'"

Neil Bogart had expressly requested that the band rerecord "I Love Rock 'n' Roll." The existing version was fine, but he insisted, and the Blackhearts agreed, that there was a lot more that could have been done to it than the Pistols team had dreamed of. Things that producer Baker, best known at that time for his work with the likes of Queen, the Cars, and Journey, was the ideal man to capture.

But Baker was tied up with another project and would not be available until Jett's sessions were over. So Kolotkin took matters into his own hands. One morning before Laguna and Cordell arrived at the studio, he had the band perform it for him. "And they really played it!"

He set them up to record it immediately.

It took us almost no time to get a basic track of "I Love Rock 'n' Roll." I thought it was a smash hit from the beginning. Then Laguna came in and Cordell came in and they were as knocked out as I was, and we finished the record up in one day. It just came together. We just kept building it up and up and up. I knew it was right when the hair stood up on the back of my neck.

At last he could hear a hit.

The album sessions complete, the Blackhearts began preparing for their next round of live shows—but with one major adjustment, as Eric Amble departed to commence his own career as a (swiftly successful) producer.

He was quickly replaced by New York guitarist Ricky Byrd, but the remainder of the band—Jett, Gary Ryan, and Lee Crystal—were faced with a dilemma. Should they allow the new album to go out as it was, with their former guitarist in the spotlight? Or should they rerecord it and capture the raw sound of the latest incarnation of Blackhearts?

One tryout later, recording "I'm Gonna Run Away" with the newcomer, they opted for the latter course, and just a week after Byrd arrived in the nest, the team was reconvening at Kingdom Sound, out in Syosset, Long Island. And the change hit them all immediately. "We [were] about

three-quarters finished," Kolotkin recalled, "and for some reason, everything sounded so much more ballsy, loud and real crunchy."

Byrd slipped effortlessly into the band, a guitarist since his early teens
who was inculcated with many of the same formative influences as Jett
but shot through with a love of the blues that informed almost everything
he played. The Rolling Stones, the Beatles, the Dave Clark Five, Cream—
fondly he recalled seeing Eric Clapton's Derek and the Dominoes perform
on the *Johnny Cash Show*. Stunned, he found himself a cheap acoustic
guitar, took lessons from his Hawaiian guitar-playing grandfather, and "it
took off from there."

"The Faces, the Stones, Otis Redding, Al Green, the Kinks, that's
what Ricky Byrd brought to the Blackhearts," he reflected thirty years
later. "We didn't make that sort of music, but it was there."

His induction into the Blackhearts, too, was seamless. His wife, Carol
Kaye, was a publicist at Steve Leber's management firm Leber/Krebs, where
Jett and Laguna had their offices. He had just returned home from a tour
with G. E. Smith when Carol told him that Jett was looking for a new guitar
player; laughingly, he admitted that he wasn't especially familiar with her
music, but he attended the audition "and everything worked out."

Punching through the album in the studio, amazed at just how easily everything came together, he even found time to pull out one of *the*
all-time great guitar parts.

> The solo from "I Love Rock 'n' Roll," I tried a whole bunch of different
> things, and the only thing I came back to was something that Leslie
> West used to tell me—"Just play the melody." So I took the guitar break
> all the way over here to the right, cut back, and it's a classic break now.
> It's so simple, so easy, but it's so memorable.

Back on the road, September 1981 saw the Blackhearts fire the first
shots in an outing that was destined to keep them on the road for the
best part of the next year—Australia and Europe were both on the itinerary, while the American dates were so all-encompassing that the tour
was divided between two separately exhausting scourings of the East and
West Coasts.

Not all of the scheduled shows were headliners, but that didn't matter. They creamed the opposition regardless. In Kansas City in March

1982, they opened for the Police in front of seventeen thousand people, and that was just one of dozens of similar billings. "We did five nights at Pine Knob with J. Geils," Ricky Byrd recalled. "We were on such a whirlwind, we were rock stars for that amount of time, and you get so swept up in the glamour. Joan usually went back to her room after the gig, but the rest of us went out, went out to the bar, hung out, drank."

Besides, the Blackhearts had long since stopped caring about the need to convert another band's audience. It happened regardless, automatically.

"We did great in the big places," Byrd continued.

> We played giant gigs. But our real house was playing the really cool little joints, that's the kind of band we were. We were a club band, and I don't mean that as a put down, we played intimate punky rock 'n' roll, and we were thrown on bills . . . When everything blew up, we were like the Pistols on some of those bills. We were playing with Journey and Loverboy and we were coming out wearing leather, bandanas, I was wearing eyeliner.

The set continued to evolve as the tour wound its way on around the country—but it wasn't the new album's contents that were being shoehorned into place, it was more favorite oldies. Years later, Jett's *The Hit List* album would give her the chance to preserve her vision of ten favorite cover versions. But she'd been preparing it for years, every time she walked into rehearsals to announce that she wanted to play something else. No, she was nothing like Gary Glitter in his prime. But she still put on the best live show since he was at his best.

"Joan Jett is more than another feeble American concession to punk rock," the *New Musical Express* announced. "Sure she's succeeding where the likes of Holly and the Italians and Pearl Harbor and the Explosions failed," and reference to those bands cannot help but awaken the memory of all the other early '80s female-fronted new wave hopefuls: the Motels, Martha and the Muffins, the Plasmatics.

But unlike so much of her supposed competition—again, it came down to authenticity: a reminder, if you will, why rock 'n' roll is so important and, more pointedly, why it was worth falling in love with. "Now, there's a lot of things I like," Jett would announce to the audience as the

Blackhearts stood poised on the edge of that song's intro. "A *lot* of things I like. But there's only one thing I love."

Titled for what Neil Bogart continued to insist was the album's most obvious hit single, *I Love Rock 'n' Roll* was released on schedule, just in time for Christmas 1981, and just in time for the critics to realize there was a lot more going on here than an ex-Runaway with a nice line in cover versions. While journalist Ira Robbins warned *Trouser Press* readers "there's a fair amount of hackneyed and failed material," he also assured them that "as long as this album is accepted in the uncomplicated and unpretentious spirit in which it was evidently intended, everyone goes home happy."

He praised the album's cover versions, noted that "I Love Rock 'n' Roll" sounded "appropriately raunch-and-rabble," and concluded that while Jett "may not be the greatest . . . there's certainly room for her on my turntable, and yours too."

Rolling Stone, too, denied that *I Love Rock 'n' Roll* was targeted at the kind of people who might habitually have read their magazine. But maybe their readers should start listening to Jett. "Jett fuses both the yearning of girl groups and the slapdash ferocity of garage bands to the power and beat of heavy metal," wrote critic Tom Carson, "[and] hooks up rock's underground (i.e., punk) to its mainstream (i.e., kids) with a populism that almost nobody is trying for anymore." Maybe, he cautioned, "this LP wasn't made for me;" wasn't made for anyone who wasn't fourteen and fighting. But for as long as somebody was capable of remembering how it felt to be that age, *I Love Rock 'n' Roll* was a clarion call to arms.

Besides, who cared what the critics say? They didn't buy records. It was out on the streets that *I Love Rock 'n' Roll* needed to make its most lasting mark, and for a few days at the beginning of its lifespan, maybe a few eyebrows were raised in a worried fashion. Sales were slow, even in cities where Jett and the Blackhearts had sold out the biggest halls, and radio was certainly hemming and hawing about whether or not to air the album; one of Boardwalk's radio reps even returned to the office to announce that "I Love Rock 'n' Roll," in particular, was running up against considerable resistance, with most programmers insisting that the song was simply too hard-hitting for rock radio. Too loud, too heavy, too *real*.

But a handful of DJs stuck their necks out regardless, and they were rewarded by phone lines that lit up like Christmas. And then came the day when the Blackhearts hit Florida, soundchecked at the venue, and then jumped back into the van to make their way to the hotel. Somebody turned on the radio as "I Love Rock 'n' Roll" faded out, and in came the disc jockey to remind his listeners what they'd just heard. The #1 most requested record on the station's playlist.

On February 6, 1982, with *I Love Rock 'n' Roll* already on the LP charts (it eventually reached #2), its title track entered the *Billboard* Top 100, and Jett watched it every step of the way.

"I Love Rock and Roll" was unstoppable. Its first week on the chart saw *Billboard* give it a "superbullet," a sure sign that it was doing well. A week later, it had jumped close to forty places up the chart. The week after that, another thirty-seven. Now she was at #17 with a superbullet, and she was convinced that it would slow down sometime. It had to.

But it didn't.

Thanks to yet another of those peculiar little quirks of fate, "I Love Rock 'n' Roll"'s author, Alan Merrill, was in Florida at the same time as Jett, playing guitar with Rick Derringer now. "Joan Jett was to play the same club the next night, and [they] came to see us that night. I thanked her for recording the song and I wished her the best." He laughed.

> She has these perfect teeth and smiled a gorgeous big smile at me. Up close she is as attractive as Angelina Jolie—they are very similar and both have a gorgeous and at the same time a "don't mess with me" vibe. Her guitarist Ricky gave me an "I Love Rock 'n' Roll" pinback, which I still have. I thought it was funny. My song was having a new life with new players.

And the next time the pair met, it would be even funnier. Because now the song was #1.

"Kenny Laguna invited me, through Rick Derringer's tour manager, to attend a Joan Jett show in the New York area somewhere. Maybe Connecticut." Of course they'd be playing the hit, so Mark Roman, Merrill's road manager and companion that evening, suggested Alan ask if he could join her onstage for it. He shook his head—no thanks. But Roman wouldn't be dissuaded; next, he asked Kenny Laguna.

"A simple and rapid shake of the head sideways back and forth, meaning 'no way' was all Mark got in response."

Merrill didn't mind.

She played "I Love Rock 'n' Roll," and the place went bananas. It actually made me a bit misty, but happy at the same time. It was so much like the Arrows' live shows back in 1975 and '76. It gave me a chill. All these young girls singing along on the chorus, just like when we were doing the Suzi Quatro/Arrows tours. It was a very good feeling.

I felt that, at last, my musical concept had reached people on a wide level. I had worked hard and endured a lot of animosity during the Arrows years to get to this place where the music was being accepted and embraced, and finally it was—thanks in large part to Joan's intuition, and her weird loving synchronicity with my song.

A video was shot—Jett's first. "It's fun to do a video about one of your songs," she reflected. "Look at your song in a different way, or try not to look at it too specifically . . . you don't want to tell too much of a story, you don't want it to be too exact."

Maybe not. But "I Love Rock 'n' Roll" did everything it was supposed to, regardless. It made people fall in love with the song, with the performer, and with the notions that the performer was placing into the song. And it almost never got screened.

They took over a New York club, Private's, for the shoot, and Jett had already decided on the jumpsuit she was going to wear for the occasion: a nifty, tight, red number that looked great when she first saw it. "But I didn't get the outfit until literally a couple of hours before we did the video and I put it on and I was horrified, the way it looked."

Director Arnold Levine's cameras rolled, the video was cut, but Jett remained unhappy. The shoot itself was a stylistic disaster, colors and extras mashing together in a Technicolor soup, band members looking awkward in their own chosen outfits . . . "It just looked weird. It didn't look right, it didn't match up." Her eyes fell on the work reel of the shoot, a black and white echo of the "finished" thing.

"We're sitting there looking at the playback in color, which was horrible and totally didn't match, then we're looking at this thing in black and white that looked like an old movie, an old TV show from the '50s, and we said 'That's it! Do it in black and white.'" The color video would remain archived for the next twenty years, until Jett and Laguna finally let it loose on her *Real Wild Child* video anthology. And they were correct. The red jumpsuit *was* ugly.

But the video worked regardless, shockingly monochrome amid the sea of ever-brighter colors in which the average MTV favorite wallowed, even as the direction itself drove straight toward the most then-fashionable tricks and quirks of the era—the way Jett's top lip would curl in precisely the same manner as Billy Idol's was prone to, the moments where the Blackhearts looked like they'd just stepped out of an Adam Ant shoot.

On March 20, 1982, "I Love Rock 'n' Roll" commenced a seven-week run at #1, knocking the almost equally successful (six weeks) J. Geils Band's "Centerfold" out of the way in the process. By the end of May, the single was #4 in the UK as well; and when journalist Sandy Robertson, still as voluble a Jett supporter as he was in the earliest days of the Runaways, told her that he finally felt vindicated by her success—that the years he'd spent insisting that Jett was destined for superstardom, while his colleagues simply laughed, had not been wasted—Jett knew exactly what he meant.

"Vindicated, that's the word! It feels good after playing all those dates and selling the albums ourselves." She laughed. *I Love Rock 'n' Roll* had just been certified double platinum by the Recording Industry of America (RIAA), the monolith that effectively controls the American music industry, but it had got there so fast that they had not even had time to prepare the intermediary awards—the silver, gold, and platinum discs that traditionally chart a record's rise. "So I'm not supposed to get the gold and silver discs in-between, but I want them all! See, even if I lose all my money, I'll still have those. It's something they can't ever take away from you." Indeed, Kenny Laguna professed himself astonished at just how little Jett did appear to care about the money that was now pouring in—or soon would be.

In June 1982, the Blackhearts were in England to perform alongside Queen, Heart, and the Teardrop Explodes at the Milton Keynes Bowl, a massive gig in front of a massive crowd. Four months later, they were back in Britain for a tour that carried the band around the clubs and colleges of the island. But it made no difference to Jett. Laguna told the *New Musical Express*, "She goes from like forty thousand people in a stadium to playing to a couple hundred, and she don't mind. She loves it! I really admire her for that. She don't care about the money."

"I don't really need that much in life," Jett agreed. "Material things don't mean that much to me. As long as I can travel and play in front of people—whether it's a sweaty little club or a big place—to see those people smiling is what it's about. I live for that hour-and-a-half on stage. That's where my dreams all come true."

"It's so hard to even think of being famous, of having that responsibility," she continued. "It's really weird. I mean—me!!—a rock star! Hey, are you a rock star? Gotta Rolls Royce, or a Cadillac? Oh my God—wake up! I must be dreaming." And what would she do if she did wake up?

Right now, she had no time to find out.

"I can't give you an answer why ["I Love Rock 'n' Roll"] became so big," Laguna confessed to the *New Jersey Record*'s David J. Spatz years later. "I've recorded a hundred other songs with her that I thought were going to be huge, but they weren't. There are just some intangibles, and we can't explain why some songs become hits and others don't."

Jett, however, kept her feet firmly planted on the ground, then and years later too.

> You'd see *Billboard* and things like that and it was exciting—but you didn't really know what was going on or how people's views of you were changing. The Blackhearts were this punk garage band that nobody would even deal with; then, all of a sudden, we have this #1 song and we're mainstream. It's all perception. We didn't change a thing.

But it did change the level at which the band operated. Instead of traveling around in the beaten-up old van they had grown so accustomed to, suddenly they had a tour bus or even a private jet. Instead of people barely nodding as Jett passed them in clubs or offices, they would descend and demand her attention, or at least some sign that she had noticed them. And instead of sneering when she talked about her music, they nodded enthusiastically and told her how they'd always been fans. All of them, even the ones she knew had sent her packing a few years before.

Fake Friends, she called them.

EIGHTEEN

Everyday People

"I Love Rock 'n' Roll" had literally just slipped from the #1 slot in the week that Neil Bogart died, on May 8, 1982. It was displaced by the theme to the movie *Chariots of Fire*, but it was proof all the same, as *Rolling Stone* remarked in Bogart's obituary, that "the man who had been labeled the Bubblegum King and the Disco King could also help turn an oft-rejected rocker into a star."

Jett attended his memorial at Hillside Memorial Chapel, Los Angeles, on May 11, just one of the dozens of stars who turned out to remember him, but she was the one singled out by *Rolling Stone* as "the most visibly shaken of all."

No matter that she and Laguna had complete control of their music. Without Bogart and Boardwalk to distribute that music and guide their vision, it was unlikely that any of the last twelve months would have happened.

Now, however, it was time to start looking ahead to the next twelve. Laguna would be busy throughout the summer, negotiating with MCA Records for Jett-Lag to be granted their own record label—to be called Blackheart of course. Jett's next album, then, wouldn't only be following up one of the biggest hits of the decade so far. It would also be inaugurating a brand-new business enterprise.

There was no question that Jett was at the top now; and if there was, then *Playboy* magazine answered it with her inclusion in a feature depicting celebrities in the raw, published in the magazine's May 1982 edition.

The photo showed a young woman sitting in a bathtub clad in nothing more than fishnet stockings, a fringed vest, and a lot of bubbles.

Jett was angrier than most people had ever seen her before.

Of course she had expected some intrusion into her private life by a media that, spotting her on the top of the pile, would now be desperate to figure out how she got there—or fabricate something that their readers would find believable. That, after all, is the nature of both beasts: success and the press. But she could also rest assured that there really wasn't much for them to find—as a teen in the Runaways, she may have had access to a better class (or quantity) of drink or drug than most kids her age, but that was hardly breaking news.

Neither—although it would be 1994 before she gave the *Advocate* interview that seemed to answer any lingering questions—had she made any attempt to disguise the fact that she was gay. Some of Kim Fowley's comments had let that out of the bag long ago, while back in the heyday of the Runaways, friends of Jett and her Hollywood-days companion Lisa Curland, were also well aware of where her "interests" lay.

Dig deep enough into anybody's past and a resourceful hack could probably find *something* to score a few salacious thrills with, but even the most hateful gossips on the old LA punk scene had little more than a disinterested shrug to offer up when they were quizzed on her background.

Until, it seemed, until now.

The problem was, the girl in the picture didn't look anything like Jett, because it wasn't Jett. Published in the magazine's Grapevine column, alongside images of Grace Slick, Ted Nugent, actresses Pia Zadora and Linda Gray, and tennis star Jimmy Connors, the photograph was, in fact, of that most short lived of former Runaways Laurie McAllister, miscaptioned somewhere between the photo shoot and the Retna picture library and now hauled out in a move that was surely far more embarrassing to *Playboy* than it was to Jett.

She responded anyway. She had contacted *Playboy* back in March to let them know their mistake, and received no response. Now her lawyers were filing charges, a $6.5 million libel suit against the magazine for publishing a photograph of her "engaging in deviant sexual behavior" (taking a bubble bath is deviant?) and causing her to "be shamed, held up to public disgrace in the community in which she lives, and injur[ing] her reputation."

Playboy didn't seem to have a leg to stand on. But it would take seven long years for the case to be completed—a period during which *Playboy* issued a heartfelt retraction and Retna went so far as to destroy the offending image, as Jett maintained her complaint and finally the legal system had had enough. With Retna's lawyers accusing that the only reason for the suit to drag on was "to obtain continuing publicity for . . . Joan Jett, while forcing the defendants to run up unwarranted legal bills," Jett did her case absolutely no favors when she failed to show up for a court-ordered deposition hearing, and then neglected to appear at a second in May 1989. Finally, New York State Judge Eugene Nardelli threw the suit out.

While one controversy raged, another was birthed, this time by Jett and Laguna themselves. "I Love Rock 'n' Roll" topped the charts; "Crimson and Clover" reached #7; "Do You Wanna Touch Me," resurrected from her debut album, reached #20. It was time, the pair decided, to unleash the song that many people—Laguna included—agreed stood out as Jett's most dramatic statement of intent: "Bad Reputation." With a video to match.

They had teamed up with English director David Mallet now, one of the original pioneers of the entire music video explosion. In 1979, at a time when few people even imagined a day when music could be seen as well as heard, he directed David Bowie through a triptych of shoots that certainly influenced the future course of the industry: "DJ," "Boys Keep Swinging," and "Look Back in Anger." He filmed an entire album's worth of songs—for a video album, of course—based around Blondie's *Eat to the Beat* album; worked with the Boomtown Rats, Peter Gabriel, and the Rolling Stones; and oversaw another Bowie video, the immortal "Ashes to Ashes."

Now you could barely turn on the television without catching one of Mallet's superstylized and superbly realized videos on the screen, and his recruitment into the Blackhearts' camp was another indication of just how huge the band had become.

Mallet bristled with ideas. Asked to come up with a concept for "Do You Wanna Touch Me," he originally suggested taking over an aircraft carrier, for a video that would probably rival *Anchors Away* for nautical novelty. A deposit was put down on just such a craft, lying at anchor in the Hudson River, but no sooner had Mallet arrived in New York than he changed his mind.

Now he wanted a beach, with its glimpses of Jett alternating between a tough nut who was capable of laying out the current Mr. World (which she proceeded to do, walking up and delivering an unscripted punch by way of introduction) and a cheesecake centerfold who flashed her bra and panties every time the chorus came around. It was a magnificent effort, but "Bad Reputation" would leave even it in the shade.

Documenting Jett's video history on the *Real Wild Child* video anthology, Kenny Laguna recalled, "We did 'Bad Reputation' after we had three hits . . . [as] our kind of way of saying 'fuck you' to the record labels. We just wanted to go on record . . . annoy[ing] the record companies."

They succeeded, too. Opening with the Blackhearts playing their song in a backstreet alleyway, while Jett is thrown out of sundry clubs and bars ("Come back when you're dressed like a lady," bellows one disgusted barman), "Bad Reputation" spooled on to a succession of record-company suits, each of them disdainfully waving the Blackhearts away, while captions to the side of the screen named and shamed the guilty organizations.

Chrysalis, Island, Magnet, EMI, Warner Brothers, Virgin . . . twenty-three different labels turned down the Blackhearts before Neil Bogart stepped in, and the "Bad Reputation" video not only called them out on it, it also reflected on the denials that followed.

"We were with you all the way, Jett," another caption insists, as the assorted bigwigs dance to the music. But there was no mistaking the message of the video, not among its public viewership and certainly not among the suits that suddenly found themselves reeling from the assassins' bullet. No sooner had MTV aired the video for the first time than the complaints began pouring in, from aggrieved label heads who couldn't seem to understand why anybody would want to make them look so stupid.

MTV backed down; the film was ultimately dropped from even partial rotation. But Jett didn't care. By the time her twenty-fourth birthday rolled around, on September 22, 1982, even *Rolling Stone* was happily conferring the status of "rock celebrity" upon her. She spent the evening at a Who gig at the Capital Center in Landover, MD, as the band crunched through their first farewell tour; and as she walked into the backstage area, Roger Daltrey fell to his knees before her and serenaded her with a chorus of "Happy Birthday."

Europe beckoned, and with it the opportunity to become the first Western rock band ever to play in what was then East Germany since shortly after the Berlin Wall was erected. Indeed, discount Blood Sweat and Tears' 1969 visit to Romania, and Jett and the Blackhearts were the first American act ever to venture behind the Iron Curtain. And wherever they played, the show was as tight as a buckle, with even the intro tape crowned by another Laguna triumph. He had been recruited by Malcolm McLaren to produce the old shopkeeper's latest managerial discovery, Bow Wow Wow, and promptly handed them a monster hit, a remake of the old garage classic "I Want Candy."

Still, the itinerary was tiring. The *New Musical Express* was not the only magazine to notice the toll that the strain was taking: "To be blunt, [that] Joan Jett is far from the healthiest looking [twenty-four] year old on the planet." She was, the paper mused, "drowsy, fumbling, and forgetful." Maybe that was why Kenny Laguna sat in on a lot of her interviews—not to try and detract from any negative impressions that Jett might leave with passing journalists, but to make sure that the kind of snap judgments that particular breed is prone to make were not necessarily their most lasting ones. Although it's just as likely that he had a lot to say as well.

He and Jett were business partners in the most musical sense of the word, and the inevitable questions that wrapped themselves around Jett's current success were just as well directed to him as to her. So Jett talked rock, Laguna talked history, and they both came together to laugh about the struggle that had finally paid off so handsomely.

The only question was, would it continue to do so?

1983 was to become the season of *Thriller*, Michael Jackson's megamillion selling monstrosity, and the cue, at last, for MTV to finally kill off one of its detractors' loudest complaints, that it only showed videos by white acts, and open its doors to the rising tide of black music that was also riding the video boom. Which, given the cyclical (if not bandwagoning) nature of the station, in turn ensured that an entire new breed of video-starring talent was about to drench the cable waves in R&B and funk. The new wave was dead, and the question was, who would survive the tsunami?

The key to what would become Joan Jett and the Blackhearts' third album, the utilitarianly titled *Album*, was a conscious decision to strip back the sonics that gave *I Love Rock 'n' Roll* so much of its flavor, and punch instead toward an even more organic sounding record.

It was a bold decision. Few artists ever dare to change a winning formula while it's still winning; and many don't even make a change once it starts losing either, which is why a lot of bands vanish up their own rectums, still churning out the same sounds that they were making when they were hot. But it was precisely *because* of that heat that the Blackhearts knew they needed to change. Hit records are great for an artist, but they're great for other artists as well, who get a sniff of the direction the wind is blowing and immediately back-engineer the whole thing, to see what they can appropriate.

Suddenly there was an awful lot of stamping, pounding glam rock being made . . . Twisted Sister were pushing forward, and Quiet Riot, an LA band that had apparently been living with its collective head inside Jett's own record collection, were recreating old Slade with slickening guile. Then there was Slade themselves, stepping back from the brink of absolute obscurity that had almost always been their American fate (and, for the last few years, their British doom too), with a revitalized vision of the old glitter stomp.

Nobody would ever have been foolish enough to suggest that there was a full-scale glam revival going on, not even when Gary Glitter landed a new record deal and had his first UK hit in a decade, not even when Alvin Stardust followed him back into contention. But David Bowie was back for the first time in years, with his *Let's Dance* confectionary dragging him round the stadium circuit, and while he was probably the least glam of them all (his latest image was surely borrowed from the waiters at his favorite Italian restaurant), still there was a moment in 1983, which managed to squeak itself out for a few months thereafter, when nobody would have been shocked if the last ten years all turned out to be a dream, and Bobby Ewing was still in the shower after all. Wearing the most spangly catsuit and the highest-heeled platform boots that he could find, of course.

Album retrenched. Ricky Byrd recalled, "We were touring so much that we would tour, do interviews, and do a record, but there wasn't a lot of time to think. It was either touring or recording. All bands say the same thing, the record companies want you to put out another record. So when we recorded *Album*, it was off the road and into the studio."

The recording itself wasn't rushed, but the December 1982 sessions were certainly crushed in between a lot of other stuff, and the sheer rawness of *Album* confirms that. "You won't hear a lot of echoes and over-dubs on the LP," Jett warned on the eve of release. "I wanted the record to be very basic sounding. We're a rock 'n'roll band and that's how I wanted it to sound."

A tip of the hat to all those fascinating people who emerge when you're famous, and claim to have been your best pal forever, "Fake Friends," the first single from the upcoming new album, sashayed out sounding more like the early Stones than the Stones had in years, and the garage roar grew heavier when you flipped it over and found the Blackhearts grinding through "Night-time" . . . *not* the old Strangeloves hit from 1966, but an original that had just as much period charm, a slow, sexy pulse about a breakup.

The actual album sessions had seen the Stones invoked even more obviously with the long-threatened cover of the live favorite "Star Fucker." Left off the album, its place was taken by Sly Stone's "Everyday People," a song that may or may not have knowingly sensed the directions in which the commercial winds were blowing, but with which one needs to be very, very careful, so borderline annoying is its melody and chorus ("Different strokes for different folks").

Jett pulled it off. The Blackhearts sounded almost threatening, Jett spitting out Sly's peerless manifesto for utopia. "Tossin' and Turnin'" wrapped up the album's oldies contingent—that and a look back at the Runaways' *Queens of Noise* staple "I Love Playin' with Fire."

In other words, there was not even a spangle of glam for the revival to ride, but a solid rock LP that could—and certainly *was*—designed to continue Jett's drive into the stadium circuit whose pictorial highlights were spread across the album's gatefold sleeve, photo after photo, to make it clear not only how big the Blackhearts were now, but how far-reaching their fame had become. In fact, Jett celebrated the release of *Album* with her biggest live show yet, as the Blackhearts stepped out at a jam-packed Shea Stadium on August 18, 1983.

Seventy thousand fans were inside, for an afternoon of music that was headlined by the Police, as they celebrated their own newly released *Synchronicity* album; and opening the bill, an all-but-unknown act from Athens, Georgia, called REM, which happened to share management with the Police.

It was not an altogether happy occasion. The headlining lawmen had arranged for the concert to be relayed around the vast stadium on a massive video screen, but it was a privilege that they reserved for themselves.

Even after Jett's entourage offered to pay for their share of the facility, the Police remained adamant. They alone could be seen on the big screen . . . their contract with the equipment's owners, they insisted, left them with no alternative. But Jett and the Blackhearts blew them offstage regardless, turning in a high-octane performance that left the Police sounding weak and facile in comparison.

Yet America was already in denial. The sassy swagger of "Fake Friends" stopped selling at #35—although given the song's subject matter, a bitter harangue about, indeed, all the fake friends that had suddenly begun latching onto Jett and the Blackhearts, that is perhaps not a surprise. Especially when it was nailed to a David Mallet video that hammered the point home even harder by lining up a cast of shadowy cardboard cutouts to represent the one-dimensional nature of this aspect of Jett's sudden fame. "It was about my experience with dealing with unreal friends," Jett mused. "Yeah, showbiz," Laguna quipped back.

"Unless you're really cautious," Jett explained to the AV Club website, "it's easy to lose touch with everything because of the workload, because you're always on the move, because you're never home, because people blow smoke up your ass to your face and then turn around and say things behind your back. This is reality. It's what happens." But it is not necessarily the best thing to sing about, when some of those same fake friends are in charge of the radio, TV, and distribution networks that you rely on.

"Fake Friends" flopped then, but worse was to come. Although it would go gold, *Album* passed out at #20. "Everyday People" stopped selling at #37 and that, again, despite Mallet shooting a characteristically stylish video for it, a succession of domestic disasters taking place in the day in the life of an everyday person. Even Jett, however, admitted that there was a certain dry irony to the fact that the video upon which she and the director lavished the most attention, and budget, was for a song that was not even destined to become a single. They were given a $200,000 budget to lavish across all three videos, and according to Laguna, three-quarters of that went to "The French Song."

Shot in London's Soho district, in the shadow of the world-famous Raymond's Revue Bar, the video rehomaged the close-up lips sequence from the *Rocky Horror Show*, before rounding up a small club's worth of extras to accompany the distinctly steamy nightclub-and-elsewhere action. "[Mallet] had been working on 'Let's Dance' by David Bowie," recalled Laguna, and he moved that entire cast of thousands over into our video, and all of us, except [Jett] and Mallet, were horrified that they spent all the money on the song that wasn't going to be the single. And the two singles. "Everyday People" and "Fake Friends" . . . "Fake Friends" he spent about ten cents on. That's when he had me in the video.

"But what's interesting," Jett countered, "if you look at the three videos with a director's eye, you can get a sense of what Mallet's vision was, that 'The French Song' would be the most conducive to the extra money . . . [It] was shot on film, on 35mm, which at the time was a brand-new thing."

It was rarely seen regardless—largely, Laguna concluded, because "MTV wasn't keen on a song about sex between three people"—or, as the song says, *J'aime faire l'amour sur tout a trois.* "I love to make love, especially with three." The French translation was provided by Jett's guitar tech, Mike Winter—five years before, he'd been a member of one of the biggest French punk bands of all, Shakin' Street.

But while you could blame the album's comparative failure on the lack of another "I Love Rock 'n' Roll" from the proceedings, you also need to remember that Jett purposefully designed the album not to have one. She pointedly refused to play the traditional industry game—the same game that the Runaways had refused to go along with five years earlier.

That band, she told writer Alan K. Stout in 1996, had the enthusiasm to talk about "the music and people always got around it—I guess [they were] threatened by teenage girls that wanted to play rock 'n' roll . . . as soon as we let people know that it wasn't a phase—that this was something we wanted to do—that's when people got strange."

Now they were getting "strange" again, wondering why Jett was less than enthusiastic about some of the photo opportunities that were offered to her, glamour-puss sessions that would reinvent her as America's kid sister; wondering why she'd rather talk about baseball than boyfriends; wondering why she was never available when another journalist asked her to share her makeup tips with the teens.

"A lot of people have made their mind up about me one way or another," she continued.

I'm sure there's a certain segment of writers who won't ever give me the time of day, hate me, don't get me, don't think I'm good, or what-

ever. I guess that's fine. It's only an opinion. There are other people
who do get it, and can be objective. I could be wrong, but a lot of
people, except for really young people, have made up their minds one
way or the other.

The album's fate barely touched Jett's live appeal, of course. The
sensibly titled World Tour II kicked off in July 1983, driving through the
expected arsenal of sold-out performances wherever it touched down.
But the following year, the sublimely titled *Glorious Results of a Misspent
Youth* album—recorded during what seemed to be another impossibly
brief break between one tour and another—slipped even further from
view than its predecessor.

Joan grabbed the title from late night television. She was watching
the episode of *The Honeymooners* where Ralph claims his pool skills are
"glorious results of a misspent youth," and she knew that no other phrase
best captured the mood of the music they were making. Wrapping up the
usual bevy of blistering Blackheart originals—"Long Time," "Push And
Stomp"—behind the positively venomous "Some Day," *Glorious Results
of a Misspent Youth* was *American Graffiti* for the '80s—the compulsive
shuffle and mad harmonies of "Love Like Mine," the maniacal rhythms of
"Hide and Seek," the teen-angst anthem "Frustrated," and all topped off
with an uproarious version of Gary U. S. Bonds's "New Orleans," featuring Bonds himself on backing vocals.

One of the most exciting American performers of the early 1960s
("New Orleans" was just one of a string of signature hits), Bonds was
also using the Record Plant studio that day, and when the Blackhearts'
own conversation turned to his signature hit, it only took a moment to
approach the great man and ask him to write down the lyrics for them.
And then place him at a mike and have him sing them as well.

"That was a real thrill," Jett said. "That was a lot of fun." Even if it did
mean they had to drop a similarly mach 10 rush through the Everly Brothers' "Bird Dog" (and "Hide and Seek" too) to accommodate it. Still, this
was an album of vintage rock 'n' roll classics, furiously updated to remind
everyone that Jett meant everything she'd said over the previous eighteen
months. She loved rock 'n' roll.

Maintaining Jett's policy of resurrecting one Runaways song per
album, *Glorious Results of a Misspent Youth* also reached back to what

was probably that band's best-known number of all, the seething statement of intent that was "Cherry Bomb," realigned for a spunky brunette in a black leather jacket, slower and a lot more menacing than the prototype, but more defiant, and more explosive too—even if the original plan of igniting real fireworks and cherry bombs at the end of the performance didn't work out. Having trailing mikes and cables through the stairwells of the Record Plant studios, the explosions simply didn't sound real enough. So they slowed down the track instead, and built the bang up with technology and good old-fashioned volume.

An apparently inevitable choice for a single, director J. J. Martin's accompanying video was a shot at Tower Records' uptown branch in New York City, at what was designed to be the biggest record in-store appearance ever staged. And that is what it became. Jett and the band spent close to eight hours on the premises, signing autographs for anything up to ten-thousand people and saying hello to just as many. Spliced with some live footage and a snatch of "New Orleans'" most raucous chant, Jett still recalls it as "a really fun video . . . with the best fans in the world."

But it lacked the vicarious immediacy of the record itself, and it was no surprise when what could have been the most obvious choice of single on the entire album was passed over for, in Europe, the dramatically '50s-styled "I Need Someone," and in America, another Gary Glitter classic, the semiballad "I Love You Love Me Love"—which arrived, shuddered Jett, complete with the most hateful video of her career, a fantastical David Mallet–concocted combination of concert footage and a goofily staged string of nursery rhyme characters. Little Bo Peep meets the Muppets, quipped Laguna. "It was my idea, as well. I thought it was really good, and then I played it for the head of MTV and they watched it with really long faces, then said 'well, did you do any other ones?'"

They didn't. This time, however, it was business, not commercial problems, that really sent the record spiraling. Two years after Neil Bogart's death, Boardwalk Records had gone bust, taking its artists with it . . . or at least, their product. No matter that Blackheart Records owned the actual rights to their music, the tape on which that music had been recorded was the property of whomever was overseeing the label's funeral rites, and they weren't budging.

"The whole Boardwalk situation went into bankruptcy," Jett told writer Amy Ray in 1997. "So we never got [money] for any of that. The whole 'I Love Rock 'N Roll' thing went totally out the window. So we had to start over again."

"They're all a bunch of assholes," Laguna spat, not only of the accountants who were holding Jett's music to ransom, but of the record company staffers who had carried on fiddling while the boardwalk burned down. "Guys who couldn't get laid in high school."

Boardwalk's parent company, MCA, shut everything down. It was because of them, Laguna revealed, that every expense the band faced, including their next video shoot in London in December 1984, needed to be paid for in cash. Ten thousand dollars' worth in that particular instance. And it was they who inspired Jett to one of the most brutal covers in her repertoire, going back to the Sex Pistols' "EMI," recorded when that band was peremptorily dropped by its first UK label, and rerecording it as "MCA." Archived until it appeared on 1993's *Flashback* compilation, "MCA" took all the bile and spite of the Pistols' original, then updated it for Jett's own fury.

Touring alone sustained the band. When the Blackhearts hit New York to play their first-ever show at the legendary CBGB, on October 11, 1984, over three thousand people descended on the venue to see them, and tour manager Elliot Saltzman recalled, "They closed the streets off. We had New York's finest and the Hell's Angels helping us out . . . a nice mix."

Matters weren't helped by the officious police lieutenant who determined that the only way to calm the situation would be to have the show shut down by 11:45 pm—just fifteen minutes after Jett was scheduled to take the stage. The alternative, he continued, would be for him to arrest everybody.

Somehow common sense prevailed, and one song recorded at that frenetic show, "Talkin' bout My Baby," would later show up on the B-side of Jett's "I Love You Love Me Love" single to remind everybody of the night Joan Jett conquered New York.

Similar scenes unfolded elsewhere, although audiences didn't always want to see Joan Jett. Sometimes, they wanted to hurt her.

NINETEEN

Good Music

In October 1984, Jett and the Blackhearts hooked up with the Scorpions for a month-long tour that took them through Germany, the Netherlands, and Scandinavia, but spent the majority of its time in Spain and Italy—"very macho countries," Jett shuddered, "and they don't like to see women." She told *Micromag*'s Anne Tangeman, "They totally couldn't understand what I was doing—didn't like it. The crowd was just hateful. They were screaming 'you cunt, you fucking cunt,' and they were working up these loogies and spitting on me. I was covered in spit from head to toe. It was hanging off me."

Everybody, it seemed, was watching her, waiting for her to walk off the stage in disgust and dismay. But she didn't. If they wanted her off the stage, they'd have to carry her off, and she was no stranger to that either.

> I've had that happen too—getting hit with batteries and shit like that. Getting ribs broken and stuff. It became personal between me and them. It was like, "Fuck you guys! I am not going anywhere. You'll have to fucking kill me to get me off the stage"—which they tried to do. Which is really weird when you see people trying to hurt you so bad for playing guitar. It was not an experience I would want to repeat.

Finally taking their leave of the Scorpions back in the saner pastures of Western Europe, the Blackhearts flew to London for a one-off show at the Marquee Club on December 6, 1984. The group had already been through the country once that fall, an outing that was somewhat less successful than might have been hoped. Talking with British journalist Mick Sinclair, Laguna remarked how the British tour encompassed twenty different cities, "[and] that's about how many people came."

But Ricky Byrd was thrilled to be playing the most historic venue in the country, the boards once trodden by so many of his past rock heroes. "That was great, a great, smelly, smoky club. It was an honor to play, a great gig to play." And all of London, it seemed, turned out for the night. The "House Full" sign went up hours before showtime, and on the streets outside, Wardour Street reverberated to the perennial question, "Hello John, gotta spare ticket?"

Inside, meanwhile, you could not move, you could barely breathe. But you *could* dance, and the floor was a forest of outstretched arms as Jett unleashed the primal glitter songs she had made her own—"Do You Wanna Touch Me," "Star Fucker" . . . "Hey lady," quipped *Melody Maker*'s review, "this is *our* culture you're playing with. It's okay, though—Joan was always more British than American and, after the stadium shouts and the Springsteen bounce, all roads lead to Blighty."

A bootleg tape preserves the madness of the night, the microphone almost melting in the heat, but still picking up the sound of the audience singing along with every song the band pulled out, and the entire place going mad for "I Love You Love Me Love." Standing there fighting off heatstroke, even the cynics who asked how Joan Jett had ever made it so huge had their question rolled up and shoved back in their faces.

Back home later in the month, the Blackhearts rang in the new year by headlining MTV's New Year's Eve extravaganza, and that blazed as well. The first live concert ever broadcast by the network, it saw the group augmented by the album's guesting Uptown Horns brass section, and seeing 1984 out with a concert for the decades.

1985, however, marked the first year during which they did not release a new album, as the Blackhearts underwent their most significant realignment since their formation.

Gary Ryan and Lee Crystal both departed the band, to be replaced by a new rhythm section. Kasim Sulton was a bassist whose past credits included Todd Rundgren's Utopia and David Bowie's late 1970s setup;

Thommy Price was the drummer who, five years before, had been Laguna's first choice for the Blackhearts' back line, and who had followed his time in Mink DeVille with stints alongside Patti Smyth and Billy Idol. Sultan, in turn, was an old friend of Price's, and together they bonded to create one of the most intuitively powerful rhythm sections of the age.

There was another reason for the layoff, however. Jett and the Blackhearts certainly had been dented by the comparative failure of their last pair of albums, and they were painfully aware that the marketplace had changed much in the past four or five years—with Jett's own core constituency of teenagers now growing into altogether different kinds of music.

The lineup for the biggest live event of the year, the charity Live Aid extravaganza in London and Philadelphia, proved that. While the likes of Spandau Ballet, Adam Ant, the Hooters, and the Cars all scraped themselves out of different dimensions of musical redundancy to cavort across the twin stages, the Blackhearts did not even receive an invitation to perform.

Jett remained defiant of course. "Popular music is splintered into several different media terms," she mused, and the Blackhearts remained strictly "a rock 'n' roll band . . . straight down the line." As long as there was still a demand for that, she shrugged, she'd do okay. And when there wasn't, she'd stop.

Jett's first album to be produced solely by Kenny Laguna after Ritchie Cordell bowed out of the industry once again, 1986's *Good Music* came together slowly and carefully, not only roping in the traditional collection of oldies (the Beach Boys' "Fun Fun Fun," Jonathan Richman's "Roadrunner"), but also recruiting some surprising assistants.

Jett and Laguna had recently befriended Beach Boy Carl Wilson, and initially called him up to ask whether he'd play some guitar on "Good Music." Wilson agreed, and as the session continued, somebody had the idea of replicating the Beach Boys' own traditional harmonic style. And maybe inviting other members of the legendary surf group down as well.

That idea was going nowhere; the Beach Boys' own management insisted that the group would never agree to stand in the same room as one another. But Wilson mentioned to Bruce Johnson that he was working with Jett, and Johnson asked if he could come over. Then Mike Love got to hear about the gathering, and he wanted to be a part of it. Followed by Al Jardine. Suddenly, four of the men who sang all those great old Beach Boys songs were lined up in the studio, and Laguna marveled, "They're all singing and they sound like the Beach Boys. And all of a sudden, Bruce goes, 'We're going to show you how to make a Beach Boys record.'"

He did, too, although there was a lot more to "Good Music" than quintessential harmonies, as Laguna and Jett dug through their own storehouse of musical memories to isolate those little moments in song that they considered made good music, and then recapture them and write them into their own melody. Most other artists would have simply reached for the sampler, but Laguna and Jett had no interest in that.

"It was just a little homage, we'd take just a tiny bit, not long enough to get sued, but just little bits like the rhythms or melodies," Laguna told the website dutchbeachboys.blogspot.com.

> The bells are from "Rag Doll" by the Four Seasons—if you listen carefully, it's the exact same part. We took a bit from "Take It Easy" by the Eagles. We had the Rolling Stones, we had "Bang A Gong" by T. Rex. We had "Layla," if you listen carefully you can hear a little bit of "Layla" in the fade. We also had "Lean on Me" in it.

They also had Darlene Love on it. The Spectorsound legend was working again with Laguna, over a decade after their first collaborations, but she had once recorded with the Beach Boys as well, adding vocals to a chain of their greatest records. Now she was a part of another one.

If "Good Music" was locked firmly in the past however, "Black Leather" catapulted Jett firmly into the present, as she linked up with the New Jersey rap group Sugarhill Gang, Scorpio and Melle Mel, to record the song, a furious statement of personal intent that slashed through the average rock chick's wardrobe to lionize Jett's own favored mode of dress—"black leather, I wear it on stage, black leather, I'm gonna wear it in the grave"—while the Gang did their thing around her.

Aerosmith's groundbreaking collaboration with Run DMC had still to be born when Scorpio let Jett know that "he had this great song that was a combo of rap and rock and wrote it for me. The lyrics were so cool and rhythmic that being a rhythm guitarist, I was immediately turned onto it." Maybe it was bad timing that saw the Aerosmith rap through "Walk This Way" topping the chart before *Good Music* was even released, but nobody ever suggested that one act had a clue what the other was doing at the time. The difference is, Aerosmith had to be convinced to participate before they helped birth the rock-rap hybrid that "Walk This Way" ignited. Jett did it because she already liked the music.

A stronger album than its predecessor, *Good Music* simply danced from highlight to highlight. Maybe "Outlaw" did plod a little (despite utilizing another of Laguna's sly borrowings, a hint of the Who's "Baba O'Reilly" over the fade). But "Fun Fun Fun" returned the Beach Boys to their own roots in classic Chuck Berry, and "If Ya Want My Luv" was heartbeat-paced seduction, a sultry summer night set to an almost Spectoresque wall of drums and guitars. "Contact" swaggered over choppy guitars, and the strident stomp of "Just Lust" fit the title so tightly that the lyrics were almost secondary to the sound.

The highlight of *Good Music* was, nevertheless, Jett's take on Jonathan Richman's "Roadrunner"—not only because Jett put so much power into performing what was already one of those archetypal rock songs whose lineage stretches back to "A Wop Bop A Loo Bop," but also because she added a great deal to the song's own iconography.

One of the all-time greatest motoring songs, immortalizing New England's Route 128 in the same way that the old R&B acts used to immortalize Route 66, "Roadrunner" was once a part of the Sex Pistols' repertoire as well (they can be heard rehearsing it in the film *Great Rock and Roll Swindle*), and Jett's take fell somewhere between the two, transferred from Bean Town to New York City, via a damp West London rehearsal studio.

Richman's original was set exclusively, and proudly, in his hometown of Boston, circling the city on the darkened highway, seeing the lights of the city as they first come into view, walking to the Stop 'n' Shop. First recorded for the Modern Lovers' debut album in 1973, but left on the shelf when that release was cancelled, Richman returned to the song in 1975 for the *Jonathan Richman and the Modern Lovers* LP, his first for Kenny Laguna's old friends at Beserkley.

The *Modern Lovers'* debut album was finally granted a release later that same year, and in 1977, both versions of "Roadrunner," jokingly retitled "Roadrunner Once" and "Roadrunner Twice," were paired for a UK hit single. "Roadrunner Thrice" would then appear as a live B-side in 1978, with Kenny Laguna sitting in the producer's seat. Now, Jett was preparing to unleash "Roadrunner" in no less than *forty-eight* different versions, each one highlighting a different regional landmark or highway around the country.

She told the AV Club,

> There's this section in the song where it says, "I'm headin' east on St. Mark's Place over to Tompkins Square Park down by the power lines." Maybe in Chicago it was, I can't remember right now, but it was probably like, "I'm headin' . . . wherever, on some, like, famous road there. Over to da da da da da." I did that for a lot of major cities and a lot of smaller cities. It was sort of a way to really personalize it. It was easy enough to do. It was exciting, I thought. How many times do bands do that? Hopefully, people got a kick out of it in each town when they heard it broken down like that.
>
> It was kind of fun, because I only had to do each one once. I got on the phone with a radio person from each place, and we talked about the streets and the places. It wasn't boring or a pain in the ass. I pretty much wrote the stuff down and did it in one take. It was fun.

It was also a brilliant marketing strategy—albeit one that was then derailed slightly by the fact there was no accompanying video or even a regular single. Instead, copies were pressed up for promotional purposes only and mailed to radio stations in the mentioned markets, places as far afield as Alaska and Philadelphia, to try and push the album out even further.

The hard graft in the marketplace, meanwhile, was left to the title track, a song whose message was perhaps as simple as any subtext could be. Jett outlined, "There's music that everybody can relate to, that they turn up really loud or when they're depressed, there's certain songs that they go and listen to, and that's good music. So what the song is saying is that you need that good music. It's as plain and simple as that."

Another nod to "good music" was delivered by the accompanying video, shot at CBGB in New York City. Meanwhile, Jett had a far meatier role to fulfill, as she headed out to Cleveland to begin work on what she personally regarded as her true motion-picture debut, *Light of Day*.

We're All Crazy, the projected movie about the Runaways that Jett
had started shooting in the desert in 1980, had never been completed.
Instead, Jett's later fame had seen a few of her sequences dusted off and
included in a new film, documenting the tribulations of a director trying
to *complete* a movie about the Runaways. But even Jett's fans remained
largely unaware of *Du-beat-e-o* following its 1984 release, and that was
probably just as well. With fresh material introduced by the Eldon "El
Duce" Hoke, vocalist and drummer with the controversial California
punk band the Mentors (controversial because they styled themselves
"Rape Rock") and actor Ray Sharkey in the newly created title role, *Du-
beat-e-o* emerged a very different creature than any that Jett would have
okayed.

"They intercut some porno footage with it," she told *Micromag*. "So
it's now a porno flick. I've never seen it. I've never wanted to see it."

Sharkey's character has no illusions over the movie's quality either.
As one of the luckless crew charged with completing the movie (or face
some brutal underworld consequences), he screens Jett's performance of
"You Don't Know What You've Got" while bemoaning, "This is my fucking assignment, take that shit footage and make it into a fucking movie."

"I suppose people who are fans might want to see it out of morbid
curiosity," Jett concluded, "but personally I don't think there's anything
worth seeing, except you'll see me very out of it."

This time around, there would be no such rejection. *Light of Day*
starred Michael J. Fox—then still fresh from his own wholesome sitcom
Family Ties and the *Back to the Future* franchise—as a would-be young
rocker, Joe Rasnick, playing in a band called, with typical Hollywood inge-
nuity, the Bar Busters. Although there probably weren't many bar bands
that had to get to grips with a brand-new, specially commissioned, Bruce
Springsteen song. The Boss composed the movie's title track.

"This is one of those movies where, every time you get a certain thing
licked, there's another dragon in the closet that you gotta tame," Fox confessed to *Rolling Stone*. For him, that was the job of singing lead vocals
in the band, although his pay check probably compensated him for that.
According to director Paul Schrader, Fox's demands had shifted a comfortably low budget movie into "a medium budget movie"—Hollywood
terminology for one that needed to do very well at the box office to even
think about breaking even.

Elsewhere, Cherise Haugen, Miss Teen USA, 1984, played one of Fox's girlfriends, while there would also be a brief glimpse of the young and then completely unknown Trent Reznor, as his band of the time, the Exotic Birds, was recruited to the shoot, appearing as a rival act, the Problems. Their appearance in the film is fleeting; their one song, a cover of Buddy Holly's "True Love Ways," is lost beneath dialogue; and journalist Jo-Ann Greene later remarked that they appeared on screen for no purpose other than to be disparaged, dismissed by one character as "cut rate specials" and by another (Michael J. Fox) as "A Flock of Seagulls."

Light of Day was not a new project. In fact, Schrader first envisioned it in the very early 1980s, as a way of exorcizing some of the family conflicts that he'd experienced in his youth. At that time, it was called *Born in the USA*, and it might have retained that title had Bruce Springsteen not come up with a similarly titled song in the meantime.

It was no coincidence either. Springsteen was the first performer approached to write the music for the movie, an offer he turned down. But when he took the title, he not only made sure to thank Schrader on the ensuing album sleeve, he also took him out to dinner to apologize and make an offer. Either Schrader could keep his old title and use Springsteen's song as its title theme, *or* the Boss would deliver a new title tune.

Schrader took the latter course, and with filming on the movie having already begun, he was handed a song called "Just Around the Corner to the Light of Day." Judicious editing cut *that* mouthful down.

To get her ready for the role of Fox's sister Patti, Jett was assigned to work with drama coach Sondra Lee (just as Fox was handed a guitar teacher, Paul Hanson), and asked about her role while filming was still underway, she was adamant. They were *not* making a rock 'n' roll movie, "although it seems to me an awful lot of people are looking at it that way."

In fact, she explained, it was the plot lines that avoided rock 'n' roll that first appealed to her. For her first-ever serious movie role, "I didn't want to play a rock 'n' roll star. Even when I heard it was a really good script." Reading it, though, "I realized that it's a family drama."

And what a drama it is. The character she had to move in to, Patti, is a teenaged wastrel, an unmarried mother who adopts a borderline-criminal existence in order to earn enough money to feed her illegitimate son. Her brother Joe (Fox), meanwhile, has dedicated his life to shielding his nephew from the social dregs and deadbeats with whom Patti is forced to consort, while their mother (played by Gena Rowlands) is dying of cancer.

The only thing the siblings can agree on is their band, the Barbusters, but as their personal conflicts build, so the band suffers, and Jett pointed out, "Music is [only] a big part of [the film] because it's a big part of these peoples' lives. So once I could tell that 'wow, I'm gonna be an actress,' then I was interested in it."

Jett was not Schrader's first choice for the role of Patti. It was originally offered to the singularly named singer Fiona; Schrader later confessed that he was so intent on giving the role to her that even Michael J. Fox was cast on the strength of a passing resemblance to the "Talk to Me" hit maker. But Fiona was off making another movie, *Hearts of Fire*, at the time, so Schrader took a chance on Jett, particularly after actress Jill Ireland—Charles Bronson's wife—began singing her praises.

She and Jett had recently become friends, and there was talk for some time that Jett might make her debut in a Bronson flick. Ireland was convinced that Jett should act alongside Bronson, to give him a naturally strong female character to act against. That particular scenario never came to pass, but Ireland remained convinced that Jett was destined for movies, a conviction that Schrader seemed to share.

In fact, the director later admitted, "That piece of casting just did not work." Part of the problem, he explained, was that he could never put his finger on what made Jett tick from an acting point of view. "Hers is a performance that, at least from this vantage point, seems to be extremely good," he told *The Morning Call*'s Cheryl Wenner as shooting came to a close in late 1986. "But I really don't know where it's coming from. With most actors and actresses, you can discuss motivation and technique and so forth. With Joan, you do so at the risk of losing it. It's the damnedest thing, I've never dealt with a performance this good that I didn't feel I had access to."

Michael J. Fox, too, confessed to being in awe of his costar. He told *Rolling Stone*:

> She's got an intensity that's real frightening. When you're working with her, you have this feeling that she could haul you off and belt you. Not that she isn't a real sweet person—that's the paradox. She really is

a sweet, generous person, but she's got this armor. So what Paul had to do was selectively help her take off plates here and there.

There was also the matter of making the Barbusters believable, and that was something that the cameras couldn't fake. So Schrader sent them out to play. With the group's lineup completed by *This Is Spinal Tap* star Michael McKean, the band played a pair of unannounced shows in Chicago, just to see how convincing they could be.

Two months of rehearsal, Jett said, had made them about as good as they were ever going to be; the key to the success of the performances, then, would be making certain that the trio was able to retain its anonymity. And they succeeded. Fox recalled, "When we came out to play, people said 'God, that looks like Joan Jett.' And they were so busy deciding if it *was* Joan Jett, that they didn't notice the guitar player lurking in the dark. It was a strange kind of anonymity because it was so public."

Accompanied by a brilliant video shot by Rob Cohen, director of *Miami Vice* (and producer of the movie itself), the single "Light of Day," with Jett handling the vocals, was released in early 1987 and made its way to #33 on the US chart, just as the movie opened to somewhat less impressive numbers in theaterland.

For all Fox's personal ambitions to shake off the "cute kid" imagery that had pursued him throughout his career so far, his audience was clearly not ready for him to do so. He later acknowledged that the scene in which he is seen smoking a cigarette was one that could probably have been left on the cutting room floor. He had hoped it would make him look tougher. In fact, it just looked wrong.

Reviews were seldom less than harsh, and Schrader himself later admitted that the movie had been a mistake. "I had progressed from being a person with a literary vision to a person with a visual vision, and in that film I tried to . . . suppress my new literacy," he admitted. And of Jett's role, he remarked simply, "it's a good performance, *but.*"

But *Light of Day* is not forgotten. In 1998, friends of the music-industry veteran Bob Benjamin, recently diagnosed as suffering from Parkinson's Disease, rallied to form a fundraising organization named after the film. Michael J. Fox's own battle with the same disease was made public that same year. The Light of Day Foundation continues to fight, and its events are traditionally closed by a performance of "Light of Day."

TWENTY

Up Your Alley

The filming of *Light of Day* was complete, and by late 1987, Jett was ready to go back out on the road. She'd missed it during the months she was cooped up in Cleveland, missed the nightly shot of adrenalin, and she could not wait to get out there again.

But the portents were not good. The 1980s were fast running out of the hourglass, and American rock was running out of balls.

MTV had a lot to do with it, as it did with most domestic musical developments that decade, but the cable network's embrace of the grating pop metallics of Winger, Nelson, and assorted other long-haired cuties with a taste for saccharin power ballads really was a dictate too far.

Neither was Joan immune from the prevalent mood. Back in the studio at the end of the year, she was writing with Poison producer Ric Browne and creating a pair of songs—"Riding With James Dean" and "Just Like in the Movies"—that really weren't much different from everything else being thrown at the rock marketplace at that time, and were even happy to look backwards as well; "Just Like In The Movies" *must* have known that ZZ Top had exhausted that particular guitar sound five years earlier.

But maybe that's what the public wanted, a Joan Jett album that didn't leap off the commercial precipice, daring all comers to knock it over; an album that kept its hand firmly on her traditional tiller but would follow the current currents regardless.

Murmurs from around the studio told of a more fractious affair than the Blackhearts had ever experienced before. *Up Your Alley* wasn't *quite* the Pat Benatar album that the label heads had wanted Jett to make back in 1982, but it was certainly the most conventional and considered record she had ever made, a succession of renta-snarl rockers layered in swooping keyboards, treated drums, and all the rest. And while tales of Jett's disillusion with the proceedings were never confirmed by the star herself, listen to "You Want In, I Want Out," and her disinterest is palpable.

She revolted. Behind those grisly flagships, *Up Your Alley* bucked furiously against the studio stereotypes. "I Still Dream About You" came close to becoming one of the greatest Glitter songs that Gary never wrote, while a signature take on Kenny Laguna's decade-old triumph with the Steve Gibbons Band, the raucous "Tulane," rocked like the Stones rewiring Chuck Berry through the cheapest amp they could find. And there was a dip into the Stooges songbook that proved that Jett's instincts were as sharp as ever.

A decade had elapsed since every punk band worth its safety pins had taken on the Stooges' catalog, but even New York poet/rocker Richard Hell floundered when he went head to head with "I Wanna Be Your Dog," a song of such apparent lyrical and musical simplicity that the nuance necessary to actually convey its message escaped nearly everyone who attempted it.

Jett, however, nailed it, not because she sounded like she really *did* want to live the lyric, but because you knew that beneath the words, she didn't. The second cut on the Stooges' twenty-year-old debut album, "I Wanna Be Your Dog" is a song of defiance and disobedience, and like Iggy Pop voicing the original recording, the tone of her delivery let everybody in on that secret. The fact that she didn't try to out-Iggy Iggy helped as well—the curse of the Pop cover, after all, is the performer's all-consuming need to prove himself (or less frequently, herself) a worthy mouthpiece for the music.

With Ricky Byrd's scorching guitar leads taking as significant a role as Jett's brittle vocals, extending the groove out over twice as many minutes as the Stooges ever managed, the old protopunk anthem was rewired as a shattering, echo-laden psychodrama, shifting mood and tempo with the same kind of deliberate dissonance that once outraged Jett's mother when she first heard "Whole Lotta Love."

No matter what other indignities may (or may not) have been perpetrated on Jett's sense of self as *Up Your Alley* rambled on, "I Wanna

Be Your Dog" proved that—like the song said—she was still ready to lay down in her favorite place . . . "and you know where that is," she ad-libbed with an audible grin.

"I Hate Myself for Loving You" was the flip of the coin, and that despite starting life beneath the distinctly less radio-friendly title of "I Hate Myself Because I Can't Get Laid." Kenny Laguna later described "I Hate Myself for Loving You" as one of the four key songs in Jett's career; the others, not surprisingly, are "I Love Rock 'n' Roll," "Bad Reputation," and "Do You Wanna Touch Me (Oh Yeah)." Ricky Byrd would add that it features one of his most quintessential guitar solos—"When you hear that break, you can hear what my influences are, Leslie West, Jeff Beck." The moment the track was complete, the studio hushed in amazement. They had their next hit single.

The song had parentage that could not do wrong; Jett cowrote it with Desmond Child, one of *the* most accomplished American songwriters of the '80s.

A decade had passed since he made his debut in the KISS camp, cowriting the band's descent into disco-dom, "I Was Made for Loving You." Since then, he had worked alongside some of the hottest names in American metal—Bon Jovi had Child to thank for their first-ever chart-topping single, "You Give Love a Bad Name" (he also cowrote "Living on a Prayer" and "Bad Medicine"), and when Aerosmith launched their 1987 revival, Child was in on "Dude Looks Like a Lady."

"The guy's a fucking genius," Aerosmith frontman Steve Tyler exclaimed. "The first time we met, we wrote 'Angel' in about an hour and forty-five minutes—and I'm not bullshitting."

Neither did Child's collaboration with Jett halt there. Another song they wrote together, "House on Fire," was promptly covered by Alice Cooper (whose entire latest album, *Trash*, was a Child cowrite), and gave the old ghoul a Top 20 smash in 1989. "I Hate Myself for Loving You," meanwhile, became one of Jett's biggest-selling records ever.

Codirectors Jean Pellerin and Doug Freel's original concept for the accompanying video, on the other hand, left a lot of people scratching their heads, and that was before Jett put her foot down and declared that she was having nothing whatsoever to do with it.

Shot after Jett and the Blackhearts had filmed their own elements of the video, and then delivered as a fait accompli on the eve of the single's release, it showed a leather-clad biker pulling up outside a

Catholic school, to be joined on the pillion by his clearly underage girl-friend. "Coming onto little girls at school?" Jett snapped. "You bet I was pissed."

The problem was, the single was so close to release that it would require a miracle to salvage something usable from the footage and have the video ready for distribution at the same time as the record. But they got one. Abandoning all but the most fleeting glimpse of the biker's bike, the live footage that had been interspersed with the original shoot was reedited and expanded, to create, ironically, one of the most vicariously volatile videos of Jett's entire career—watch it, and every emotion that had filled her heart as a concert-going teenager became a tangible emotion. "It was," Joey Ramone exclaimed, "probably the only time I've ever watched a straightforward concert video and felt like I was actually at the gig."

Buoyed by a Top 10 chart placing for "I Hate Myself for Loving You," *Up Your Alley* pushed the Blackhearts back into the Top 20 for the first time in six years, while a tour with Robert Plant, the old Zeppelin war dog riding his hit *Now and Zen* album, kept the Blackhearts' momentum going strong. Even when the outing was interrupted after Plant's drummer broke his foot roller-skating in the dressing room, there was no respite. The band simply utilized the break to shoot their next video, "Little Liar."

Another Desmond Child cowrite, "Little Liar" rewarded the band with their second consecutive Top 20 hit, and that despite being an even more calculatedly power ballad–shaped confection than its predecessor. Sales of *Up Your Alley* passed the two million mark. Joan Jett was back, she was hot, and she had no doubt as to what the next album should be. The ultimate jukebox, a nonstop tear through her all-time favorite songs.

Recorded at the Hit Factory in New York, *The Hit List* would pull its contents from across the musical spectrum. "Usually they're just songs that I'm a fan of," Jett explained.

> To some degree, the message has to be something I can live with, something I believe in. I try to be little bit obscure, and try not to pick songs that are really obvious. I think it's fun. People might bitch about cover songs, but, hey, I write songs, too. A lot of the songs I've

recorded are songs I write. But why not? I've got no ego involved here.
I don't have to prove myself as a writer to myself or anyone else.

Besides, she added, "Even though I'm in a band, I'm a fan, too, and it's fun to be able to play some of these songs just for the hell of it. If it's a message that you believe in and a riff that you like, why not?"

The Blackhearts did not initially set out to record an all-covers record. Rather, they were working toward a regular new album and, as usual, started out by recording the selected covers "because they're the ones we know best." It was only as the sessions went on that they were inspired "to do a whole album full of songs like that. We did it just for the hell of it."

Few people could argue with the eventual selections. "Love Hurts" was a country-tinged ballad that had been given fresh legs by the Scots hard-rock band Nazareth; "Pretty Vacant" peeled out of the Sex Pistols' catalog; ZZ Top's "Tush" was beautifully redirected to a woman's point of view; the Chambers Brothers' "Time Has Come Today" transformed into a punching-party rocker; and so on.

The Doors' "Love Me Two Times" paid tribute to one of the Runaways' predecessors at the top of the Hollywood hit list; Jimi Hendrix's "Up From The Sky" gave Ricky Byrd a chance to dance with one of his instrument's greatest acolytes. And while a stab at Alice Cooper's "Be My Lover" would not make the final cut, it slashed with almost autobiographical intent through Jett's own love of rock 'n' roll. (Among the album's other outtakes, the soundtrack to the movie *Flashback* resurrected a fabulous romp through the Ritchie Cordell oldie "Indian Giver.")

There were moments of sublime brilliance, those occasions when you could cut through everything that the band and the Blackhearts did to a song and hear it from Jett's point of view, a fifteen-year-old dancing around her bedroom, singing along with the record player.

That's who snarls through the Rolling Stones' "Let It Bleed," that most gorgeously sleazy of all the band's late '60s masterpieces—an adolescent would-be rocker, practicing for a dream that might never come true, but knowing she'll be ready if it does. And that's who almost lets her emotions get away from her during a beautifully heartfelt recasting of the Kinks' "Celluloid Heroes."

"That's my personal favorite on *The Hit List*," Jett declared. Written and recorded back in 1972, with Hollywood still the theater of grimy dreams that Jett remembered from her own teens, "the song talks about . . . walking down Hollywood Boulevard and looking at the names on the stars" embedded in the sidewalk. She told *Bad Reputation Nation*,

> Those are all things I did when I first moved to California. When I was doing the record, it reminded me of when I was fourteen years old and dreaming about becoming famous. That song really brought back memories about all that stuff. "Celluloid Heroes" became special to me because I was able to go back mentally and think about walking up and down the street, dreaming of being famous.

"I was in a restaurant," recalled Alan Merrill,

> and Joan Jett's *Hit List* album came on and I listened to how well the record was produced. The percussion sitting in the right place in the mix. The voice right in the middle of the mix, and in your face, as it should be. Crunchy guitars and tight simple bass and drums. Simple guitar solos. Jett makes great rock records. Her vocals are easily identifiable and very rock 'n' roll, with a dry discernable snarl curled around every syllable . . . I really like her version of "Road Runner" a lot.

A signature demolition of AC/DC's "Dirty Deeds Done Dirt Cheap," crashing the Top 40 in January 1990, was the first indication that *The Hit List* was going to be something special. The title track from AC/DC's third album, recorded shortly before they left their native Australia for a new career in London and the world in 1976, "Dirty Deeds Done Dirt Cheap" was AC/DC *in extremis*, a declaration of demented degradation that in the days before the band found their heavy metal feet, almost had them poised on the edge of the UK punk scene. Certainly Bon Scott, the band's vocalist until his untimely death in 1980, had no hesitation in claiming that AC/DC were at least as great an influence on the burgeoning scene as the Sex Pistols and the Clash, and playing back through their earliest records, it was not difficult to understand where he was coming from.

Since that time, of course, AC/DC had become established as one of the world's most compulsive, and successful, metal acts. But when Jett tracked back to *Dirty Deeds Done Dirt Cheap*, she not only recalled the subversive promise that the band once posited; she also recaptured it. In musical terms, "Dirty Deeds Done Dirt Cheap" might well have been the most successful cover version she has ever recorded.

Commercially, however, the album's most successful inclusion was the Blackhearts' reworking of Creedence Clearwater Revival's "Have You Ever Seen the Rain?," a recording that became one of Jett's biggest hits ever—in Southeast Asia. "The record was #1 for the year in Thailand, Singapore, and Malaysia," recalled an astonished Kenny Laguna.

Topping the charts throughout the region, the record's success opened up an entirely new market for Jett and the Blackhearts. "It was this humungo hit," Laguna continued, and suddenly the Blackhearts were "playing to like sixty thousand people in Taiwan, Bangkok, the most incredible places, Jakarta . . ."

That December, and the following year too, the band would be touring the region with Jett enthusing, "We had a blast! It was so great! They were really into rock 'n'roll and they knew the songs! It was ninety degrees and the land was all jungle. It was really nice. We got to run around the jungle. The people there are really into rock 'n'roll and nobody ever goes there. We're one of the few bands who have played there."

Her enthusiasm knew no bounds. She talked of undertaking a full world tour, visiting Australia, New Zealand, and Japan, returning to Malaysia and Indonesia, scouring Europe and the Americas. She wanted to show the world what "real rock 'n' roll" sounded like, "and thank God it's The Blackhearts and not one of these fake fuckers."

But they didn't overlook their homeland. On the road around *The Hit List*'s release, Jett realized that the Blackhearts were the only band she'd heard of who had played at least eight cities in every state of the union—which may be an exaggeration (are there even eight cities to play in Delaware or Rhode Island?) but it does give an indication of just how devoted to the road she was.

Her own latest tour was, she declared, her largest production yet. And no sooner was that outing completed than she hit the road again, this time opening for Aerosmith as *they* continued their own revival. "I think it'll be a lot of fun," she said ahead of time. She certainly shrugged off *Bad Reputation Nation*'s questions about having to go back to being the support band again.

I don't have any head trips about opening or headlining. I always pre-
fer to headline, but I've been opening shows and headlining all my life.
I'm looking forward to the two bands playing together. Sometimes,
when you play with other bands, it can be really special and something
that the fans can remember for years. I remember shows that I went
to and I guess everybody does.

The Hit List, and its accompanying tour, also welcomed Thommy
Price back to the fold—although few people realized he had actually
departed. Shortly after completing *Up Your Alley*, he left to concentrate
on the band that he and Kasim Sulton had put together, the very sensibly named Price/Sulton. But no sooner were the Blackhearts back in the
studio to record *The Hit List* than Price was returning to the fold, just to
help out at first but becoming increasingly more involved until, finally,
he was a full-time member once again. And when Sulton left the band,
Price quickly filled the gap by introducing another of his friends, Phil Feit,
in time to record a new song for the movie soundtrack *Days of Thunder*,
"Long Live the Night."

The Hit List was still new on the shelves when Jett's friend Jill Ireland
passed away. Fifty-four years old, Ireland had been battling illness since
1984 when she was diagnosed with breast cancer; she was still fighting
when Jett and Kenny Laguna wrote "Don't Surrender," a song expressly
dedicated to Ireland's struggle. "We [were] great friends," Jett mourned.
It was Ireland who turned Jett on to crystals, a fascination that she has
nurtured ever since; "[She] taught me a lot during our friendship."

Ireland died on May 18, 1990; and although another year would elapse
before it could be released, "Don't Surrender" was earmarked immediately for inclusion on Jett's next album.

Originally to be titled *Out of Bounds* but eventually changed to *Notorious*, work on that set—her eighth—began immediately following the
band's return from their latest visit to Malaysia and Southeast Asia. Jett
told her fan club, "We went in the studio once we returned from Malaysia
in January and we worked on the album until it was completed at the end
of June. We were in the studio everyday—all day long."

"We really grooved in the studio this time," she bubbled.

I think it's a great record. Everybody always says that their new
album is the best thing they've ever done. I really believe this is the

best one we've ever done. The reason I feel that way is because a lot of times when we finish a record, even though I've always loved all the songs, there were always one or two that I wasn't as crazy about like I was about the others. I don't feel that way about this record. I really love every song and every note on the album. I also think that I've sung better that I ever have before. I don't know why, maybe it's because of all the vocal exercises that I've been doing. That really helped.

She was still writing with Desmond Child. Five new songs came out of their partnership: "The Only Good Thing You Ever Said Was Goodbye" was a neat little rocker with plenty of scope for some dirty guitar; "Lie to Me" was a sultry rhythm with a hint of exotica pulsing around its well-constructed corners. "Ashes in the Wind," "Don't Surrender," and "Goodbye," however, were power ballads one and all, and following firmly in the footsteps of "I Hate Myself for Loving You," et al., were either thrilling or disappointing, accordingly.

But there would also be another glance back toward the primal energies of Gary Glitter and Suzi Quatro, thumping through the dramatic stomp of "Treadin' Water" and "Machismo," songs that saw cowriters Jett and Laguna peel back to the earliest energies of their partnership as if to balance the slicker sensibilities of the Child compositions, while "I Want You" played that particular riff even harder, by resurrecting one of the songs they wrote at the very dawn of their partnership.

Perhaps the most revealing inclusion, though, was "Misunderstood," revisiting "Bad Reputation" with an autobiographical romp through school, the Runaways and after, through the prism of an outlaw status Jett never set out to court. In terms of making a point, of course, it said nothing that she had not repeated in countless interviews for the past fifteen years. But the fact that Jett still felt the need to defend herself for simply following her own instincts lifted "Misunderstood" high above the usual bad boy/girl posturing that has been a default setting for rockers since the dawn of time. Because she was right to do so, and if anybody doubted that, there was the pointed resignation of "Backlash" to pinpoint the source of her dissatisfaction.

"Backlash" was cowritten with Paul Westerberg, the frontman of the Replacements—a band that Jett had adored since the first time she heard them, crashing out of Minneapolis on the tail end of the early 1980s hardcore movement, but swiftly establishing themselves among the most contrarily melodic and musical bands of the decade. At the forefront of the so-called college rock scene that prefaced the industry's catch-all adoption of the "alternative" tag, the Replacements were nearing the end of their lives now—released just months after *The Hit List*, their latest album, *All Shook Down*, would be their last, as Westerberg prepared himself for a solo career.

He and Jett had often talked about writing a song together; now the time was right. At least partially inspired by the commercial and critical changes in fortune that Jett had suffered over the years, "Backlash" was recorded with Westerberg himself in the studio, playing the distinctively dirty guitar that had always characterized the best of his own recordings, and singing alongside Jett.

He appeared, too, in director Paul Rachman's video, shot on the roof of the studio by the 59th Street Bridge in Queens, while a huge screen behind the band unfurled all of Jett's past videos and a few other old favorites as well. Vintage Who and Hendrix can both be glimpsed as the video marches on, solid-state declarations of precisely where Jett stood in the annals of rock.

But it was a foothold that Jett would retain for just a couple of weeks longer. *Notorious* was released in August 1991, well received by the music press and well anticipated by the marketplace. But nobody could have foreseen that less than a month later, *all* predictions and expectations for the remainder of the year were to be upset by the sudden arrival of a new band, a new sound, an entire new lifestyle, hurtling out of the backwoods on the fringes of Seattle and destined to rewrite the rock rule book for the next five years.

Nirvana and Grunge were coming, and from the moment "Smells Like Teen Spirit" hit the airwaves in early September, it was as though no other new release even existed. The media scramble that followed then to discover further bands from the suddenly seething hot-bed of the Pacific Northwest didn't simply push an entire generation of post-'80s rockers down the pecking order. It pushed them off it altogether. Suddenly all was grunge, all was flannel, and if you didn't have a Western Washington (or at worst, Northern Oregon) zip code on your press pack, then it was scarcely worth plugging in your guitar.

So she did what she always did in moments of adversity. She went on tour.

THREE

Pure and Simple

TWENTY-ONE

Activity Grrrl

As the corporate ogre expands its creeping influence on the minds of industrialized youth, the time has come for the International Rockers of the World to convene in celebration of our grand independence. Hangman hipsters, new mod rockers, side street walkers, scooter-mounted dream girls, punks, teds, the instigators of the Love Rock Explosion, the editors of every angry grrrl zine, the plotters of youth rebellion in every form, the midwestern librarians and Scottish ski instructors who live by night, all are setting aside August 20–25, 1991 as the time.

—*The International Pop Underground Convention manifesto*

It was not a good time to be on the road, but Jett didn't care. The American touring industry had been hit hard, but not by the seismic shock of Nirvana. Countrywide, a recession had walloped the music industry, forcing tours of every description to either cancel or downscale drastically. Unlike many performers, however, Jett was not going to let it get her down.

"You have to be realistic about what's going on in the country," she told the fan club.

> You can't just go into any arena because your ego dictates it. You can't play a twenty thousand seat place when you're not capable of doing that. If you can't fill all twenty thousand seats, then you

shouldn't be playing there. We've decided to go into the smaller places and do our shows on a more intimate level, and have a really good time with it.

But there was, perhaps, another reason behind Jett's decision to scale back her visibility. After close to a decade alongside her, Ricky Byrd had quit the Blackhearts for a solo career. Bassist Phil Feit too was gone; alongside Jett and Thommy Price, the band now lined up with bassist Kenny Aaronson and guitarist Tommy Byrnes.

Byrd's departure hit hard. After a decade in the band, the last surviving member of the team that scored with "I Love Rock 'n' Roll" was, in many fans' eyes, as much a Blackheart as Jett herself. His guitar was certainly an intrinsic, crucial and—simply because it was impossible to imagine anybody else filling his shoes—irreplaceable component in the Blackhearts' sound.

But he was tiring of the road, tiring of the constant movement. Looking back on his years "at the top" in 2010, he was horrified to discover that he simply didn't remember a lot of them, that an entire decade of his life had flashed past in a sea of hotel rooms, stages, studios, and photo ops.

It's a sad story, and I've kicked myself ever since, but I was more interested in being a rock star. I'm twenty-two years sober, but previous to that, I wasn't. When I should have been learning and experiencing in the studio, I was sitting in the lounge watching TV. I was twenty-four, twenty-five, and how many musicians pay attention? That's why you have a producer and an engineer. When it was my parts, I'd be there, but it seemed such a long process that I didn't spend as much time in the control room as I should have. Twisting knobs? Fucking pointless.

He would remain friends with Jett, of course—"if we saw each other today, we'd be all hugs and kisses," he admitted in 2010—and he would make a guest reappearance on her *Pure and Simple* album. But he had his own career, and music, to think about now.

I've never had a cross word with Joan. I was in the band for twelve years, a long time, and I wanted to do some other things. There was internal shit all the time, me and Joan got along great, and I'm friends with Kenny also, but there were discrepancies with publishing, song-writing, all the usual crap, and on top of that, then I found myself thinking, "I'm onstage in front of fifty thousand people and I'm wondering what am I going to have for dinner." So I got myself a publishing deal and it was time to go.

In 2010, Byrd spoke proudly of the solo debut album that he had completed that summer. It had been a long time coming, but he'd put a lot into it, too.

The man with the unenviable role of replacing Byrd, Kenny Aaronson, was, once again, a Thommy Price recommendation, although he also had a strong connection with the Blackhearts' own history. Back in the early 1970s, Aaronson's Brooklyn-based hard-rock trio Dust were signed up by no less than Neil Bogart and signed to Kama Sutra. Changing their name to Stories, they then scored a massive hit with "Brother Louie," which, for fans of the six degrees of separation, became a European monster for Suzi Quatro's RAK labelmates Hot Chocolate.

He moved on. Hall and Oates, Sammy Hagar, Rick Derringer, Billy Squier, Billy Idol, Bob Dylan . . . one of the most reliable session players of the 1980s, it was during one such session that he first met Thommy Price and heard that the Blackhearts were growing tired of the apparent merry-go-round that the bass slot had become. As a drummer, it was especially frustrating for Price, and while Aaronson admitted that he was scarcely familiar with Jett's music, he was happy to meet the band, play a little— and that was it. He was in, and relishing every moment of it.

The only question was, would anybody listen?

Not everything was lost in the new musical climate. A flurry of fresh interest percolated around "I Love Rock 'n' Roll," following its inclusion in 1992's *Wayne's World* movie—there was even a new video produced for it, splicing elements of the Mike Myers and Dana Carvey movie into a new Jett and the Blackhearts performance. The effort helped push the remixed song to #75 in the UK, and that despite Jett and Laguna loathing both the video and its director. "They destroyed it," she shrugged.

And there were glimmers of a fresh future to be found as well, if only an artist knew where to look. Grunge, like punk fifteen years earlier, was a remarkable leveler, setting a new common denominator for musicians to aspire toward and then ensuring that it was open to everybody who cared, and not just whichever exclusive club of well-coiffed stylists could afford to climb aboard.

A musical antidote to the absurdities of the late 1980s, a stylistic rebellion against the hairspray and spandex that had become the self-proclaimed rocker's most basic uniform, grunge was built around guitars that growled and clothes that didn't simply come off the peg; they were best left on the ground beneath it, to be scruffed and trampled and generally battered before you would even dream of putting them on. Lumberjack shirts. Dirty jeans. Old boots.

Anti-glam, anti-glamour. Anti–Guns N' Roses, anti–Bullet Boys. And for however long the look could survive intact before the high-street fashion stores commenced transforming it into high chic, it represented the most exciting sound that rock had heard in more than a decade, aurally and visually. It was a new beginning, one that echoed the corrosive impact of punk rock in terms of resetting the historical clock to what future historians would regard as Year Zero, but one that—like punk—also drew its heroes from where it needed to find them, as opposed to the places that the history books normally placed them.

For almost fifteen years, Jett had been adamant that one day, the Runaways would be recognized for what they truly were—an all-girl group, of course, but one that was created, and executed, for all the right reasons. They had never been overtly feminist in a political sense; they were feminist because they were female, carving a swathe through a universe that had hitherto been utterly male dominated. And while critics preferred to point to Patti Smith, and to a lesser extent Blondie, as the harbingers of any new sense of female consciousness, they told only half of the story.

Patti was art, Blondie was pop, but it was the Runaways who rocked, and for every teenaged girl who looked at la belle Smith and strummed a guitar behind her poetry (Alanis Morrissette, P. J. Harvey, Tori Amos, and so forth, take a bow), there were others who didn't give a flying fuck for boys who looked at Johnny, or dancing barefoot because the night told them to. They wanted to plug in, turn up, and blast the fucking shit out of everything.

The new wave of female musicians and bandleaders who began to surface in the early 1990s were hardly likely to be original Runaways fans. Age alone dictated against that. But they had certainly danced around their bedrooms playing air guitar to "I Love Rock 'n' Roll" and "Bad Reputation," in precisely the same manner as Jett danced around hers to "All Right Now" and "War Pigs." And the end result was the same as well.

The Riot Grrrl phenomenon was a peculiarly American creation—cringingly, British viewers may recall catching the Spice Girls on television's *Top of the Pops* one evening, early on during their ghastly reign, and hearing the show's female host announce them as delivering some Riot Grrrl action. But its roots *were* at least partially British, female-fronted bands like X-Ray Spex and Penetration, or all-woman concerns like Nirvana frontman Kurt Cobain's favorite Raincoats—acts that employed their femininity neither as a sexual nor a stylistic concern, but because that was what they were.

Add the Runaways, Chrissie Hynde, Exene Cervenka, Lydia Lunch, and Sonic Youth's Kim Gordon to the brew; add too Canada's Mecca Normal and San Francisco's Sugar Baby Doll, and by the time the Olympia, WA, radio station KAOS began broadcasting Lois Maffeo's *Your Dream Girl* show in 1991, and knotting that into the thriving DIY music scene being pioneered locally by K Records, a distinctly feminist punk ethos was both breaking through and making itself heard.

External politics, most publicly centering around the Christian Coalition's Right to Life assault on legal abortion, but also around the media's mocking response to sexual harassment charges brought by Anita Hill against Supreme Court Justice Clarence Thomas, focused further attention on the movement, while the arrival of the *Riot Grrrl* fanzine gave it a name.

Published by Allison Wolfe, Molly Neuman, Kathleen Hanna, and Tobi Vail, *Riot Grrrl* was the point around which so much disparate underground activity was destined to coalesce, with two bands—Hanna's own Bikini Kill, and Wolfe and Neumann's Bratmobile—moving inexorably, if not necessarily enthusiastically, to the forefront. Both groups furiously denied any credit for "creating" the subsequent movement. But both were something more than midwives regardless.

It was K Records' International Pop Underground Convention, in late August 1991, that confirmed the validity of the Riot Grrrl movement (should the outside media have demanded proof of such a thing). A weeklong festival, the first night of the Convention, August 20, was given over exclusively to what the organizers called Love Rock Revolution Girl

Style Now, an all-female billing that brought in more bands than most observers had even imagined existed—Bratmobile, 7 Year Bitch, Heavens to Betsy, Nikki McClure, Lois Maffeo, Mecca Normal's Jean Smith, and Kathleen Hanna's Suture side project.

It would take some months—even years—before the alternative music media finally picked up on what was already a thriving community and pushed it into the spotlight. But the notion that something called Riot Grrrl existed as a rambunctious little sister to the all-conquering grunge scene was one that even the mainstream could comprehend. Hence *Top of the Pops'* subpoenaing of the term for the Spice Girls; hence the arrival of a few dozen other acts into the swelling ranks of the genre. And hence, a growing sociopolitical awareness that the seeds the Runaways first planted were finally beginning to blossom.

For Jett, Riot Grrrl offered more than simple vindication, however. In common with a lot of other music fans, both within and without the industry itself, she had been growing increasingly weary of the stagnation that the late 1980s and early 1990s described as rock 'n' roll. She welcomed Nirvana, not as the destroyers of an old way of life, but as the harbingers of a new sense of consciousness, musical and otherwise—one that promised representation not only to the kids who were sick of listening to bland corporate rock but whose roots reached down to the disenfranchised politics that those same kids felt in their hearts.

For the first time in too long, a spokesman had arisen, and no matter how unwilling Kurt Cobain may have been to accept that mantle, he adopted it nevertheless and he used it well. Plus, as Jett said following his suicide, "He was a great guitar player and a great singer."

Nirvana's success, and Cobain's wide-eyed enthusiasm for so many other performers and causes, opened doors that the industry itself would never have permitted be unlocked, and if the rapid spread of grunge-styled music swiftly proved that this idea was as wide open to dilution as any past movement, still the handful of bands that did remain true to their original notions ensured that it would, literally, take death to snatch away the glory. Cobain died in April 1994 and the grunge scene folded up almost immediately.

Riot Grrrl was not immune to the dilution. Indeed, by the time Jett penned her own tribute to the movement, 1994's snarling "Activity Grrrl"—written the day after she saw her first Bikini Kill gig—its original progenitors had already seen many of their own founding ideals either wholly subverted or else ruthlessly coopted. When Jett lamented the fact that she was not even invited to perform at the first Lilith Fair festival— an ostensibly woman-centric operation whose inspiration, if not its content, was wholly drawn from the Riot Grrrl example—her regrets came not from a commercial angle but from the realization that, once again, the market had missed the point.

"I'm still always fighting the [idea that playing rock 'n' roll] is some kind of phase or something," she told writer Amy Ray in 1997.

> Like I'm some kind of freak, like other girls can't grow up to be what I've done. Like it's a one-off thing. No, wrong. There's gonna be other ones behind me. I think because a lot of times I'm gregarious, I like people to feel like they can approach me. But certainly, I'm rebellious. I am not the way . . . well, I guess the way I was taught girls should grow up. I don't know how they're taught today. I don't know what they think. But I still see a lot of girls not claiming their power. Just sort of letting other people tell them what to do, and that's a learning process, like it was for me. I let many people tell me what to do, until I said, "No. Now it's my turn."

Suddenly, it appeared, a lot of women were making that same declaration.

It is one thing, however, to be feted as an icon and a figurehead of a movement, another to actually become involved in the movement and even help to shape it. But that is what Jett proceeded to do. By showing her interest in what was happening, and graciously acknowledging that her example at least had something to do with things, the sense that she "approved" of what was happening was a tangible thing.

> I think all the women, and the girls who are out there playing music, really inspire me. Anybody that I'm aware of, that I am lucky enough to come across, regardless of whether I'm really into it or not, just the fact that they're out there doin' it, because there were no women doin' this when I started. There are now, [but] I can never take that for granted. I can never let that go. I have to always appreciate that. But within that, there are probably too many women to name that inspire me.

She started attending shows, talking with bands, establishing a rapport that developed into friendships. And she agreed to produce the next single by Kathleen Hanna's Bikini Kill—a band, she enthused, that simply didn't care what anybody thought. They just went out there and played.

"What makes a difference to me is that bands like Bikini Kill are at the heart of the movement, like me. Kathleen Hanna thought the Runaways were valid. That's all I care about, not what some fanzine says, or what self-appointed 'cool people' say."

Jett had already dipped a toe back into the waters of outside production, for the first time since the Germs, when the Washington DC–based band Circus Lupus invited her to oversee their upcoming "Popman" single.

> I went to see them someplace in New York. They were on Dischord Records, which is Fugazi's label. [The members of Fugazi] are friends of mine, and they let me know that this great band was in town. We met and hung out, and got along really well. They were going into the studio to do a single, and they asked me if I would do it. And I said, "Yeah, I'd love to." So that's how that happened.

Now she was returning to the studio with Bikini Kill, to cut what would become the three songs that, led off by the self-defining "Rebel Girl," are often regarded today as that band's finest hour.

Jett's friendship with Hanna would ultimately develop into one of the most important working relationships in her career. The pair still write together today, with Jett explaining, "It was only natural that I sort of tried to write songs with her. Kathleen is very sort of outside the box, and forced me to write in a different way. I just thought it was a lot of fun to give that a try."

"We have to hear woman playing rock 'n' roll on the radio," she told *Micromag*.

> Which is not the case now. It's all lip service and it's all pop records. I'm not saying that's not valid—it is valid, it's very valid. But women, playing sweaty, screaming, aggressive rock 'n' roll is valid too. It's all lip service that "women are equal now" and "we've arrived" and all that shit until you hear L7, Bikini Kill or bands like them, or me, consistently on the radio the way Jane's Addiction [and] Nirvana [are].

The Bikini Kill session was still fresh in her mind when Jett was back in the soundproof booth with L7, recording a new version of "Cherry Bomb" for inclusion on the latest *Rock for Choice* benefit album, *The Spirit of 73*. And when the album was launched with a special benefit concert, Jett was there as well, leaping onstage to join L7 as they ran through that same song.

There was one band, however, that she never got to play with—at least in their original state—but whose story was to dominate Jett's mid-1990s regardless.

The Gits formed at Antioch College in Yellow Springs, Ohio, in 1986. Singer Mia Zapata, guitarist Joe Spleen, bassist Matt Dresdner, and drummer Steve Moriarty were originally known as the Snivelling Little Rat Faced Gits, a name they lifted from an episode of television's *Monty Python's Flying Circus*. They'd already shortened it to the Gits by the time they self released a cassette of their earliest scramblings, *Private Lubs*, in 1988, and the following year, the band relocated to Seattle. There was, they'd heard, something of a music scene bubbling around there, which was more than you could say for Yellow Springs.

They established their headquarters in the city's Capitol Hill district—the rental that they quickly rechristened the Rathouse became one of the emergent local music scene's key hangouts and party places, and as both grunge and Riot Grrrl began emerging from the hinterland of local labels, zines, and scenes in the Pacific Northwest, the Gits managed to steer a musical course that bound them to neither—and both.

"There was a real vibrant music scene here, in all aspects," Steve Moriarty recalled, and Zapata flourished within it. "I just liked the urgency and the honesty of her vocals. Her art and the music were the most important things to her, and everything else, who cares."

When they toured Europe in 1990, at a time when the continental underground was first getting excited about the so-called Seattle sound, the Gits were feted as highly as the headlining Tad. But when you actually listened to them, they clearly had roots and intentions that went far beyond the average wall of mogadon guitar sludge—intentions that existed in a bubble almost wholly of their own making, musically beholden to neither of these but grateful, of course, for the helping hand that the media's misinterpretations lent them.

A clutch of new releases over the next couple of years paved the way for the Gits' debut album, *Frenching the Bully*; that European tour was financed almost wholly by the band's now-burgeoning reputation and of course, their uber-hip place of residence. And because it was the peak of Nirvana's years of fame, and Pearl Jam and Soundgarden's too, there was scarcely a record label in the West whose eyes were not firmly fixed on the rain-swept streets of Seattle in search of the Next Big Thing—few labels, too, that had not established at least a local presence, if not a full-blown office in the city, to make certain that nothing escaped their gaze.

Some truly dreadful music made it out of there. Exciting though it seemed at the time, hindsight has done terrible, terrible things to the grinding guitars, throat lozenge vocals, and mastodon riffery that was grunge's raison d'être. But the Gits rose above it all. A major label deal was imminent; their second album, *Enter: The Conquering Chicken*, was underway.

And then Mia Zapata went out for an evening at the Comet, a bar on Pine Street where she often spent time, and she never came home.

The Gits had just returned to Seattle following a West Coast concert tour, although they did not necessarily return in triumph. Moriarty continued, "[Mia] said for some reason, 'I don't wanna be back in Seattle. I really have a bad feeling here.' She was a real intuitive person. Extremely intuitive."

Her body—raped, beaten, and strangled—was discovered in a nearby alleyway, early in the morning of July 8, 1993.

She was twenty-seven years old.

The city was paralyzed. Nobody could believe what had happened— even people who had never thought of the Gits as anything more than just another local band playing around a scene that was brimming with the things, were shocked and horrified by the sheer brutality of Zapata's murder. That, and the sense that things like this simply didn't happen to rock stars. Zapata was no John Lennon after all; she had no deranged fans stalking the streets armed with Salinger novels and loaded guns. She was simply a singer in a band.

The police disagreed. Their initial inquiries were focused almost exclusively upon Mia's immediate circle of friends and associates, and their suspicions only made matters worse, as friends began looking at other friends and wondering—*Did you do it?*

The rumor mill went into overdrive. Reports that Zapata's body was discovered with arms outstretched, perpendicular to her body, in some gruesome parody of the crucifixion, gave rise to the belief that she was the victim of a cult killing, and eyes for a while settled upon the city's gothic and industrial community.

Logic struggled to take over. Few within Zapata's own circle, or beyond for that matter, ever truly believed that the police's suspicions were on anything remotely approaching the right path. Increasingly, the conviction that the police were wasting time chasing grunge-shaped ghosts began to take hold, and with it the knowledge that with every passing day, the real killer was getting further and further away.

He left no evidence of the remotest value, just a broken body dumped unceremoniously in the street and a fragment of saliva where he'd bitten Zapata's breast. But DNA technology was still in its infancy. There could be no help from that direction.

Zapata's friends rallied. Maybe the police were content butting their heads against a wall of unfounded suspicion, but they weren't. The idea of hiring a private investigator was raised and acted upon—benefit concerts were being staged to raise the necessary funds.

Further funding and awareness was raised around the formation of Home Alive, a nonprofit self-defense group designed to teach women how to protect themselves on the street, how to fight back.

A bevy of bands that played the same circuit as the Gits added their own voices to the furor. 7 Year Bitch's next album was titled for Mia, *Viva Zapata*; Everclear's latest, *World of Noise*, was dedicated to her. It was Jett, however, who delivered the highest-profile message.

Jett was spending a lot of time in Seattle that spring and summer, hanging out with Kathleen Hanna and Kat Bjelland of the band Babes in Toyland. As always, she kept a low profile—journalist Amy Hanson recalled

> hearing from different people that she was in town, but she really didn't broadcast it. Seattle was so hip at that time, a lot of [rock stars] were coming through simply to be seen—you'd go to a club and they'd be leaning against the back wall waiting to be recognized. Joan just blended in, she'd be in the mosh pit with her friends, and if you did see her, you'd wonder if she knew how much she looked like Joan Jett.

"I had never heard of the Gits," Jett told Amy Ray.

[But] a friend of mine told me about this band, the Gits, and this lead singer, Mia Zapata, who had just been found raped and murdered, and everybody was all freakin' out. It was such a tragic thing. You'd go see bands, and people were really depressed about it, and they talked about it. I was able to see firsthand the response of her friends. I told Kathleen Hanna about this, and she also knew some of these people, and we decided to write a song about it, but instead of writing a song about feeling powerless, we wrote a song about beating a stalker, you know, kind of like, being stalked, and being attacked, and knowing enough to get away, and live. So we wrote this song.

It was called "Go Home."

TWENTY-TWO

Love Is All Around (Again)

With Tony Bruno, ex of the New Jersey hard rockers Saraya, stepping in as the Blackhearts' latest guitarist, *Pure and Simple* was released in June 1994. A dynamic set, built around crunchy Sex Pistolian guitars, animal percussives, and Jett's harshest vocals in a long time, *Pure and Simple* was clearly influenced by her recent experiences in the maw of the new movement.

The very title, she insisted, hit the nail on the head. The Blackhearts were playing it pure and playing it simple, the same as they always had. They had, however, refocused that objective somewhat. For the first time on a Joan Jett album, there were no cover versions included, as Jett instead targeted the record's contents wholly at her own, most immediate, preoccupations.

L7's Jennifer Finch stopped by the studio to contribute some backing vocals, Finch's bandmate Donita Sparks cowrote the song "Hostility," Kat Bjelland shared the credits for "Here to Stay." And no less than three high-energy Kathleen Hanna cowrites, "Go Home," "Spinster," and "Rubber and Glue," so flavored the album that taken alongside the seething "Activity Grrrl," *Pure and Simple* could not help but remind listeners that many of the attitudes that hallmarked the Riot Grrrl movement were ones that Jett had shared for almost twenty years.

It was Jett's idea to try collaborating with these other performers, although she admitted that at first, she had no clue what form a collaboration might take. There was talk that she might produce them. A notion of going out and performing together was floated. But she slipped most naturally into songwriting mode, and the results were spectacular. Too often when a new musical movement rises up and starts to pinpoint its heroes, the relationship remains that of teacher and pupil—over in the UK at the same time, bands like Blur and Oasis were feting past masters Ray Davies and Paul Weller, but one could never shake the feeling that the brief partnerships that followed were media stunts as much as anything else, the older man grabbing at the fame of his followers, the younger seeking the historical validation that a legend's patronage could confer.

Joan wrote with her friends because they were her friends, and because she was a fan. There was no sense of passing on some mythic musical torch, no patronizing pat on the head and a condescending "aren't you doing well."

"I'm a fan of each one of those bands," Jett elaborated. "I've gone to see them play over the last couple of years. I've seen L7 in New York, Washington DC, and Los Angeles. I started hanging out with them and really getting to know them. I just thought it would be nice to work with these people at one point in some kind of capacity."

Of course there was some tutelage required, and some reassurance too. Her new cowriters were not accustomed to working with somebody outside of their most immediate circle, and they found it correspondingly difficult to relax. Once that happened, however, the music flowed.

Pure and Simple continued to expand. There were guest appearances from Mike Howe and John Marshall of the band Metal Church, and Ricky Byrd was back to layer some of his so-characteristic guitar across "Eye to Eye." And Desmond Child was on hand to ensure that the mood didn't become too hardcore. But the key to the album remained Jett's own musical taste. She set out to make a record that sounded like something she'd have bought herself, a record that pulled its influences and textures from the kind of records and bands that she most loved at that moment—Fugazi, Bikini Kill, L7. A record that sounded like the Blackhearts on stage.

The *Pure And Simple* world tour kicked off on June 25, 1994, in Albany, New York, with these same goals in mind. It had been three years since the last Blackhearts tour, and that was far too long, she declared. "I'm so psyched to be back out on the road," Jett enthused as the opening night loomed, and even more so because the support act, the Baltimore-based Lungfish, was another band with which she'd been in love for years. Plus, she laughed, it made a change from the usual support acts she was saddled with, "bands that we are totally unfamiliar with, or in some cases we're not into it at all. I really wanted to go out on the road this time with a band that I was aware of and I liked their music."

The only problem, she said, was that she was going to have to start getting to her own shows early so she could catch their opening act.

Mia Zapata and the Gits, meanwhile, remained on her mind. "Go Home," the song that she wrote with Kathleen Hanna in the aftermath of Zapata's murder, was set to become Jett's next single, and when she traveled to London to shoot the accompanying video with director Julian Temple, she did so knowing that this was her opportunity to raise her voice even louder.

Jett and Kenny Laguna had known Temple for over a decade; they first met him in London around 1980 while he was still riding the success of his directorial debut, *The Great Rock and Roll Swindle*. Since then, he had continued to create some of the most talked about, and vivaciously talk-*worthy* videos of the age—minimovies, in a way—and that is what Jett wanted for "Go Home": a shadowy black-and-white thriller in which a barely recognizable Jett is being followed from a club and attacked by a stalker.

Except this time, the story had a happy ending—Jett got away from her would-be assailant. But the video's message was hammered home regardless. A stark caption at the end of the video reminded viewers that "Mia Zapata was brutally raped and murdered in July of '93. Her murderer has never been found."

"So, we were trying to inform people that way," Jett explained. "But since the video never got any airplay, nobody saw it."

In fact they did. Zapata's bandmates caught sight of it and contacted Jett, just to thank her for showing concern. Steve Moriarty continued,

> She wrote back a couple of weeks after, a really nice letter from a hotel in Germany [the latest stop on the current Blackhearts tour], saying that she'd love to do anything to help and to contact her management immediately. So I did, and one thing led to another . . . and we would in essence form a band with her and do some benefit shows.

A lot faster than anybody could have expected, a plan began to take shape—a new band, three Gits and Jett, playing their way through a selection of songs by both the Blackhearts and the Gits.

"I could feel that it was a little bit of a strange proposition," Jett admitted. "But I think that they realized that my heart was true about this. It wasn't a publicity stunt." In March 1995, eighteen months after Zapata's slaying, a series of three benefit shows, at RCKNDY and the King Theater in Seattle, and La Luna in Portland, were set up to continue raising funds for Home Alive: Pearl Jam, the Posies, and Seven Year Bitch had already agreed to appear. Now there was a new name on the posters, Evil Stig—Joan Jett and the Gits.

The shows, Jett continued, "were pretty heavy," any sense of celebration deadened by the sheer weight of the tragedy that inspired them. At one, Jett noticed a fight breaking out in the audience. Whoever was on stage at the time, she told writer David Snowden, stopped playing to remind them,

> "Hey, that's not what this night is about." It was really amazing to see that sort of awareness. People took the initiative to want to find out about it and seemed genuinely interested. They weren't just there to see a band, watch a show, and leave. It was a little bit more than that. That was real special and it was something that all of us felt.

Kenny Laguna arranged for both of the Seattle shows to be recorded on 24-track, but it was only once the band played the tapes back that the idea was born of issuing a souvenir of the occasion, taking the original live tracks into the studio in Vancouver, Canada, and then overdubbing, replacing, and adding to the performance to create what Steve Moriarty described as "kind of a cross" between a live album and a studio set.

"It has the live energy that Kenny wanted to capture, but also has the attention that we were able to pay by going back into the studio and redoing stuff, and fine-tuning, and adding backing vocals and strings."

It also furnished them with an opportunity to muse on how the whole project had suddenly taken on a life of its own, as Jett reflected. "It started with a couple of benefits to raise some money in Seattle and Portland. We recorded the gigs and took the tape recordings we did to the studio, which became an album—that wasn't expected. The whole thing just snowballed," and it kept on snowballing, because now she was back talking to the musicians about the possibility of a full tour.

The Gits had reconvened as a new band, the Dancing French Liberals of '48, and had their own career to be getting on with, and Jett continued, "We didn't plan to do a tour like most bands would when they have an album come out, because we didn't know what was going to happen or what kind of reaction it would get. The tour just kind of came. It was something that people wanted to see . . . there was excitement, so we decided to do a tour."

Again, it was intended as simply a one-off event. "It's really hard to say if it will continue because Evil Stig was The Gits' music," she said at the time—just two of Jett's own "classics," "Activity Grrrl" and "Crimson and Clover," would appear on the finished record. "To keep going, we'd either have to record more Gits material or decide to write some things . . . which then ultimately wouldn't be the Gits stuff which Evil Stig is. Evil Stig is 'Gits live' backwards, so for me I would have to rectify that in my head somehow."

The project was allowed to slumber once the tour was over, but still, the outing was an unqualified success. "I had a blast!" Jett confirmed. "It was a lot of fun." Evil Stig presented her with a whole new way of singing, and she didn't even have her guitar to hand, at least for the Gits numbers in the set. "It was really different for me trying to be just a lead singer. I don't mean that to belittle it, but not having the guitar in my hands, and more or less something to hide behind, was a lot different."

In some ways, it was a liberating experience—touring with the Blackhearts, after all, always presented its own set of challenges and responsibilities, the pressure that comes, she said, from knowing that "ultimately it is my job and I want to do a good job at it. With the Evil Stig project, I still have responsibilities, but it wasn't like I had to worry about sales, or things like that." She could just go out and enjoy herself.

Meanwhile, the search for Zapata's killer continued—or, rather, it didn't, as time passed and other cases took precedence, cases that actually presented the police with leads to follow and clues to chase up. Occasionally there would be a flurry of activity, usually when the case came to the attention of such national television shows as *Unsolved Mysteries*, *American Justice*, *Cold Case Files*, *City Confidential*, *48 Hours*, and *America's Most Wanted*. But these, likewise, fell on stony ground. A CBS news report in 2005 pointed out that the Seattle Police Department had no less than three hundred unsolved murders still on its books, including the killing of an assistant United States attorney.

But it also had one of the most tenacious cold-case teams in the country, a department that had solved twenty of those outstanding murders in just three years. It took seven long years to finally apprehend Zapata's killer, and when a break in the case did finally come, it was completely by chance. Precious little evidence of any description had been left at the murder scene, but that tiny trace of saliva from the bite on Mia's breast had been collected and stored, on the off chance that DNA profiling might one day advance sufficiently for such microscopic materials to be of use.

That day had now arrived and, finally, a random DNA check pointed investigators towards a Cuban-American fisherman named Jesus Mezquia. Recently arrested for a burglary in Florida, Mezquia had lived in Seattle for a short time in the early 1990s. On March 25, 2004, almost *eleven years* after he killed Mia, a jury convicted him of murder. He was sentenced to thirty-six years in prison, the maximum allowed under Washington state law.

Joan described Home Alive:

What they do is teach self-defense courses. They teach you things that can give you that split second to get away, like how to set boundaries and yell at people. Too many people feel funny to yell at somebody if they feel threatened. Sometimes people will back down and say, "Do whatever you want, just don't hurt me." Those people are afraid to say, "Hey what do you want? Don't come any closer." Some people feel embarrassed to yell. Look, you're dealing with your life. It's a scary world we live in and that little hesitation could mean your life. A little bit of embarrassment is worth it.

People should know something about protecting themselves and doing things like stepping down on someone's instep, whacking at their eyes, hitting them in the throat, a knee to the balls. Little things that sound insignificant such as screaming like you're some sort of nut case might make an attacker go away, and save your life.

Even as she and Laguna worked toward the Evil Stig album, work on Jett's own next album was already underway. Falling in with songwriter Jim

Vallance, they took over his Armoury Studios in Vancouver, recruited producer Bob Rock, and began recording fresh material with him. She was also reunited with Paul Westerberg, whose song "Androgynous" (from the Replacements' *Let It Be* album) had recently moved into the Blackhearts' live set, and was one of the first songs pinned down for the next album.

A new guitarist was recruited. It was one of the Mia Zapata benefit shows, at La Luna in Portland, that introduced the latest member of the Blackhearts, bassist Sean Ray Koos, to the audience. Born in Hawthorne, California, on March 13, 1961, the son of a Bourbon Street jazz trumpeter, Koos was in the audience one evening when Tony Bruno gave one of his solo shows. The two knew one another, and when Koos went up to say hello, Bruno asked if he was interested in auditioning for the band. "'It's in two days.' He gave me a tape that night and I said, 'Yeah, I'm into it.'"

He knew Jett's music, of course—he'd been a fan since the first time he saw the Blackhearts opening for the Who a decade before. "Even back then, I was going, 'God, if I could just be in a band like that.'" Now he was, and reaping the immediate benefits too. The first track he recorded with the Blackhearts, at A&M Studios in Los Angeles in December 1995, was a version of the old J. Geils' Band hit "Love Stinks" for inclusion in the movie soundtrack *Mr. Wrong*. And the second was the theme to television's *Mary Tyler Moore* show, "Love Is All Around," commissioned from Jett by the Women's College Basketball organization as a theme for the upcoming Sweet Sixteen championship.

There were other projects percolating too. A call from the music supervisor of the upcoming movie *Tank Girl* gave Jett the opportunity to voice the Cole Porter song "Let's Do It," with the LA punk veterans Bad Religion alongside her, and afterwards Laguna told the fan club that

it came out a lot better than anyone had dreamed. [But] when we got done with it, Bad Religion's manager decided he didn't want it to come out as a single. He never thought it could be that good. We like the guys from Bad Religion, but they wanted us to put another voice on it, so we called our friend, Paul Westerberg. He was really into it and did it. So the guys in Bad Religion are playing the backing track with Thommy Price . . . and Tony Bruno playing bass. So you have Bad Religion, who also did all the background vocals, Jett, the Blackhearts, and

Paul Westerberg on one track that Cole Porter wrote. That probably won't ever happen again.

For the most part, however, the Blackhearts simply got on with their job, headlining venues that crammed in up to ten thousand kids at a time, hitting the summertime festivals around the US, throwing a sharp version of "Real Wild Child" onto an Iggy Pop tribute album . . . "I had a real hard-on for 'I Wanna Be Your Dog,'" Jett recalled. "But I don't know." "Real Wild Child," the mid-1980s rocker that gave Iggy his first-ever hit single, had been in the Blackhearts' live set for a while, "and it was a lot of fun," she said. "You know—why not do something different?"

The accompanying video was just as exciting. With Jett nursing a shoulder she had injured the previous evening in a bicycling accident, but biting back the pain to celebrate the appearance in the shoot of Joey Ramone, it also allowed Jett to unveil her new hairstyle to the cameras— short, blonde, and spiky replacing the familiar lush darkness. It seemed somehow appropriate.

Meanwhile, what about that new Joan Jett and the Blackhearts album? Almost two years had elapsed since it was first formulated, at Armoury Studios in Vancouver, and it was, apparently, still gestating.

But it was also snared within a succession of bear traps, only the most easily resolved of which had anything to do with Jett and the band.

The Bob Rock sessions had been mothballed after Rock became involved in the latest Metallica project. Of course it drew him away from the Blackhearts, and while there were initially plans for him to simply pick up where he left off, once Metallica was complete, Jett shrugged, "We couldn't wait anymore. It sort of slowed us down a bit, but now we're back in the flow."

Now the band was working with Ted Templeman, a veteran whose resume stretched back to the Doobie Brothers and Van Morrison in 1971, then moved on to the likes of Van Halen, Aerosmith, the Bullet Boys, Damn Yankees, and Cheap Trick.

"Bob's a great guy," Jett explained as the Templeman sessions got underway. "He's a very good producer and a really nice guy, but for some reason things didn't sound right. I don't think it had to do necessarily with him; it's just everything sounded a bit soft. It just wasn't coming across the way we wanted it to sound. It didn't sound raw or aggressive enough, so we decided to change producers."

She reeled off her songwriting collaborators. Jim Vallance was back, and so was Kathleen Hanna. She had laid down some favorite covers and was looking forward to the album's scheduled release date in September 1997. "I'm excited about that."

In fact, she would have a lot more time than she thought. Having already scrapped the bulk of the Bob Rock sessions, the Templeman recordings, too, were archived. September 1997 came and went with no sign of the album; in its place, Blackheart Records released a hits collection, *Fit to Be Tied*, with bonus track–stuffed reissues for *Bad Reputation* and *I Love Rock 'n' Roll* to follow. And eighteen months later, Jett was still awaiting a berth on the new release sheets, and growing increasingly frustrated by the delays.

Talking with the fan club that summer of 1999, Kenny Laguna sighed,

> Every time Warner Brothers goes through a change of management, they're all excited about Joan, and they stick their nose in it, and we're still trying to cooperate with these guys . . . they've got a really good guy in there now, so we'll see how it is. They're talking a good game, so let's see if they walk it like they talk it.

There were, he said, some twenty-five songs in the can, drawn from both the Rock and the Templeman sessions, and the album would certainly be created from that stockpile. In the meantime, the gap would be plugged with yet another compilation.

Fetish, Laguna declared, would draw together "the very best songs that are sexually adventurous, that Joan's done." "Handyman," "Black Leather," "The French Song," "Star Fucker," and "Do You Wanna Touch Me" were all rounded up, together with a thunderously explicit "XXX" version of "Fetish"—XXX because there really can't be many songs where the opening verse concludes with a reflection of tying up your lover "while I fuck your head." Up there with the Headcoatees' tantalizing revision of the old ballad "Come into My Life," rewired as "Come into My Mouth," "Fetish" is one of those songs that can liven up the dourest party, and

Laguna had no doubt that the full CD would have a similar effect. "It's going to be a really cool album, and it flows well."

Fetish was, he said, an idea that they'd been batting around for a while, and there is little doubt that it was the protracted drama over the "real" new album that pushed them to release what amounted to another compilation.

But that wasn't the only reason. Themed compilation albums were an unusual idea, and it was one that Laguna wanted to act upon before anybody else came up with the same notion—particularly as there was also a sense that the Blackhearts had inadvertently passed some very good ideas on to other Warners acts in the past, and they had no intention of that happening again.

> It was a unique idea and I just had a feeling that somebody was going to steal the idea. It had been sitting around too long, people were talking about it, we'd been getting hundreds of letters about the song live, we had it on the Internet for a while, and it was getting a reaction, we were getting a lot of requests from clubs all over the country for copies of it. And I thought, you know what, we sit around long enough, somebody's going to copy this song, copy the idea. So that's why we did it.

Fetish would be released in June 1999, five long years after *Pure and Simple*, and its X-rated subject matter certainly drew in a few curious ears that might not otherwise have listened to a Joan Jett album. Which certainly made a pleasant change from the other Jett-related scuttlebutt that was hanging from the grapevine that season . . . the imminent Runaways reunion.

More than a decade had passed since the band's name was last sighted on the release schedules, as part of a postscript that left every past member of the band feeling cheated. In 1986 Kim Fowley had pieced together a new Runaways lineup, around teenaged singer/songwriter Gayle Welch and (male) guitarist Bill Millay, and an album, *Young and Fast*, followed in 1987. It did little beyond raise some scornful eyebrows among critics who couldn't believe that Fowley had not learned his lesson with the last lineup, and it was quickly forgotten. But as the Riot Grrrl movement and its successors continued to draw the original Runaways' legacy into the daylight, so more and more business-oriented minds began to wonder if the time was not right for the real thing to reconvene.

Jett was adamant that it wouldn't.

It will never be like it was. To me, it is like why? Why do it? Someone's gotta tell me a good reason why. We would be creamed in the press, creamed. A bunch of almost forty-year-old women trying to recapture their youth, and it didn't work the first time and da da da da da . . . It just leaves us wide open and I can't deal with that. The Runaways were so special to me, and I can't take that. I would rather not do it at all. I don't need to do it. It would have to be totally fun, no head trips from anyone, no bullshit . . . perfect.

And she knew that wasn't going to happen . . . or be allowed to happen.

What she didn't acknowledge, at least to begin with, was how close it came to taking place. According to Cherie Currie, the original idea came from Lita Ford. "Lita approached us . . . had us all write letters to Joan, begging her." And suddenly, Jett agreed. "So we had like a million-dollar record deal right then."

A telephone conference call was arranged between Currie, Sandy West, Lita Ford, Jett, and Kenny Laguna, just returning home following a Blackhearts show in Hong Kong. They were exhausted, and according to Currie, it showed. "Lita didn't last three minutes on the phone. Joan had just flown in from Hong Kong; she was exhausted. Joan's very Zen. And Lita gets so pissed off."

"I want you to be doing fuckin' double back flips over this," Ford demanded. "I want you excited."

Jett was astonished. She was excited. "Hey, Lita, man, you know, chill out. I'm tired, I just got off a plane after fifteen hours."

But it wasn't enough. "Sorry—I can't do this. I'm out."

Currie picks up the thread. "It was like, 'wait wait wait, Lita! Lita, wait!' She goes, 'No, sorry, fuck all you guys, forget it' and she hangs up the phone."

That was the first reunion attempt. Shortly after, a second swam into view as the band was offered a forty-date reunion tour, this time for three-and-a-half million dollars. There was talk that Suzi Quatro had been approached to fill the bass-playing slot and had not said no; "Joan was interested," Currie continued, "We're all into it. And Lita freaks out again and says, 'You know what? I don't need the money. I'm moving into my two-million-dollar house in the Caribbean—have a nice life, everyone. Goodbye.' And it was just like, 'what the hell?'"

Neither could they simply go ahead without Ford—the contract demanded there be four original members of the band on board, and both Vicki Blue and Jackie Fox had already made it clear that they no longer played bass. ("And Jackie never really could play," added Currie.) The dream died; instead, Jett launched into a tour with Def Leppard, and just as she had so many times in the past, shrugged off the critics who wondered how her brand of garage punk could ever sit comfortably onstage with a band best remembered for sundry metal anthems.

"I think the music works well together because both bands write three-minute rock songs with melodies and big choruses. There might be a different tilt, but the music works well together and the audiences work great together too." Besides, anybody who missed the glam influences that were as pointed in Def Leppard's music as they were in Jett's surely had their ears stuffed with prejudice; it would be a few years more before Def Leppard released a covers album of their own, the solid gold *Hey*, but one glance at its track listing could have paired it with any of Jett's own adventures with the music of her youth.

Almost. But even Jett was astonished when she received the call asking if she'd be interested in appearing in a revival of one of the most precious of all her teenaged memories. *The Rocky Horror Picture Show* was coming back to Broadway, and this time, it was going to be enormous.

TWENTY-THREE

Do the Time Warp

A s the twentieth century finally ran down, Joan Jett seemed to be every-where. Switch on the television and "Bad Reputation" was pumping out, the theme music to NBC television's hit *Freaks and Geeks* series.

Open the fashion pages, and her still shockingly cropped blonde look was popping up on a lot of other heads.

And read the news, and there were the Blackhearts performing at a NOW benefit in Washington DC in front of two hundred fifty thousand people, and grabbing further headlines when they played for the troops at the Gioia del Colle Air Base in Italy on May 19, 1999. Jett was by no means a fan of warfare, but she was also smart enough to draw the line between the people who serve and protect their country and those who make the often asinine decisions to send those people to war.

The Italian job was, she revealed to NBC, simply the latest in a long line of similar projects stretching back for a decade or more.

I don't remember the exact circumstance as to how I got involved. We have gone all over the world, from the DMZ in Korea to parts of Eastern Germany, I think even some stuff in Hawaii, but I am not sure if it was USO.

We have been all over the place, to a lot of places that just, well . . . aren't very pleasant. I just never publicize it, because I don't want people to misinterpret the reason why I do it. The reason I do it is because, if people really look into it, [the soldiers are] just kids. The people I usually play to anyway, that is my audience. They are in a very uncomfortable situation. I personally don't publicize it because people will misinterpret that I am supporting government policy.

Her hairstyle, meanwhile, was already old hat so far as she was concerned, because New Year's Eve would see her go one step further by shaving it all off. Now, she proudly proclaimed, "I'm bald to the skin." She told writer Jaan Uhelszki,

> I had been planning it for six months, figuring if I shaved my head on the millennium, I'll sit and contemplate my life, and what it means to be alive during this time, and my hopes for the future, for humanity, for the earth, and just to really be present in that. So that was all attached to this head shaving. I just figured come hell or high water, I'm shaving my head. So I did, and I love it.
>
> I'm obsessive about it. I don't want to feel any fuzz. I just want to feel smooth skin. It feels great and I think it looks great. But no one said a word. About my blond hair, they said, "Oh, your hair looks great," or "I like your hair blond." But [this time] no one said a word— not the fans, my friends. Nobody said anything.

Jett was midway through filming a martial arts scene with actor Chuck Norris when one of the most surprising calls she had ever received came through. She was no stranger to the occasional cameo role on television or film—an episode of *Highlander* in 1992, a small part in Craig Hammans's *Boogie Boy* movie in 1998. Now she was battling Norris in the season finale of *Walker, Texas Ranger*, when she was invited to audition for a role in *The Rocky Horror Picture Show*, as the excitable groupie girl Columbia. She "jumped," she said, at the chance.

It was twenty-five years since Joan and her friends had made a point of catching every screening of the *Rocky Horror Show*, learning every line of dialog and cheering or hooting the action as it unfolded; twenty-five years, too, since the first New York production of *Rocky Horror* fell so flat on Broadway, and director Christopher Ashley admitted that they were taking a chance with the revival. "When the play and the film came out in the early '70s, a guy putting on a dress was really cutting edge," he explained. But thirty years later, "How many times have you seen RuPaul on network television?"

Still, a strong cast came together—Dick Cavett, the grand old man of American music television, would appear as the play's narrator, Tom Hewitt as Frank-N-Furter, Alice Ripley as Janet, Raul Esparza as Riff Raff . . . And Joan as Columbia.

Her audition was plain sailing; she probably knew most of her script by heart, anyway, after so many years of watching and rewatching the *Rocky Horror Picture Show* movie. She was asked to read the scene where Frank-N-Furter's cruelty finally causes Columbia to snap; then was called back to try out with a choreographer, to make certain that she was able to follow direction.

She could, but it was frustrating work. "I've never danced," she admitted to writer Mary Campbell. "I'm a perfectionist. I expected to get the dance steps right the first time." Still, she grasped the role, and now she was plunged into some of the most intensive rehearsals of her entire career. "It's been pretty demanding," she understated at the time. "I'm pretty sore and tired, and trying to catch up on sleep and stuff."

Some revisions were made. Writing the play back in the early 1970s, Richard O'Brien gave the character of Columbia a tap-dancing sequence, as a reminder of when he'd been asked to portray a tap-dancing King Herod in *Jesus Christ Superstar*. Would Jett too be forced to sublimate her rocker persona for the joys of tap?

Would she hell. Instead she grabbed a convenient guitar and soloed the guts out of it, a moment that the watching *Entertainment Weekly* proclaimed the highlight of her entire performance. "Jett never quite adapts her proto–riot grrrl rock persona to the role of Columbia, if only because she's not trained for this kind of stage. [But] when she plugs in a guitar and shreds a few chords, she's on home turf."

The Rocky Horror Show opened on Broadway on November 15, 2000, a $3.5 million show that squeezed into the Circle in the Square Theatre and was an instant hit.

"I know her fellow actors saw that Joan was the toughest," Kenny Laguna exclaimed later. "She was the last man standing, she never missed a show until her six months were up. She had the mandatory Actors Equity week off, and then never missed a show. They begged her to stay on, and she did, though we had to do some dates [with The Blackhearts]."

Jett herself learned much from the production, he said. "She learned a great deal about projection and performance by doing that show every night with those very talented people. I see a vast improvement in her on stage, although she was already one of the best rock performers who ever lived." Alan Merrill agreed. "Joan invited me [along] to see her and I enjoyed her performance a lot."

In the months that followed, Jett and Laguna would link with *Rocky Horror* costar Jared Emmick, penning a handful of country-tinged songs for him and also rearranging "I Hate Myself for Loving You" as a country ballad. Jett would not, however, appear on the obligatory cast recording of the play's soundtrack, after locking horns over a number of the proposed terms and then resolutely refusing to be pushed into accepting them.

Laguna told the fan club what happened next.

> They are so used to bullying people with the paycheck, they never dreamed Joan would call their bluff. The people in the show work from paycheck to paycheck. They can get pushed around because of that. But Joan wasn't there for the money, so they couldn't push us around. They found out the hard way. They were arrogant. The joke was on them, and the whole record business knows it.
>
> We didn't care about that bullshit. We didn't need their money, and we sell more than they did when we have a bad selling release on Blackheart. If they had lived up to their word and Joan was in the cast CD, they would have sold many times more then they did. I'm sure they were shocked when they got slapped in the press; that someone could actually fight back. People on Broadway were secretly calling us and cheering us for standing up to the plantation system that exploits Broadway actors on a regular basis.

Jett would remain with the production throughout the next year, until the Broadway slowdown in the wake of 9/11 caused *Rocky Horror* to finally close its doors on September 23 2001 . . . It would be back the following month for a final burst of shows, but Jett had already moved on. In October, playing a 9/11 benefit in Red Bank, New Jersey, she joined Bruce Springsteen onstage for the first time, to perform a triumphant "Light of Day"—afterwards, she described it as one of the greatest moments in her entire career.

Weeks later, she was in rehearsal for one of the furthest flung of all her tours, as she undertook a scouring of the US military's newly created bases in the post-9/11 Middle East, an outing that she and Laguna christened the "Stan" tour—because "we were all over the place, and every place ended in "stan" (Uzbekistan, Pakistan, Turkmenistan, even Afghanistan).

She did not necessarily agree with the reasons why the troops were in such places, but she was determined to support them however she could. Many of the kids in the armed forces, she reminded people, were just that, kids, "and they need the moral boost a lot of the time. Depending on what is needed at the time and my availability, I do different things. Most of the time, I like to go to different parts of the world and perform for the troops. It's really a way to give back because it's important."

Back home, Jett's next project was also be stage oriented, appearing alongside actresses Gina Gershon, Jennifer Esposito, Jane Adams, and Shelly Cole in *Prey for Rock & Roll*, an adaptation of an off-Broadway play about an all-girl band trying to make it big in the Los Angeles rock 'n' roll scene. Although it sounded, from such a brief description, like one more stab at the Runaways story, cowriter Cheri Lovedog in fact based the play upon her own experiences of putting together an all-girl rock band in the early 1980s. Shooting, with director Alex Steyermark, was scheduled to begin May 16, 2002, in Los Angeles—just a month after Jett performed at the Rock 'n' Roll Hall of Fame.

She was not being inducted. That honor, it seemed, required connections that journeyed far beyond the requisite quarter century of rocking service, and a soft spot in the heart of the nominating committee. You needed somebody out there going to bat for you on a constant basis; it was no coincidence, for example, that two of the acts being inducted that year, the Ramones and the Talking Heads, were both Sire Records acts. Jett, on the other hand, was merely appearing at one of the organization's fundraising events. And today, more than a decade after they qualified for inclusion, the Runaways remain Hall of Fame outcasts.

There were further honors in the pipeline, however, as the Runaways were inducted into the Guitar Center Walk of Fame and granted their own star on Los Angeles' Rockwalk—a musical version of the Hollywood Walk of Fame. Jett celebrated with the release of a limited-edition single, pairing her and Cherie Currie together for the first time in twenty-five years, dueting through "Cherry Bomb" at the Sun Theater in Anaheim on August 18, 2001.

"I'd like to bring out a very special old friend of mine," Jett announced to the packed auditorium. "We haven't been onstage together in about twenty-four years, it's a long time." And afterwards, she admitted "[Cherie] sounded as good as she ever did." The joy on Jett's face as the performance got underway, incidentally, was priceless. "That was a great moment," enthused Kenny Laguna. "It was magic! They have such good energy together. There's never been anything except love between them."

Prey for Rock & Roll never happened. Jett did, however, have a role in another movie, *The Sweet Life*. Kenny Laguna explained, "She got into it through Chris Stein from Blondie. His wife was starring in it, they needed somebody beautiful and tough, and Chris suggested Joan, and we liked it and we like these guys. So we wrote some new songs for that."

In fact, the only thing that they didn't seem to have was a release date for the new album. "So we chucked it," shrugged Kenny Laguna. It was time to begin work on the next one.

TWENTY-FOUR

AC/DC

J ett and Kenny Laguna alike were sick and tired of answering questions about the new album, just as they were sick of having to ask them. "We're always working on new stuff," Laguna explained. But they needed to get out of their deal with Warner Brothers before they could do anything with it. Things had changed a lot since the days of the *Joan Jett* album, when you could just press up a few thousand, stick them in the trunk, and sell them at gigs. An act of Jett's visibility and magnitude needed an organization to match gearing up behind her, to make sure the music was heard where it needed to be, was available where people wanted it to be. And right now, none of that was possible.

More stopgaps would appear in 2001. A concert DVD, capturing a brilliant VH-1 performance from Telluride, Colorado, three years earlier, became Jett's first-ever official live document. And *Unfinished Business* was a five-song collection of sports-related songs led off by "Love Is All Around" and Jett's version of "The Star Spangled Banner," recorded six years earlier at Cal Ripken's historic game: to those gems, Jett added her take on Iggy Pop's "Real Wild Child"—ESPN's choice for the theme to the first X-Games, and another of that same station's requests, "I Left My Heart in San Francisco." The video for songwriter Ray Castoldi's title track, meanwhile, was shot at Madison Square Garden at the opening day of the new women's basketball season.

But it would be 2004 before a new Joan Jett album appeared, and even then it was only available in Japan. The creation of *Naked*, as a relieved Kenny Laguna explained,

> was quite an odyssey. Now that we've reached our destination, I believe we have made the best Joan Jett and the Blackhearts CD ever. Of course, I always think that when we finish, but sometimes I'm right, like this time. After working on the recording for so long, we realized we had before us a work with many textures, recorded in several countries and many cities.

No single set of sessions dominated the record. Rather, *Naked*'s contents were drawn from close to a decade's worth of beginnings. The title track, for example, dated back to Jett's time in Seattle producing Bikini Kill and touring with Evil Stig; a clutch of other songs were either written or recorded with Katherine Hanna. "Bad Time" was cut with another of Laguna's '60s bubblegum cohorts, Joey Levine; "Right in the Middle" was written with Linda Perry. She and Jett had been friends for years, dating back to Perry's time in the band Four Non Blondes. "She's always been a great songwriter. She stopped performing live and just focused on writing songs, and we just had an opportunity a couple years ago to sit down and try to write songs."

That deliciously seductive take on Paul Westerberg's "Androgynous" finally made it onto disc, and so did a riotous punk version of the song that opened every performance of *The Rocky Horror Show*, "Science Fiction Double Feature"—further salt for the wounds of the powers-that-be that missed out on Jett appearing on the stage show's cast album.

A mere two songs apiece from the Bob Rock and Ted Templeman sessions hinted at the album (or even albums) that might have appeared in the late 1990s; but they included a fabulous version of "Season of the Witch," a Donovan composition from the late 1960s that has rightfully ascended to the ranks of the greatest songs ever written. Jett followed in footsteps as disparate as Julie Driscoll and Courtney Love when she cut it, but her version stands alongside them with ease.

There was "Kiss on the Lips," a slash of savage dissonance set to the sultriest rhythm, the dirtiest lyric, and the loudest guitars that Jett had

unleashed in years. And in the midst of this, there was "Turn It Around"
. . . the kind of Joan Jett song, said Kenny Laguna, "that made the Runaways famous." And it arrived at exactly the same time as a few of that
band's other qualities were revisited, this time on the big screen.

The Runaways reunion that consumed so many discussions in the
late 1990s never happened. But the notion did start a very different set
of wheels in motion, as director Victoria Tischler-Blue, the Runaways'
Vicki Blue, began planning a documentary about the entire Runaways
phenomenon.

Blue had been involved in movies for far longer than she was ever a
musician. Back in 1984, she even had a role in *This Is Spinal Tap*, alongside Jett's *Light of Day*–bandmate Michael McKean. She switched from
one side of the camera to the other, and began work on *Edgeplay* in 1998,
when she discovered a box of old super-8 footage, TV recordings, and
videos that she had collected over the years of her time in the Runaways.
The result would become her directorial debut and an opportunity for the
rest of the band—Sandy West, Jackie Fox, and Lita Ford—to join Jett and
Cherie Currie (whose *Neon Angel* autobiography was published in 1989)
in telling *their* side of the story.

It *was* their side, as well. Jett had no interest in the documentary,
no thought of participating—to the extent, Tischler-Blue later revealed,
of actively blocking the inclusion of any original Runaways music in the
film. "My original cut of *Edgeplay* focused largely on the Runaways' history and music. Unfortunately, as is so often the case, not everyone in the
band saw eye to eye on the use of our music, and ultimately I was denied
music sync licenses for it." (It fell to Suzi Quatro to deliver the movie's
theme music, and Tischler-Blue and Quatro would later collaborate on a
film of their own, *Naked Under Leather*.)

The loss of the Runaways' original music could have been a cata-
strophic blow. Instead, "It turned out to be a tremendous gift, for after
sitting with this footage for several years, I began to see another story
emerge, a story initially revealed only through the body language of my
bandmates as they spoke about specific events . . . a story of impulse,
denial and abuse."

Watching *Edgeplay* is a little like watching a car accident. It pulls no
punches: about the boot camp regime that the musicians were faced with

when they first hitched up with Kim Fowley, about the pressures and torments that they underwent on the road, about the nightmares that their parents endured as they discovered—often long after the fact—that none of the safeguards they had been assured would be in place around the girls was actually enacted.

Past arguments were revisited—and although the intrigues that surrounded the band were scarcely different from those with which any five teenaged girls might consume themselves, of course the spotlight and the stakes were a lot bigger for the Runaways:

Lita's belief that although she scarcely believed a word out of Kim Fowley's mouth, she never let go of the very first dream he offered her, that the Runaways were set to become superstars.

Cherie's anguish at being forced to choose between her bandmates and her family, not only at that final showdown at the photographer's studio but before that as well, as her father began asking Fowley awkward questions about the way the band was being treated. "Tell your dad to back off," her bandmates told her after hearing Fowley's side of the story, but without really knowing precisely what was being discussed.

Jackie's growing suspicion that a lot of people were making money from the Runaways, at a time when they barely had enough ready cash to take a taxi someplace.

And so on.

"I think there are a couple of things people respond to," Tischler-Blue said of the Runaways.

> First, [they] captured teen spirit. I have the double-edged viewpoint of having watched them as a fan, and later having been part of the band. When I used to watch them, I thought they epitomized all the things that I was about and loved—the rebel thing. When I made *Edgeplay*, I tried to capture that same rebel feeling.
>
> Also, I think people like to watch teenage girls morphing into middle-aged women.

Edgeplay followed the Runaways' career in largely linear fashion, an approach that, according to Tischler-Blue, would prove of immense value to the cast of the later *The Runaways* movie. Scout Taylor-Compton, who played Lita Ford in the Floria Sigismondi production, visited Ford while she and Tischler-Blue were filming their own latest project, the television reality series *The Gillettes: An Extreme American Family.*

> She said that the way the actresses learned about the Runaways . . . was that they sat down together, on their own, without the director, and learned about everybody from watching *Edgeplay.* In fact, even the director mentioned . . . that she pulled the film's most talked about and anticipated scene—the Joan/Cherie lesbian pussy bump—from *Edgeplay.*

And *Edgeplay* received all the attention that it deserved. An official selection at 2004 film festivals as far apart as London, Santa Cruz, and Beverly Hills, *Edgeplay* could have been one of the great rock 'n' roll documentaries. It turned into a helluva lot more than that.

Jett was, as always, either on the road or in the studio as *Edgeplay* moved through production and release. After all the problems occasioned by their stint with Warner Brothers, and with that eight years of confusion receding ever further into the distant past, Blackheart Records was stable again and signing new acts; over the next couple of years, the Eyeliners and the Vacancies would join the label just in time for Blackheart Records' twenty-fifth anniversary celebration at Webster Hall in Manhattan.

She launched her own radio show, *Joan Jett's Radio Revolution*, through Steve Van Zandt's *Underground Garage* on Sirius, playing the music that influenced and impressed her over the years and, she laughed, "turn[ing] people on to different things." She toured the Blackhearts as relentlessly as ever, and all the while, she was preparing for the release of the American version of *Naked*, 2006's *Sinner*.

Reviews for *Sinner* were minimal, and while she remained a reliable draw on the live circuit, it was apparent that Jett had very much fallen into that peculiar hole in the music business that awaits most performers, the point where they are no longer expected to, or even want to, compete with the brightest young stars of the day; are content simply to make their music, play to their fans, and leave the hullabaloo to a younger generation.

Which is not to say that they've given up. In interviews, Jett remained as hungry as ever, and *Naked/Sinner* was certainly no slouch in musical terms. But she was no longer a competitor, in the strict business sense of the term. She was much more than that. She was a veteran—a status that she embraced that summer when she joined the touring Warped caravan, playing alongside bands that were half her age and giving each of them a run for their money.

"Oh, I know she'll be fine. Joan grew up playing in bands that drove around in vans and worked hard," said Warped founder Kevin Lyman.

> She knows all about the grind. And she's tough. I bet she's tougher than a lot of these Emo bands we get on the tour. I know she'll spend a lot less time on her tour bus playing video games than they do. Joan is committed for the whole tour. She'll play every date, and she's also interested in talking to kids at each stop. She wants to talk to the girls who come out, who want to start bands. I mean, Joan was in a group when she was fifteen, so she can give these girls some great advice

"Joan is in her element on Warped," Kenny Laguna agreed. "Throughout her career she's toured with everyone from the Ramones to the Kinks to Foreigner. And she's done arenas, but this tour is what she was made for."

"It's exactly what I thought it would be," Jett simply laughed.

> It's like a punk-band circus, full of summer fun. Warped Tour has been a blast! The kids seem to respond really well to it. You'd almost never know that some of them weren't even born back then. They've been really welcoming and accepting of the band, and all the other bands on Warped have just been really awesome to us as well.

"I can honestly say that I haven't seen a band that sucks yet," Joan told *Big Wheel Online*. "I've got my little BMX and I just go crazy riding around from one stage to the next checking out all these great new acts. Mostly, though, I would have to say Anti-Flag, the Casualties, Bouncing Souls, and NOFX are some of my personal favorites. Oh and of course Against Me! I absolutely love that band." Another of the bands on the tour, the Dollyrots, would later join Blackheart Records.

"I keep my eyes open [for new acts to sign] all the time when I'm on the road," says Jett. "We made Blackheart Records what we wanted it to be. It's a place where girls can feel comfortable to be—both in a work environment and on an artistic level."

A live album, recorded at the tour's Portland berth, captured the Blackhearts in full flight. Yowling through a solid-hits set, with guitars on stun and Jett in full howl, the best of *Live at Warped* can be compared to any past Jett live recording, both in terms of excitement and audience response. Twenty-five years had elapsed since her first tours pushed her out in front of a predominantly teenaged, predominantly punk-minded crowd, but it might as well have been twenty-five minutes.

Warped was particularly significant, however, in that it reunited her with a band, she readily admitted, that she never expected to see or hear again.

The Germs had re-formed, with new frontman Shane West replacing Darby Crash. And, Jett enthused,

> I thought they were still great and were very tight. I think Shane did an excellent job of filling in for Darby as well. I felt that he really kind of channeled Darby, because if you're going to do this you got to be the best and I think Shane did about as good as anybody could do of filling his shoes. I was really looking forward to seeing all of them as well because it had been so long since I had spoken to any of them, and it was like a reunion of sorts.

But stepping out of the spotlight that had followed her through the 1980s and '90s had allowed her to take stock of her life outside of rock 'n' roll—the private existence that even her most devoted fans had no business looking into, and now she could relax into it.

She turned her attention to wider issues, flowing beyond even her work for Home Alone and NOW. A vocal supporter of Democratic candidate Howard Dean during his ultimately ill-fated run for the presidential nomination, she spoke angrily of the media furor that surrounded the so-called roar he delivered to a roomful of students and many said was responsible for finally derailing his campaign. "Mick Jagger would sound pretty stupid as well, if you took away the background noise," she reminded people.

She spoke too of her vegetarianism, a cause that she initially espoused simply because, she told *GoVeg*, "I was on the road eight months a year, and meat was too heavy to eat late at night," but which rapidly became a moral stance too.

> I slowly lost my taste for meat, and at the same time, I experienced a slowly dawning awareness that it is unnecessary to eat animals in order to live in this world. To give into the urge to eat flesh just because you can—now that's weak! It's like eating your dog or cat. It may take something like bird flu or mad cow disease to convince people to stop killing animals for food.
>
> I hope that soon we can make sure that everything we do is earth-friendly. I've always appreciated nature—trees, grass, birds, sun, and even insects. I obsessively recycle. I almost never turn on lights; I pretty much live in the dark. I don't use a lot of water. I'm a vegetarian, so I avoid contributing to the major environmental damage that the meat industry creates. I try to minimize my needs.

She had stopped drinking. Alan Merrill spent some time with Jett after one of her *Rocky Horror* performances, and recalled, "Joan and Kenny drove me home, and I remember Joan stopped for an orange juice. She really is very sober, it's no act. I respect that a lot. She's sharp and focused. No cloudy head there. She's dedicated to health."

It was this awareness, and discipline, that flavored much of *Naked /Sinner*.

> I really wanted it to be organic and coming from my heart. So, I think maybe the initial thought of wanting to go in that direction, I had to wait until things happened in our world and in our country that fired me up enough where the words came out organically. Something like [the song] "Riddles," when you look at what's gone on in this country in the last five years, I don't even recognize it. Sometimes I think the thoughts that we're having at the time: "Has anybody seen this? Days go by and people don't seem to get upset? Am I crazy? Are people seeing what I'm seeing in this world?"

At the same time, however, it was perhaps no coincidence that the gossipmongers should be thrown a bone or two around the same time as

Sinner was released. Jett had steadfastly avoided playing those games in the past, refusing to sacrifice an iota of her private life for the enrichment of her public persona. But she remained strangely tightlipped over tab-loidese reports that she was spotted being a little more than friendly with actress Carmen Electra following a concert at the Music Box.

The two women had starred together in Jett's latest video, *Sinner*'s cover of Sweet's old rocker "AC/DC," itself a lyric armed with more than a little gay innuendo. The ubiquitous "eyewitness" source told *Star Magazine*, "[They] got hot and heavy and they certainly were not trying to hide it. They were fully kissing and going at it. They were very physical with hugging and kissing and touching. It looked like the real thing for them— like they were totally in love."

Electra added further fuel to whatever fire the tabloids were trying to ignite when she looked back at the video for "Do You Wanna Touch Me (Oh Yeah)" and recalled, "Remember the video where [Jett] comes out with a trench coat on and she opens up the trench coat and she's wearing a bikini and then she's rocking out with a guitar? She's hot."

Jett was back in the bikini for the "AC/DC" shoot, romping and wink-ing through a song that thirty-plus years earlier had been rejected as a possible Sweet single for precisely the same reasons that it proved such an irresistible one in 2006. The gay angle that the Sweet had always cham-pioned with their imagery was good for a laugh. But the lesbian triangle painted by "AC/DC" hammered the point home harder than anybody in mid-1970s Britain was comfortable with. Thirty years later, attitudes had changed dramatically, and for many observers, perhaps the biggest dis-appointment about this whole episode came nine months later, when the same magazine was reporting "it" was all over. Whatever "it" may have been.

"Joan wants more than Carmen wants to give," the obligatory "close friend" told *Star*, adding that the split was caused by Electra refusing to either slow her schedule down or go public with their romance. "Still, friends hope the two can work it out, because 'they are truly in love.'" Or, as the Hollywood Backwash website put it, "Too bad this is just a rumor, they make a smoking hot couple!"

And one smoking hot publicity item!

TWENTY-FIVE

Queens of Noise Revisited

In 2003, Kenny Laguna's old chum, songwriter Greg Kihn, invited Jett to contribute to a book he was putting together for Thunder's Mouth Press, *Carved in Rock*. A collection of short stories written by rock stars, it drew in names from across the spectrum—golden oldies like Eric Burdon of the Animals, Pete Townshend of the Who, and Ray Manzarek of the Doors; post-punk legends Lydia Lunch, Richard Hell, and Jim Carroll, and many more.

In the event, Jett cowrote her story with Kihn himself, a rock 'n' roll fable titled "Bad Reputation." It was not, in fairness, the best tale in the book, nor the most enthralling. But the idea of the power of rock 'n' roll being able to withstand even a full-fledged assault by bloodsucking vampires was definitely one to conjure with. Particularly as it was but a short leap from the teenaged twists that run through "Bad Reputation" to the not-so-doomed romances that fire the *Twilight* franchise, and on to actress Kristen Stewart being recruited to play Joan Jett in a movie about the Runaways.

The Runaways was based on *Neon Angel*, Cherie Currie's long out of print autobiography about her life both before and after the Runaways. That band, after all, consumed just three years of her career (and around one-third of the book). Since that time, Currie had moved into both a solo career and a smattering of acting, while also building herself a reputation in the art field as one of the country's leading exponents of chainsaw art, creating a dazzling array of beautifully carved creations that range from a variety of animals (she specializes in bears), to mermaids, tikis, and intricate relief carvings. When Runaways drummer Sandy West died following a lengthy battle with cancer in 2006, Cherie created her memorial.

Rather than pursue the documentary approach that sustained *Edgeplay*, however, director Floria Sigismondi preferred to take a fictional approach. There would be no place in her script, for example, for either Jackie Fox or Vicki Blue; their places would be subsumed into a composite bassist named Robin . . . an irony that Tischler-Blue was swift to remark upon. "The only two band members who actually remember anything, because they didn't get high or drink, are the two that are excluded from the story." Lita Ford, too, largely absented herself from the proceedings.

But *The Runaways* had something that *Edgeplay* didn't. The involvement of Joan Jett.

"It was actually a long process," Jett explained to cinematical.com.

> It started with Cherie Currie's book. She had written a book about her life in the Runaways and then some things that occurred to her afterwards. Kenny Laguna . . . was trying to help her get it published. So he'd gone around to different publishers and they had trouble, you know, getting it published or getting any sort of response. I think this was his idea of getting the Runaways into the Rock and Roll Hall of Fame or something. And then he thought, like, "What about a TV movie?" Lifetime, or something like that, and then went to MTV, thinking maybe they'll do it. They weren't really interested.

For a time, there was talk of JT LeRoy writing the screenplay; one of the hottest young authors of the early 2000s, LeRoy had written a bestselling memoir of his life as a sixteen-year-old male prostitute being whored out by his drug-addicted mother. In fact, he was none of these things, as Jett recalled. "It turned out to be two fifty-year-old women. So once that all happened, then obviously LeRoy wasn't the one that was going to write the screenplay." Laguna continued his rounds, and finally Floria Sigismondi arrived on board.

"At that point," Jett continued, "I guess I started to take it seriously and to really think about 'was I into it?' Once I decided yes, I was into it."

She enthused to *Spin Online* about Kristen Stewart's portrayal of herself.

> She's authentic. She cared about it. It wasn't just a gig. It wasn't like, "Okay, I'm gonna do this role blah, blah, blah and in a few months then go do something else." I mean, she cut off her hair. She really immersed herself in it. I don't mean to put words in her mouth, but what I get is that she feels she has to do it justice, whatever that means. She knows the Runaways have fans. She knows I have fans and she was concerned about being authentic. And I found her to be wonderful to be around.

They met for the first time on New Year's Eve 2008 at a Blackhearts concert.

> We hung out for the whole day, and I just dumped on her about everything I could think about the Runaways—I mean, the good, the bad, and the ugly. I told her all that stuff and how much it meant to me.
>
> I burned her all the Runaways CDs, I burned her several Runaways bootlegs from live shows in Cleveland in '76 or the Whiskey and the Starwood, so she could hear the onstage banter and the audience yelling. I gave her some tapes of me talking as a fourteen-year-old because I had a very Maryland/Pennsylvania drawl. Whether or not she got a chance to utilize that wasn't important. It was about just having that for her own self so she could listen and see who I was.
>
> We got along great. It was really scary when you see us together, physically. The energy is so similar, the way we move, the way our hands move, our hair, the way that we talk, the way we start and don't finish sentences. I mean it's really bizarre, you know, but in a great way.

"I was looking for raw," said Sigismondi. "This very short period of time held a big place in all of their lives. It was a very delicate thing, but it wasn't all heartfelt. There was anger. There was resentment. There was sorrow. They were breaking new ground. They were taking risks. They were doing things that brought them up against walls."

Watching that struggle play back, Jett admitted, was

pretty surreal. It's hard to judge, hard to have some distance from, but I'm working on it and it's getting better. It's not painful for me to watch, so I think that's a good sign. The only part that's painful is that I go, "Oh, man, I'd like to do it again and really pay attention." Not that I wasn't paying attention back then, but you don't realize sometimes when you're in moments how special they are until they're gone.

Jett continued:

I knew [Kristen] was watching my posture, my mannerisms, everything I did, the way I hold my hands, just everything, and she really soaked it in. When we were hanging out together on set, it was like I had a mirror image. Even just sitting around, we'd do the same thing at the same time. It was just great—and it wasn't creepy. It was wonderfully special.

The cast remained friends, too. In January 2010, in the runup to the movie's release, both Stewart and Fanning joined Jett and the Blackhearts onstage at Harry O's in Park City, Utah. They didn't sing a note, but the audience was deafening regardless, and would continue so as the band continued to tour through the movie's first weeks in theaters. Not for the first time, and probably not for the last either, Joan Jett had pulled herself back into the headlines for all the right reasons. Because some people are stars, regardless of whether they're on TV every night.

The Runaways movie was a hit—of course it was. And so Jett moved into 2010 (and beyond) again at the peak of her powers, only this time with a difference. Those powers were no longer regarded as having been born from nowhere in the early 1980s, riding the coattails of a glam-rock anthem that she didn't even write.

She is a force for positive action in the music industry, knowing that by reaching out from her station on the stage, she can change lives at the back of a room. She signed up for a few dates with the True Colors tour, a joint venture by Cyndi Lauper, the Human Rights Organization, and Families and Friends of Lesbians and Gays; she spoke on the issues that concerned her, knowing that they might also concern her audience. There was a time when the very idea of turning fifty might have struck her as the end of the road—assuming, unlike most teenagers, she even believed she would get there.

Instead it marks a whole new beginning, because just as crucial as the plaudits being ladled onto Jett's future are those that after thirty-plus years of struggle were now being laid upon her past—a past that had finally been accepted—a past that was being acknowledged for what it was as opposed to the fantasy that it started out as.

One of the greatest rock 'n' roll adventures of them all.

Acknowledgments

No less than three abandoned projects lie at the heart of this book.

The first, dating back to the mid-1980s, was a projected article for the UK rock weekly *Melody Maker*, an interview with Joan Jett that for reasons I cannot recall never made it into print. The second, a short time later, was a full Runaways history intended for the monthly *Record Collector*, but which simply never got completed. And the third, in the early 1990s, was a prototype for the book you are now holding, written and researched in the wake of Joan's most recent string of hits, but abandoned when my then-publisher proved a lot less convinced about its potential than I was.

So my first and most grateful thanks go to my editor Mike Edison, for *finally* allowing me to write a book that I sometimes doubted would ever get going; to Joanna Dalin for a peerless copyedit; and to Jessica Burr for making everything run smoothly. And thanks to everybody I spoke to all that time ago, whose stories, recollections, and time were poured into my initial researches—and to everybody I've talked with in the years since then, for this and various other projects:

Joan Jett, Kenny Laguna, Ricky Byrd, Sandy West, Lita Ford, Cherie Currie, Kim Fowley, Theresa K., Gaye Advert, Alan Merrill, Malcolm McLaren, Steve Jones, Stiv Bators, Mick Farren, Sandy Robertson, Rodney Bingenheimer, Lemmy Kilminster, Randy Detroit, Tony Secunda, Brendan Mullen, and Pat Smear.

And to Mia Zapata and the Gits, a fabulous band gathering such well-deserved speed in the same city that I was then living in, and whose music and performances were such a welcome relief from a lot of the other stuff we were hearing at that time.

Throughout this book, I have also drawn upon the writings and interviews of others, as noted in both the text and the accompanying bibliography. Special acknowledgement is due, however, to *Edgeplay*, Victoria Tischler-Blue's superlative documentary of the life and times of the Runaways; and *Real Wild Child: A Video Anthology*, Joan Jett and Kenny Laguna's own history of Jett's video career.

I thank YouTube for being home to so many classic clips of Joan Jett, the Blackhearts, and the Runaways in action and conversation; and *Bad Reputation Nation*, the online repository of All Things Joan, whose news, interviews, and fan club newsletter archives proved invaluable.

And also—Amy Hanson, Jo-Ann Greene, Oliver, Toby and Trevor, Jen W., Mike Sharman, Vaughan Funnell and Sexagisma, Dan Reed and WXPN (plus Ann and Max), Dave and Sue, Gaye and Tim, Linda and Larry, Andrew and Esther, Karen and Todd, Deb and Roger, Oliver, Trevor and Captain Tobias Wilcox, Jenny and James, Betsy and Steve, Thompsons, Lowes, and the Nyack Hansons.

Joan Jett Discography

PART ONE: THE RUNAWAYS DISCOGRAPHY

The Runaways

Released 1976

Cherry Bomb / You Drive Me Wild / Is It Day or Night? / Thunder / Rock and Roll / Lovers / American Nights / Blackmail / Secrets / Dead End Justice

Queens of Noise

Released 1977

Queens of Noise / Take It or Leave It / Midnight Music / Born to Be Bad / Neon Angels on the Road to Ruin / I Love Playin' with Fire / California Paradise / Hollywood / Heartbeat / Johnny Guitar

Live In Japan

Released 1977

Queens of Noise / California Paradise / All Right You Guys / Wild Thing / Gettin' Hot / Rock and Roll / You Drive Me Wild / Neon Angels on the Road to Ruin / I Wanna Be Where the Boys Are / Cherry Bomb / American Nights / C'mon

Waitin' for the Night

Released 1977

Little Sister / Wasted / Gotta Get Out Tonight / Wait for Me / Fantasies / School Days / Trash Can Murders / Don't Go Away / Waitin' for the Night / You're Too Possessive

Little Lost Girls

(UK title: *And Now . . . The Runaways*)

Released 1979

Saturday Night Special / Eight Days a Week / Mama Weer All Crazee Now / I'm a Million / Right Now / Takeover / My Buddy and Me / Little Lost Girls / Black Leather

COMPILATIONS

Flaming Schoolgirls
Released 1980

Intro / Strawberry Fields Forever / C'mon / Hollywood Cruisin' / Blackmail /
Is It Day or Night? (live) / Here Comes the Sun / Hollywood Dream / Don't
Abuse Me / I Love Playin' with Fire (live) / Secrets (live)

The Best of the Runaways
Released 1982

Cherry Bomb / Blackmail / I Love Playin' with Fire / Born to Be Bad / Take It
or Leave It / Queens of Noise (live) / You Drive Me Wild (live) / School Days /
Wait for Me / Wasted / Don't Go Away / Waitin' for the Night / C'mon

Born to Be Bad: Demos
Released 1991

Yesterday's Kids / Is It Day or Night? / Let's Party Now / All Right Now /
Thunder / Rock and Roll / American Nights / California Paradise / I'm a Star /
You Drive Me Wild / Born to Be Bad / Wild Thing

Neon Angels
Released 1992

Cherry Bomb / Blackmail / California Paradise / Born to Be Bad / I Love
Playing with Fire / Hollywood / Lovers / Neon Angels on the Road to Ruin /
Don't Go Away / Queens of Noise / You Drive Me Wild / Waiting for the Night

The Millennium Collection
Released 2005

Cherry Bomb / Blackmail / Secrets / I Love Playin' with Fire / Born to Be Bad /
Take It or Leave It / Queens of Noise / Neon Angels on the Road to Ruin /
Wasted / Wait for Me / Waitin' for the Night

The Mercury Albums Anthology
Released 2010

Cherry Bomb / You Drive Me Wild / Is It Day or Night? / Thunder / Rock and
Roll / Lovers / American Nights / Blackmail / Secrets / Dead End Justice /
Queens of Noise / Take It or Leave It / Midnight Music / Born to Be Bad /
Neon Angels on the Road to Ruin / I Love Playin' with Fire / California
Paradise / Hollywood / Heartbeat / Johnny Guitar / Queens of Noise (live) /
California Paradise / All Right You Guys (live) / Wild Thing (live) / Gettin'
Hot (live) / Rock and Roll (live) / You Drive Me Wild (live) / Neon Angels

on the Road to Ruin (live) / I Wanna Be Where the Boys Are (live) / Cherry Bomb (live) / American Nights (live) / C'mon (live) / Little Sister / Wasted / Gotta Get Out Tonight / Wait for Me / Fantasies / School Days / Trash Can Murders / Don't Go Away / Waitin' for the Night / You're Too Possessive

The Runaways—Original Motion Picture Soundtrack

Released 2010

Roxy Roller (performed by Nick Gilder) / The Wild One (performed by Suzi Quatro) / It's a Man's Man's Man's World (performed by MC5) / Rebel Rebel (performed by David Bowie) / Cherry Bomb (performed by Dakota Fanning) / Hollywood (performed by the Runaways) / California Paradise (performed by Dakota Fanning) / You Drive Me Wild (performed by the Runaways) / Queens of Noise (performed by Dakota Fanning and Kristin Stewart) / Dead End Justice (performed by Kristin Stewart and Dakota Fanning) / I Wanna Be Your Dog (performed by the Stooges) / Pretty Vacant (performed by the Sex Pistols) / Don't Abuse Me (performed by Joan Jett)

PART TWO: JOAN JETT AND THE BLACKHEARTS DISCOGRAPHY

Joan Jett

Released 1980

Bad Reputation / Make Believe / You Don't Know What You've Got / You Don't Own Me / Too Bad on Your Birthday / Do You Wanna Touch Me (Oh Yeah) / Let Me Go / Doing All Right with the Boys / Shout / Jezebel / Don't Abuse Me / Wooly Bully

Bad Reputation

Released 1981

Bad Reputation / Make Believe / You Don't Know What You've Got / You Don't Own Me / Too Bad on Your Birthday / Do You Wanna Touch Me (Oh Yeah) / Let Me Go / Doing All Right with the Boys / Shout / Jezebel / Don't Abuse Me / Wooly Bully

CD BONUS TRACKS

Call Me Lightning / Hanky Panky / What Can I Do for You / You Don't Own Me / Bad Reputation (live with the Remains) / Summertime Blues

I Love Rock 'n' Roll

Released 1981

I Love Rock 'n' Roll / (I'm Gonna) Run Away / Love Is Pain / Nag / Crimson and Clover / Victim of Circumstance / Bits and Pieces / Be Straight / You're Too Possessive / Little Drummer Boy

CD BONUS TRACKS

Oh Woe Is Me / Louie Louie / You Don't Know What You've Got (live) / Summertime Blues / Nag (with the Coasters)

Album

Released 1983

Fake Friends / Handyman / Everyday People / A Hundred Feet Away / Secret Love / Star Star / The French Song / Tossin' and Turnin' / Why Can't We Be Happy / I Love Playing with Fire / Coney Island Whitefish / Had Enough

CD BONUS TRACKS

Nitetime / Everyday People (dance mix) / Wait for Me / Who Can You Trust / Scratch My Back / Locked Groove

Glorious Results of a Misspent Youth

Released 1984

Cherry Bomb / I Love You Love Me Love / Frustrated / Hold Me / Long Time / Talkin' 'bout My Baby / I Need Someone / Love Like Mine / New Orleans / Someday / Push and Stomp / I Got No Answers

CD BONUS TRACKS

Hide and Seek / I Can't Control Myself / Bird Dog / Talkin' bout My Baby (live) / Bombs Away / Cherry Bomb (dance mix) I Need Someone (dance mix)

Good Music

Released 1986

Good Music / This Means War / Roadrunner / If Ya Want My Luv / Fun, Fun, Fun / Black Leather / Outlaw / Just Lust / You Got Me Floatin' / Contact

Up Your Alley

Released 1988

I Hate Myself for Loving You / Ridin' with James Dean / Little Liar / Tulane / I Wanna Be Your Dog / I Still Dream About You / You Want In, I Want Out / Just Like in the Movies / Desire / Back It Up / Play That Song Again

The Hit List

Released 1990

Dirty Deeds (shortened title of "Dirty Deeds Done Dirt Cheap") / Love Hurts / Pretty Vacant / Celluloid Heroes / Tush / Time Has Come Today / Up from the Skies / Have You Ever Seen the Rain? / Love Me Two Times / Roadrunner USA (1990 Version) / Let It Bleed (German bonus track) / Love Stinks (German bonus track)

Notorious

Released 1991

Backlash / Ashes in the Wind / The Only Good Thing (You Ever Said Was Goodbye) / Lie to Me / Don't Surrender / Goodbye / Machismo / Treadin' Water / I Want You / Wait for Me / Misunderstood (Japanese bonus track)

Pure and Simple

Released 1994

Go Home / Eye to Eye / Spinster / Torture / Rubber and Glue / As I Am / Activity Grrrl / Insecure / Wonderin' / Consumed / You Got a Problem / Brighter Day / Hostility (bonus track on LP, cassette) / Here to Stay (bonus track on LP, Japanese CD)

Evil Stig

Released 1995

Sign of the Crab / Bob (Cousin O.) / Drinking Song / Spear and Magic Helmet / Last to Know / Guilt Within Your Head / Whirlwind / Another Shot of Whiskey / Second Skin / Activity Grrrl / You Got a Problem / Crimson and Clover / Drunks

Naked

Released 2004

Naked / Bad Time / Fetish / Androgynous / Science Fiction Double Feature (punk version) / Right in the Middle / Turn It Around / Everyone Knows / Baby Blue / Kiss on the Lips / Watersign / Tube Talkin' / Season of the Witch / Bad Time (monster mix) / Can't Live Without You / Five

Sinner

Released 2006

An asterisk (*) indicates a track previously released on Naked

Riddles / AC/DC / Five * / Naked* / Everyone Knows * / Change the World / Androgynous* / Fetish* / Watersign* / Tube Talkin'* / Turn It Around* / Baby Blue* / A Hundred Feet Away / Bad Time*

Live at Warped Tour

Released 2008

Bad Reputation (live) / Cherry Bomb (live) / Change The World (live) / Do
You Wanna Touch Me (Oh Yeah) / AC/DC (live) / Riddles (live) / Five (live) /
Crimson and Clover (live) / Fetish (alternate version)

COMPILATIONS

I Love Rock 'n' Roll '92

Released 1992 (Japan)
I Love Rock 'n' Roll (remix) / Love Is Pain (live at the Ritz) / Talkin' 'bout My
Baby (live at CBGBs) / The Only Good Thing (You Ever Said Was Goodbye)

The Jett Age

Released 1992 (Japan)
Bad Reputation / Do You Wanna Touch Me (Oh Yeah) / I Love Rock 'n' Roll /
Crimson and Clover / Everyday People / The French Song / Star Star / Cherry
Bomb / Have You Ever Seen the Rain? / Love Hurts / Dirty Deeds / The Only
Good Thing / Ashes in the Wind / Don't Surrender / Backlash / I Love Rock 'n'
Roll (remix)

Flashback

Released 1993, re-released with Bonus Tracks (Japan)
All Previously Unreleased / Rarities
Real Wild Child (recorded 1997) / Hide and Seek (recorded 1984) / Indian
Giver (recorded 1990) / I Hate Long Good-byes (recorded 1984) / Cherry
Bomb (recorded 1992, live with L7) / Fantasy (recorded 1984) / Light of Day
(recorded 1986) / Gotcha (recorded 1985) / She Lost You (recorded 1987) /
MCA (EMI, recorded 1984) / Rebel, Rebel (recorded 1983) / Be My Lover
(recorded 1990) / Bring It on Home (recorded 1984) / Play with Me (recorded
1985) / Activity Grrrl (recorded 1993) / Heartbeat (1985) / Bad Reputation
(recorded live, 1981) / Black Leather (demo, recorded 1986) / I Love Rock 'n'
Roll (recorded 1979) / Right til the End (recorded 1987)

Do You Wanna Touch Me?

Released 1993 (France)
Do You Wanna Touch Me? (Oh Yeah) / Bad Reputation / I Hate Myself for
Loving You / Backlash / Little Liar / Tulane / Torture (previously unreleased) /
Wonderin' (previously unreleased) / Cherry Bomb / Roadrunner USA / New

Orleans / Have You Ever Seen the Rain? / Activity Grrrl / Gotcha / Everyday People / Time Has Come Today / Rebel Rebel

1979
Released 1995
All Recorded 1979
You Don't Know What You Got / I Want You / You Can't Get Me (acoustic version) / I'll Never Get Away / We're All Crazy Now / What Can I Do for You / You Can't Get Me (electric version)

Cherry Bomb
Released 1995
Cherry Bomb (dance mix) / A Little Bit of Heaven (recorded 1984) / Who Can You Trust? (recorded 1985) / Let It Bleed / Long Live the Night (Days of Thunder soundtrack, 1990) / Right til the End

Fit to Be Tied
Released 1997
Bad Reputation / Light of Day/ Do You Wanna Touch Me (Oh Yeah) / Roadrunner USA (alternate version) / I Love Rock 'n' Roll / Victim of Circumstance / Everyday People / I Hate Myself for Loving You (alternate version) / Crimson and Clover / Fake Friends / Make Believe / Cherry Bomb / Little Liar (live) / World of Denial (previously unreleased) / Love Is All Around

Fetish
Released 1999
Fetish (previously unreleased) / Handyman / The French Song / Baby Blue / Star Star / Love Is Pain / Secret Love / Cherry Bomb / Hanky Panky / Coney Island Whitefish / Wooly Bully / Do You Want to Touch Me (Oh Yeah) (live 1981) / Black Leather (live) / Fetish XXX (previously unreleased)

Unfinished Business
Released 2001
Unfinished Business (previously unreleased) / I Left My Heart in San Francisco (previously unreleased) / Real Wild Child / Love Is All Around / The Star Spangled Banner (previously unreleased)

Cherry Bomb
Released 2002
Cherry Bomb (live 2001 with Cherie Currie) / Don't Believe in Heaven / Long Time (live)

Jett Rock

Released 2004 (Japan)
Cherry Bomb / Backlash / I Hate Myself for Loving You / Love Is All Around /
Have You Ever Seen the Rain? / I Love Rock 'n' Roll / You Can't Get Me
(acoustic) / Bad Reputation / Everyday People / I Want You / Do You Wanna
Touch Me (Oh Yeah) / Let's Do It / Light of Day / Watersign / Good Music /
I Need Someone / Fetish / Spinster / Crimson and Clover / This Means War /
Science Fiction Double Feature

Greatest Hits

Released 2010
Cherry Bomb / You Drive Me Wild / School Days / Love Is Pain / Bad
Reputation / You Don't Know What You've Got / I Want You / I Love Rock 'n'
Roll / (I'm Gonna) Run Away / Crimson and Clover / Do You Wanna Touch
Me (Oh Yeah) / The French Song / Everyday People / Fake Friends / Light of
Day

Bibliography

Alexander, Jeff. "Joan Jett" (*Loud Fast Rules!*, October 2006).

Altman, Billy. "Confessions of a High Flying Jet" (*Creem*, February 1981).

Auslander, Philip. *Performing Glam Rock: Gender and Theatricality in Popular Music* (University of Michigan Press, 2006).

Baker, Cary. "The Runaways: How Can We Miss You if You Don't Stay Away" (*Creem*, July 1983).

Barren, Mick. "The Runaways: From Jailbait to Jes' Plain Bait" (*NME*, October 1976).

Bashe, Philip. "Joan Jett Lives Down Her Rep" (*Circus*, March 1982).

———. "Joan Jett Plays Hardball" (*Circus*, June 1982).

———. "Joan's Platinum Jett" (*Circus*, July 1983).

Bienstock, Richard. "Jett Sett" (*Guitar World*, May 2010).

Bolles, Don, Adam Parfrey, and Brendan Mullen. *Lexicon Devil: The Fast Times and Short Life of Darby Crash* (Feral House, 2002).

Chun, Kimberly. "Joan Jett Still Loves Rock 'n' Roll" (*Play Guitar!*, vol. 6, issue 1, 2007).

Coble, Margaret. "I Love Rock 'n' Roll" (*Curve*, July 2006).

Connelly, Christopher. "Joan Jett Has the Last Laugh" (*Rolling Stone*, April 1982).

Conniff, Tamara, and Jerry Lee Williams. (*Seconds*, issue 46, 1998).

Currie, Cherie, and Tony O'Neill. *Neon Angel: A Memoir of a Runaway* (It Books, revised edition, 2010).

Dadomo, Giovanni. "LA Lolitas" (*Sounds*, November 1976).

Deggans, Eric. "Love is All Around" (*Rockgrrl*, November 1996).

DeMuir, Harold. "Joan Jett Regains Lost Ground" (*Rock Scene*, May 1987).

Derringer, Liz. "Women in Rock" (*High Times*, November 1979).

Doherty, Harry. "The Runaways: You Sexy Things!" (*Melody Maker*, October 1976).

Edmonds, Ben. "Fowley's Angels" (*Mojo*, May 2000).

Edwards, Henry, and Tony Zanetta. *Stardust: The Life and Times of David Bowie* (Michael Joseph, 1986).

Farren, Mick. *The Black Leather Jacket* (Plexus, 1985).

———. "LA Punk" (*NME*, April 1981).

Fortnam, Ian. "Joan Jett" (*Classic Rock*, December 2007).

Frame, Pete. *Rock Family Trees* (Omnibus Books, various editions).

Francher, Lisa. "Are You Young and Rebellious Enough?" (*Bomp*, Spring 1976).

Gaitskill, Mary. "Joan Jett" (*Interview*, August 2006).

Galboa, Glenn. "Jett Sett Rocking" (*Beacon Journal*, 1998).

Gallotta, Paul. "Joan Jett Finds the Hit Making Touch Again" (*Circus*, December 1988).

———. "Joan Jett's Notorious Journey" (*Circus*, November 1991).

Galvin, Peter. "No Jett Lagg" (*The Advocate*, May 1994).

Garbarini, Vic. "60 Minutes with Joan Jett" (*Guitar World*, February 1998).

Gehr, Richard. "Joan Jett: Her Life Was Saved By Rock & Roll" (*Music & Sound Output*, July 1988).

Golden, Ellen Zoe. "Life of the Party" (*Hit Parader*, July 1983).

Goldstein, Patrick. "Lissome Lolitas or Teenage Trash?" (*Creem*, February 1977).

Goldstein, Toby. "Bad Reputation" (*Musician*, March 1982).

Green, Jim. "Joan Jett: Selling Records Is the Best Revenge" (*Trouser Press*, June 1982).

Guinness Book of British Hit Singles . . . Albums (Guinness World Records, various editions).

Gullo, Joann. "Joan Jett: Still a Sinner" (*Inside Connection*, August 2007).

Hall, Russell. "Joan Jett Check It Out" (*Performing Songwriter*, December 2001).

Hanna, Kathleen. "Idol Worship" (*Alternative Press*, August 2006).

Harry, Bill. *Arrows* (Everest, 1976).

Hayden, Chaunce. "Jett Sett" (*Penthouse*, October 1999).

———. "Rock Legend Joan Jett" (*Steppin' Out* March 2010).

Hendrix, Mike. "The Queen of Rock & Roll" (*Outlaw Biker*, issue 173, 2008).

Hoahing, Cheryl A. "Joan Jett & the Blackhearts" (*Metal Edge*, August 2006).

Holder, Noddy. *Who's Crazee Now? My Autobiography* (Ebury Press, 1999).

Hoskyns, Barney. *Waiting for the Sun: A Rock 'n' Roll History of Los Angeles* (Backbeat Books, 2009).

Jacobs, A. J. "What I've Learned" (*Esquire*, November 2009).

Jerome, Jim. "Teeny Queens of Rock" (*People*, August 1976).

Jett, Joan, and Kristina Estlund (ed). "Evil Stig: Cause and Effect" (*Rip*, November 1995).

Jett, Joan, and Todd Oldham. *Joan Jett* (Ammo Books, 2010).

K., Brenda. "The Runaways: A Lot More than Horny Hype" (*New Wave Rock*, February 1979).

Kaplan, Big Joe. "Biker's Rock and Roll Sweetheart" (*Outlaw Biker Magazine*, 1988).

Kubernik, Harvey. "The Runaways: Runaway Girls" (*Melody Maker*, July 1976).

Leblanc, Lauraine. *Pretty in Pink: Girls' Gender Resistance in a Boys' Subculture* (Rutgers University Press, 1999).

Lefkowitz, Ellen. "Not Too Old to Rock 'n' Roll" (*Long Island Woman*, March 2008).

Lens, Jenny. *Punk Pioneers* (Universe, 2008).

Manning, Kara. "You Can't Always Get What You Want" (*American Theatre*, February 2001).

Martin, Gavin. "Joan Jett: Whomping the Suckers with a Superball" (*NME*, April 1982).

Matheu, Robert and Brian J. Bowe (eds). *Creem: America's Only Rock 'n' Roll Magazine* (Collins, 2007).

McDonnell, Evelyn. "Girls & Guitars" (*Out*, April 2000).

———. "Joan Jett" (*Interview*, March 2010).

McNeil, Legs and Gillian McCain. *Please Kill Me: The Uncensored Oral History of Punk* (Grove Press, 2006).

Miller, Gerri. "She's Back in Business" (*Metal Edge*, March 1987).

Mullen, Brendan, Roger Gastman, and Kristine McKenna. *Live at the Masque: Nightmare in Punk Alley* (Gingko Press, 2007).

Murray, Charles Shaar. *Shots from the Hip* (Penguin, 1991).

Muso, Michael. Joan Jett Gets Tough (*US*, April 1982).

Needs, Kris. "Joan Jett: Return of the Jett Girl" (*ZigZag*, February 1980).

Newman, Margaret. "Six Questions with Joan Jett" (*Billboard*, May 2006).

Olson, Steve. "Cherie Currie" (*Juice Magazine*, issue 62).

Pappademas, Alex, and Will Welch. "Paradise City" (*GQ*, March 2009).

Perry, Andrew. "Welcome Back!" (*Mojo*, January 2008).

Quatro, Suzi. *Unzipped* (Hodder & Stoughton, 2007).

Raha, Maria. *Cinderella's Big Score: Women of the Punk and Indie Underground* (Seal Press, 2004).

Ray, Amy. "Joan Jett" (*Stomp and Stammer*, 1997).

Ridenour, Shelly. "Do You Wanna Touch" (*Nylon*, September 2001).

Robbins, Ira. "Joan Jett: I Love Rock 'N' Roll" (*Trouser Press*, March 1982).

Robbins, Julia. "She's a Rebel" (*Creem Metal*, October 1989).

Robertson, Sandy. "Joan Jett and the Blackhearts" (*Sounds*, May 1982).

———. "Joan Jett: Heart Attack" (*Sounds*, November 1982)

———. "Kim Fowley: The Dorian Gray of Rock 'n' Roll" (*Sounds*, August 1977).

———. "Runaways: A Primer for the New Runaways" (*Sounds*, September 1977).

———. "The Runaways" (*Sounds*, November 1977).

———. "Keep on Running" (*Sounds*, March 1979).

Robinson, Lisa. "Naughty Nymphets Leave Lisa Cold (*Creem*, November 1976).

Rolling Stone Cover to Cover (Bondi Digital Publishing, 2008).

Rudge, Charlotte. "Queen of Noise" (*Nylon*, June 2006).

Salewicz, Chris. "The Runaways: And I Wonder . . . I Wah Wah Wah Wah Wonder . . ." (*NME*, July 1976).

Scholosberg, Karen. "Joan Jett Unchained" (*Creem*, October 1986).

Secher, Andy. "Joan Jett, Bad to the Bone" (*Hit Parader*, November 1983).

Sinclair, Mick. "Joan Jett" (*ZigZag*, January 1985).

Sinclair, Tim. "Jett the Good Times Roll" (*Entertainment Weekly*, 24 November 2000).

Spitz, Marc, and Brendan Mullen. "Queens of Noise" (*Spin*, December 2001).

———. *We Got the Neutron Bomb: The Untold Story of LA Punk* (Three Rivers Press, 2001).

Steffenhagen, Spike. *The Runaways, Joan Jett and Lita Ford (Hard Rock Comics)* (Revolutionary Comics, 1993).

Strong, Martin. *The Great Rock . . .* and *Psychedelic Discography* (Canongate Books, various editions).

Sutcliffe, Phil. "The Runaways: Newcastle City Hall" (*Sounds*, November 1977).

Swenson, John. "No More Bad Reputation" (*Rock World*, May 1985).

Tangeman, Anne. "Joan Jett" (*Micromag*, 1999).

Thompson, Dave. *The A–Z of Glam Rock* (Cherry Red Books, 2010).

———. *Music on Film: The Rocky Horror Picture Show* (Limelight Editions, forthcoming).

Thrills, Adrian. "Return of the Runaway" (*NME*, March 1979).

Tobler, John, and Stuart Grundy. *The Record Producers* (BBC Books, 1982).

Trakin, Roy. "Live Review" (*Musician*, June 1981).

Turman, Katherine. "Jett Sett" (*Maximum Guitar*, January 1998).

Uhelszki, Jaan. "No Introduction Necessary" (*Alternative Press*, April 2000).

———. "Punk Mama" (*Guitar World*, June 2006).

Vincentelli, Elisabeth. "Joan Jett OG" (*Option*, September 1994).

Warnock, Kathleen. "Oh the Horror" (*Rockrgrl*, March 2001).

Weinstein, Emily. "Joan Jett" (*Venus Zine*, June 2006).

Welch, Chris, and Simon Napier Bell. *Marc Bolan: Born to Boogie* (Eel Pie, 1982).

Whitburn, Joel. *Top Pop Singles . . . Albums* (Record Research, various editions).

Wieder, Judy. "Joan Jett Back on Top" (*Blast*, December 1988).

———. "Joan Jett Wants to Be Your Dog" (*Creem Metal*, November 1988).

Young, Jon. "Joan Jett" (*Trouser Press*, November 1980).

Index